Terrorism and guerrilla warfare

Other books by the same author:

Across the River (as Richard Jocelyn) (1957) London: Constable.

The Long, Long War (1966) London: Cassell, and New York: Praeger.

Protest and the Urban Guerilla (1973) London: Cassell, and New York: Abelard Schumann.

Riot and Revolution in Singapore and Malaya, 1948–63 (1973) London: Faber and Faber.

Living in Terrorism (1975) London: Faber and Faber, and New York: Arlington House.

Guerrillas and Terrorists (1977) London: Faber and Faber (1980) Athens Ohio: Ohio University Press.

Kidnap and Ransom (1978) London and Boston: Faber and Faber.

Britain in Agony (1978) London: Faber and Faber, and (1980) Harmondsworth: Penguin.

The Media and Political Violence (1981) London: Macmillan, and New Jersey: Humanities Press.

Industrial Conflict and Democracy (1984) London: Macmillan.

Conflict and Violence in Singapore and Malaysia 1948–83 (1984) Boulder, Colorado: Westview Press, and (1985) Singapore: Graham Brash.

The Future of Political Violence (1986) London: Macmillan, and New York: St Martin's Press.

Kidnap, Hijack and Extortion (1987) London: Macmillan, and New York: St Martin's Press.

Terrorism and guerrilla warfare

Forecasts and remedies

Richard Clutterbuck

Routledge
London and New York

First published 1990 by Routledge
11 New Fetter Lane, London EC4P 4EE
29 West 35th Street, New York, NY 10001

Phototypeset by Input Typesetting Ltd, London
Printed in Great Britain by Richard Clay Ltd, Bungay, Suffolk

British Library Cataloguing in Publication Data

Clutterbuck, Richard
  Terrorism and guerrilla warfare: forecasts and remedies
  1. Terrorism
  I. Title
  322.4'2

  ISBN 0–415–02440–4

Library of Congress Cataloging in Publication Data

Clutterbuck, Richard L.
  Terrorism and guerrilla warfare: forecasts and remedies/
Richard Clutterbuck.
      p.   cm.
   Bibliography: p.
   Includes index.
   ISBN 0–415–02440–4
   1. Terrorism. 2. Guerrilla warfare. I. Title.
HV6431.C554 1989
303.6'25 — dc20

Contents

Contents

Contents

Contents

Part VI **Conclusions**

Preface

I had my mind directed to the future of terrorism in April 1981, when 22 SAS Regiment, in the wake of their triumph at Princes Gate the previous year, invited me to speak to their annual study period about how I saw terrorism developing in the coming ten years. This invitation was both a compliment and a challenge. Characteristically the SAS were a highly stimulating audience (there were about 200 of them there) and I learned a lot from their lively cross-examination. They are the best of all practitioners in this field, so when Peter Sowden first suggested in 1983 that I should write this book, I already had some preliminary ideas. I was, however, committed to four other books, then in various stages from early research to proof-correcting, so I turned my antennae to the subject during this enforced five-year gestation period, while the other four books came to publication in 1984, 1985, 1986, and 1987.

I began detailed research in 1985, helped by one of my former students, Shelagh Macleod, then on her way to selection for commission in the army. Her grasp of both weapons and electronics was a great asset. We were greatly helped by the Royal Military College of Science (especially Dan Raschen); also the Royal School of Military Engineering (especially Alec Wright and John Wyatt), who train the bomb search teams for Northern Ireland and lead the world in research of techniques in this field.

Ian Hogg, editor of *Jane's Infantry Weapons*, took enormous trouble on my behalf in both conversation and correspondence. Professor Richard Gregory of Bristol University, Dr John Hulbert of Cogitaire, and Superintendent David Webb of the Devon and Cornwall Constabulary gave me a fascinating insight into the microelectronics revolution, and its application to fighting terrorism and crime. Of the designers and manufacturers, Ferranti, Heckler and Koch, and Miriad International were especially helpful. On the political side I again went to see the best – Dr Peter

Janke and his team of researchers at Control Risks who, though immensely in demand from the business world, found time to help me analyse current events all over the world and to predict how they might develop. I have, however, discussed political matters only when they seemed to me to be important in the development of the prognosis of the conduct of terrorism and guerrilla warfare as a whole. I have not tried to cover every country and every political conflict in the world. Some readers will inevitably disagree with my choice, and to them I apologize.

Throughout these years I have averaged eighty lectures a year at Bramshill and other police colleges, many of them about the future, and the week-by-week cross-examination by superintendents, inspectors, and bodyguards fresh from the ground has been an exceptionally healthy and constructive dimension.

This book is not science fiction. My task, as is indicated in Peter Sowden's choice of subtitle, has been to examine current trends and to predict how they seem likely to work out in the next five to ten years. I have applied this particularly to the technology, which (apart from the occasional luxury of a flight of fancy) I have tried to keep down to earth. Above all, since no one is an expert in all fields, I have tried to make each technological chapter in itself comprehensible to the non-professional. I hope that electronics experts will be tolerant of my child's guide to computer development, but that they will find my similar child's guide to the characteristics of the revolutionary Heckler and Koch G11 assault rifle useful and comprehensible in exchange, and vice versa. Perhaps both electronics and weapons experts will pick up a bit about sniffing for explosives and neutron bombardment; maybe they will be as horrified as I was when I began to delve into the malign and world-wide influence of drug-trafficking on crime, guerrilla warfare, and terrorism.

To Peter Sowden I am especially grateful for his patience and his guidance on what you, the reader, will and will not want to read about. I hope that he and I have got this right.

Richard Clutterbuck

Abbreviations

For foreign acronyms and in other cases where it is judged to be more helpful to the reader, an English description (in parenthesis) is given instead of spelling out the words.

ACR	Advanced Combat Rifle
AD	(Direct Action) (France)
AFR	Automatic Fingerprint Recognition
AGV	Autonomous Guided Vehicle
AI	Artificial Intelligence
AIIB	Anti-Imperialist International Brigade
AISSF	All India Sikh Students' Federation
ALF	Animal Liberation Front
ARENA	(Republican National Alliance) (El Salvador)
ASU	Active Service Unit
ATF	US Government Bureau of Alcohol, Tobacco, and Firearms
AUPO	(Autopropellant Ammunition) (Italy)
BCP	Burmese Communist Party
BMA	British Medical Association
BR	(Red Brigades) (Italy)
BR-PCC	(Fighting Communist Party – a splinter group of the Red Brigades) (Italy)
BSIA	British Security Industry Association
CAWS	Close Assault Weapon System
CCC	(Combatant Communist Cells) Belgium
CCTV	Closed Circuit Television
CDRF	(Rodrigo Franco Democratic Commando) (Peru)
CGSB	(Simon Bolivar Guerrilla Co-ordination) (Colombia)
COT	Computerized Organic Tracer

Abbreviations

CRIS	Crime Reporting Information System
DEA	Drug Enforcement Administration (USA)
DFLP	Democratic Front for the Liberation of Palestine
DNA	(Genetic molecule in body fluids)
DP	Detection Probability
DUP	Democratic Unionist Party (Sudan)
EC	European Community
ECM	Electronic Counter-measures
EDP	Electronic Data Processing
EGP	(Guerrilla Army of the Poor) (Guatemala)
ELN	(National Liberation Army) (Colombia)
EPL	(People's Liberation Army) (Colombia)
ETA	(Basque Extremist Movement) (Spain)
FAA	Federal Aviation Authority (USA)
FACES	Facial Analysis Comparison and Elimination System
FAR	False Alarm Rate
FARC	(Armed Revolutionary Forces of Columbia)
FARL	(Lebanese Armed Revolutionary Factions)
FBI	Federal Bureau of Investigation (USA)
FLNC	(Corsican National Liberation Front) (France)
FMLN	(National Liberation Front) (El Salvador)
FRG	Federal Republic of Germany
GIGN	(French Anti-Terrorist Commando)
GNP	Gross National Product
GPHMG	General Purpose Heavy Machine-gun
GSG9	(German Anti-Terrorist Commando)
HB	(Political party supporting ETA) (Spain)
HED	Hydrogenous Explosive Detection
HMG	Heavy machine-gun
HOLMES	Home Office Large and Major Enquiry System
IATA	International Air Transport Association
ID card	Identification card
IED	Improvised Explosive Device
IFF	Identification Friend or Foe
II	Image intensification
INF	Islamic National Front (Sudan)
INLA	Irish National Liberation Army

IPEC	International Police Exhibition and Conference
IPKF	Indian Peacekeeping Force (Sri Lanka)
IR	Infra-red
IRA	Irish Republican Army
IW	Individual weapon
IZL	Irgun Zvai Leumi (Israel)
JAL	Japanese Airlines
JRA	Japanese Red Army
JVP	(People's Liberation Front) (Sri Lanka)
KGB	(Soviet Intelligence Organization)
KSPI	Kurdish Socialist Party of Iraq
LAW	Light Anti-Tank Weapon
LF	Lebanese Forces
LIPS	Logical inferences per second
LSW	Light support weapon
LTTE	Liberation Tigers of Tamil Eelam (Sri Lanka)
M19	(19 April Movement) (Colombia)
MCLOS	Manual Command to Line of Sight
MIK	(Military Industrial Complex) (Germany)
MNF	Multinational Peacekeeping Force
MNLF	(Moro National Liberation Front) (Philippines)
mps	metres per second
MRTA	(Tupac Amaro Revolutionary Movement) (Peru)
NATO	North Atlantic Treaty Organization
NDF	National Democratic Front (Burma/Philippines)
NPA	New People's Army (Philippines)
PCIED	Projectile Controlled Improvised Explosive Device
PFLP	Popular Front for the Liberation of Palestine
PFLP(GC)	Popular Front for the Liberation of Palestine (General Command)
PIN	Personal Identification Number
PLO	Palestine Liberation Organization
PNTA	Prompt Neutron Thermal Activation
PROD	Photo Retrieval from Optical Disc
PSP	Progressive Socialist Party (Druze-Lebanon)
RAF	Red Army Faction (Germany)
Risc	Reduced instruction set computers

Abbreviations

RUC	Royal Ulster Contabulary
RZ	(Revolutionary Cells) (Germany)
SACLOS	Semi-Automatic Command to Line of Sight
SAM	Surface-to-Air Missile
SAS	Special Air Service Regiment
SEP	Surrendered Enemy Personnel
SL	(Shining Path) (Peru)
SLA	South Lebanon Army
SLAP	Saboted Light Armour Penetration
SLFP	Sri Lanka Freedom Party
SPAS	Special Purpose Automatic Shotgun
SPLA	Sudanese People's Liberation Army
SSM	Surface-to-Surface Missile
STOL	Short Take-Off and Landing
TI	Thermal imagery
UNFDAC	United Nations Fund for Drug Abuse Control
UNP	United National Party (Sri Lanka)
UP	(Patriotic Front) (Colombia)
VDU	Visual display unit
VTOL	Vertical Take-Off and Landing

Prologue

Six years on . . .

A selection of press and radio news reports, June 1996

Gatwick, 2 June   The Air France hijack is over. An SAS rescue force raided the aircraft at 1 am today in total darkness and total silence. We long-suffering hacks were unaware that the attack had gone in until a coach-load of passengers was brought into the terminal.

All appeared to be bemused but unharmed. Mr James Garner, 56, of Wimbledon, said 'I really knew nothing about it. I woke up to find an airport official asking me to leave the aircraft. I don't know how long I'd been asleep.' Others told much the same story. Some conjectured that it might have been an incapacitating gas or low-frequency electromagnetic vibrations which induce unconsciousness. These, however, are believed to take several seconds to cause unconsciousness and it is rumoured that Air France has been testing a high-pressure pulse, a kind of silent blast, which can be operated from either inside or outside the aircraft (from the Control Tower). This is alleged to 'knock out' everyone on board for about ten seconds, and if there were a simultaneous release either of a gas or of low-frequency vibrations, passengers, crew, and hijackers might all have remained unconscious for fifteen or twenty minutes. The SAS were not available for comment. Sussex police said that two men and three women were helping them with their enquiries.

Singapore, 5 June   Millionaire Tan Yekim, 48, was rescued after he had been kidnapped outside a hotel in Orchard Road. The bodyguard had given the alarm and it is believed that Singapore Police were able to trace him by means of an active or passive electronic tag which he carried. This may have been a micro-transmitter, which he could have pushed between the seat cushions in the kidnap car before he was searched.

The police are known to have installed electronic monitors at numerous points in the city, for example on traffic islands and in cables buried under the road surface. These are mainly used to catch vehicles which have not got permits (in the form of tags under the car) to enter the restricted traffic zone. These permit tags are 'passive', that is they react to a transmission from the monitor and it is conceivable that Mr Tan may have had no more than a passive tag somewhere on his body, possibly in the form of a fluid used as a hair-dressing. When the monitor recorded Mr Tan's tag (active or passive) it would also have noted the registration number of the car, as this presumably did carry a permit tag, since without one the kidnappers' car would have been quickly tracked by the responses triggered by an unauthorized vehicle passing the monitor.

Frankfurt, 7 June Five men were arrested yesterday at Frankfurt Airport and charged with conspiracy to hijack. All are said to be of Middle Eastern origin. Along with other passengers without International Air Travel Permits (machine-readable cards now carried by the great majority of EC passengers) they were questioned for about fifteen minutes shortly before they were due to board a Lufthansa flight for Riyadh. An airport spokesman said: 'We checked eight or ten points from their passports and from our supplementary questions. These were fed into the national computer, which was able to reveal suspicious links between these five, although they were travelling separately. We called them out of the boarding lounge for further questioning and search. One had a telephone number in his diary which led us to an aircraft cleaner, who was then also questioned, and a search of the aircraft revealed a bag containing pistols and ammunition in the towel compartment in one of the toilets. Two of the others resisted search and it became evident that they did in fact know each other.' The other passengers were allowed to board and the aircraft took off an hour late.

Manchester, 8 June After a call from security staff at a computer company, police today arrested a man claiming to be a welder, Charles Thompson, employed by a firm which has a maintenance contract on the premises. His identity card appeared to be valid but a fingerprint scan, referred to the national police computer, revealed that he was not Charles Thompson but a man wanted for forgery.

London, 15 June A man riddled with bullets in Mayfair yesterday is believed to be the 125th victim of London's drug war this year and also a member of the Huallaga gang, which has been making a monopoly bid for the trade in 'crack', the popular cocaine derivative.

Dublin, 19th June   A consignment of explosives, with multiple sealed wrappings to defeat the vapour-sniffers and dogs, was detected by neutron bombardment in the cargo sheds at Dublin Airport. Like all explosives manufactured in the USA and in west and east Europe, including the USSR, it was tagged with colour-coded particles, which will enable not only its manufacturing source, but also every legal movement it has made since, to be traced on the internationally linked police computer network.

Zurich, 21 June   The system for monitoring of international bank transfer, initiated by a consortium of Swiss and Japanese banks in 1992, was further extended today with the accession of all the state banks in the USSR and China, who have recently made common cause with the west in fighting international terrorism and drug traffic. The EC countries, the USA, Canada, Australia, New Zealand, and all the newly industrialized countries in East Asia, are already members and Argentina, Brazil, and Chile have expressed their intention of joining. Using fine-grained parallel computers, the member banks can trace the most complex sources and disposals of money in a few seconds and will make this information available to the police if ordered by the Courts to do so. This has proved invaluable in the fight against crime, and especially in detecting the laundering of money from extortion and drug deals. This money is commonly dispersed very rapidly in small amounts to different accounts in different countries. Thus far, the missing links in the chain have been certain Third World banks, which are happy to take and pass on money but refuse to co-operate with the police in tracing it. After the latest accessions it is expected that all the member banks will be required by their governments to boycott any dealings with banks which do not subscribe to the scheme. It is hoped that virtually 100 per cent of banks will have joined by 1998.

And nine years on . . .

Milan, 25 May 1999   A group of top businessmen in Milan, which had one of the highest kidnap rates in the world, seem to have solved the problem of being ambushed on the road. They live in a heavily protected 'country club' containing a number of blocks of luxury flats, whose roofs act as flight decks, with their microlite VTOL aircraft stored in hangers immediately below. These are powered by four revolutionary 'Featherweight' engines, developed by the European Aerospace Corporation which weigh less than 20 kg, but the four engines produce jets powerful enough to lift the aircraft with two people on board. The engine with its fuel is delivered in a sealed package, which is exchanged complete after a stated number of hours. The makers are cagey about the design and have dismissed as 'conjectural' reports that it relies on a new process of nuclear fusion. The aircraft have easy manoeuvrability, and can hover, fly sideways, and stop as quickly as a car by rotating the jets. They are equipped with the new 'Batman' radar system. According to one regular user: 'Even when the airways are crowded, it is much easier to avoid collision than on crowded roads – or amongst yachts milling around off Cowes. And, of course, the baddies have no idea which of the birds in the flock is mine. I have never travelled so safely in my life.'

Part one

Fighting under the nuclear umbrella

Chapter one

Introduction

6 February 1989 was the 15,982nd day since the end of the Second World War, overtaking the longest previous period without an unlimited war between major powers (15,981 days or 43½ years), that is between the end of the Franco-Prussian War in 1871 and the start of the First World War. While there have been some prolonged local conflicts with horrific casualties (e.g. the Iran-Iraq War of 1980–8) all the fighting has been strictly limited and localized.

There have been many other conflicts since the nuclear umbrella was erected in August 1945, including those in Korea, Suez, and Vietnam; also the short sharp Indo-Pakistan and Arab-Israeli wars, and fairly substantial border clashes on the Chinese borders with the USSR, India, and Vietnam. All of these involved conventional operations between uniformed armies using artillery and aircraft. Although one side or the other (very occasionally both – e.g. the USSR and China when they clashed in 1969 on the Ussuri River) had access to nuclear weapons, there was never the slightest risk of their being used.

Virtually every other conflict since 1945 can be classed as guerrilla warfare or terrorism. Though some have been extremely bloody (for example, 70,000 killed in El Salvador out of a population of 6 million in eight years), the weapons have mainly been hand-held firearms or hand-placed bombs. The killing has been more personal and more calculatedly cruel than in fighting between conventional armies.

Though some of the guerrilla conflicts have been international (e.g. by the Palestinians), their primary causes have usually been internal between rival communities or by dissidents hoping to overturn their government. They have, however, been exploited by foreign powers: sometimes by neighbours bent on annexation (e.g. by North Vietnam in South Vietnam from 1959 to 1972, culminating in conventional military invasions in 1972 and 1975);

and sometimes from far away (e.g. by Cuba on behalf of the USSR in Africa and Central America, and by the USA in Nicaragua and Afghanistan). Exploitation, sometimes amounting to sponsorship, of internal conflicts has largely supplanted invasion and bombardment since 1945 as the principal means of using force to further foreign policy objectives.

Developing technology has played an increasing part in this type of conflict, both by guerrillas and terrorists, and by those fighting against them. Recent examples have been the precise time delay fuse in the bomb planted by the IRA in Brighton in 1984, heat-seeking surface-to-air missiles used by the Mujahideen in Afghanistan, and sophisticated surveillance and computerized intelligence systems used in Northern Ireland and Germany.

There is absolutely no sign of this type of conflict declining, because it is more cost effective than conventional war and because it carries less risk of escalation. And both sides will clearly continue to use any effective technological aids that they can afford.

The second chapter of Part I looks at the spectrum of political conflict which has emerged under the nuclear umbrella, ranging from 'agit-prop' and street disorder, through guerrilla warfare and terrorism, to civil war and invasion.

Part II, which amounts to about one-third of the book (six chapters) examines current and potential technological developments, as they affect weapons, choice of terrorist targets, and the means of countering terrorism by better intelligence and security.

Part III looks at the quite horrific effect of drug-trafficking on both rural and urban terrorism, amongst the producers and processors in the Third World, the international traffickers, and the consumers on the streets of affluent western societies. This part concludes that the cure lies in determined action by western governments in their own countries to cut off the demand.

Part IV examines the organization, tactics, and trends in rural guerrilla warfare, both in conducting and in countering it, and assesses the likely effects of both political and technological change.

Part V does the same for urban terrorism.

Part VI considers some nightmare scenarios of what could happen if the world fails to contain these attempts to destabilize it, and it strikes a balance between determined action to counter them and the price these could involve in the sacrifice of civil liberties.

Chapter two

The spectrum of political conflict

The bulwarks of a pluralist society

The deepest anxiety amongst ordinary people in a community arises when they perceive a threat of collapse of order and security; lest the lives of their families have no protection against armed intruders or rampaging mobs; and lest their property, their food stocks, and their savings become vulnerable to seizure or destruction without hope of restitution. This has been so for at least 12,000 years, since people first set up agricultural communities and villages, when survival and prosperity began manifestly to depend upon confidence that their crops and domestic animals would safely mature to provide their food, and that women and children would not be abducted while the men were hunting or working in the fields – in other words, that there was internal security under a rule of law with a collective means to enforce it. Then, as a village agricultural community became more prosperous than the nomadic tribes outside, external security also became essential lest the hungry tribesmen swarmed in to seize the animals and fertile fields and put the villagers to death or into bondage. Thus security and the rule of law were from the start and still remain the foundations of civilized society.

As societies developed, security and the rule of law became more complex. Villages organized themselves into mutually supporting settlements, sharing the land between them. Later they improved their defences against marauding bands with forts and walled cities. Cities grew into city states and groups of cities and settlements coalesced into nations. The larger the communities grew, the more complex became the hierarchy required to maintain security and enforce the law. These hierarchies threw up strong men as chiefs or kings, and other strong men emerged to challenge them from within. Such societies were autocratic until the Greek city states developed the idea of democracy, with the chief thereby gaining the loyalty and moral support of the majority. Rival interest groups – merchants, scholars, farmers, soldiers, priests, and public officials – consolidated to strengthen their influence and the equilibrium of pluralism emerged. To maintain control, the hierarchy needed information about the plans and intrigues of these interest groups, competing for power and influence, so a third element became essential to security and the rule of law – intelligence.

Pluralist societies, with all their instabilities, are inherently more durable than authoritarian societies because they are founded on a network of popular consents. The 1980s have provided dramatic evidence that the traditionally authoritarian societies – the USSR, China, and the Latin American countries – are moving towards pluralism, with only some of the African countries lagging behind the trend. But the short-term strengths of the authoritarian states may remain a threat to the pluralist societies for a long time to come; there is a real possibility that the development of information technology may reverse the present trend and lead some governments to become more rather than less authoritarian to retain control of their people.

The bulwarks of stability in a pluralist society are very slender. These bulwarks – security, intelligence, and the rule of law – are maintained by the security forces (police and army), the intelligence services, and the judiciary. If these become weak or corrupt, the rising tide of drug abuse, crime, political violence, public disorder, and civil war can all too easily sweep the bulwarks away, leading to an authoritarian government of the right (most commonly the army) or the left (usually a professionally organized Marxist revolutionary party).

Destabilization and terrorism

The process of destabilization has been developed over the ages and then rationalized and documented in the twentieth century. It has been used against both authoritarian and pluralist societies, the authoritarian societies being the quickest to crack: Tsarist Russia, Kuomintang China, French Indochina, French Algeria, Batista's Cuba, Haile Selassie's Ethiopia, and Somoza's Nicaragua. A few pluralist societies have succumbed, but seldom to a left-wing revolution. More often, the threat of that provokes a right-wing takeover – as in Italy in 1922 and the Weimar Republic of Germany in 1933 – but in both cases their pluralism was shallow-rooted. Peru – whose democracy also lacks depth – is currently under determined attack. Many other pluralist democracies, however, have been seriously challenged in the last half-century – including France, Greece, Italy, and the Northern Irish Province of the United Kingdom – and these challenges will undoubtedly continue. There are recognizable though overlapping phases: organization and 'agit-prop', street disorder, intimidation, terrorism, making the law unworkable, and achieving a climate of collapse.

Organization and **agit-prop**, in which members of the public are openly aroused to discontent with their grievances; the more responsive ones are then discreetly organized, initially as sympathizers, later as auxiliaries, and finally as members of clandestine revolutionary cells.

Street disorder is organized and grows as discontent gathers momentum, whether the result leads to something worse (e.g. in Germany in 1934) or better (in the Philippines in 1986 and in South Korea in 1987). Demonstrations burgeon into large-scale rioting, which usually draws an increasingly violent and repressive response, particularly if the police or army begin to fear that their lines may break and the disorder get out of control. Repression arouses further public discontent as friends and family members are arrested or come home bloody and broken. The police and the public become polarized as 'them and us'.

Intimidation of police officers, government officials, and members of the public who support them is usually organized in parallel with the street demonstrations. Police officers may get isolated from their units and lynched; others may be attacked or threatened in their homes. Collaborators may be attacked or, more commonly, intimidated by slogans daubed on their homes or victimization of their children at school: the bully-boy tactics so effectively used by Hitler's Brownshirts in 1923–34.

Terrorism is a lethal form of intimidation and, because penalties for murder are severe, it is usually done clandestinely. Selected revolutionary cells are assigned as hit squads, which target individual ministers, national and (especially) local government officials, and suspected informers. One purpose is to cow the officials into a tacit 'live-and-let-live' performance of their duties. This may, from the terrorists' viewpoint, be even better than killing them, because tolerating complaisant incumbents who give an outward appearance of exercising government authority may be preferable to having them replaced by a tougher successor who will enforce the law. In South Vietnam in the late 1960s, for example, there were many villages in which the local officials operated freely by day, issuing licences and permits and collecting taxes, but they and their policemen and soldiers all moved out to spend the night in a defended compound *outside* the village. This suited the Vietcong perfectly. Visiting politicians, bureaucrats, and journalists, seeing the local official working without any apparent worries in his office, with the flag flying outside and a uniformed guard at the door, would report the village to be 'under government control'. But the inhabitants and the official himself knew otherwise; the real control rested with the Vietcong cadres *inside* the village, who emerged after dark to cut the throat of anyone who had done anything positive against them – beyond acceptable tasks like growing food, serving in shops, or repairing the roads. In particular, anyone who was suspected of acting as a police informer was unlikely to survive more than a few nights. And if the local official himself went beyond what the Vietcong would tolerate, he would be killed (sometimes with members of his family) in such a way as to deter others from seeking his job, other than on the basis of conforming to the requirements discreetly notified to him by the cadres.

Other opinion-formers, such as journalists and teachers, may be terrorized into following – or at least not criticizing – the revolutionary line; and intimidation of employers helps to disrupt the economy. But those involved in enforcing the law are probably the most cost-effective targets.

Making the law unworkable is perhaps the most important aim of terrorism. By being targeted and seeing others die, witnesses are deterred from giving evidence ('I saw nothing'); juries and sometimes even judges dare not convict. Liberal forms of law may have to be suspended with, for example, trial without juries for terrorist offences (as has been the case in the Republic of Ireland since 1962 and Northern Ireland since 1973) and evidence accepted from witnesses not required to show their faces or undergo cross-examination. Such emergency laws are manifestly less fair than the liberal processes of law which they replace so that there is more risk of injustice and less public confidence in the judiciary and the rule of law. This is precisely what the terrorist wants.

A climate of collapse may be achieved without the revolutionaries' ever needing to advance beyond the stage of street disorder, intimidation, and selective terrorist killings. Power changed hands in Petrograd in 1917, in Italy in 1922, in Germany in 1933, and in the Philippines in 1986 without mass bloodshed or civil war. The essential ingredient of a 'climate of collapse' is for loss of confidence to spread amongst both the public and the government and its officers so that the public begins to doubt not only the ability but also the will of the government, the judiciary, and the police to enforce its own laws. Rioters and terrorists get a sense of impunity and strike out more boldly. Vigilante groups emerge to take the law into their own hands. People become alarmed at the prospect of a collapse of order, with no work, no money, no food in the shops, no water, no transport: in fact a collapse of the means of livelihood for themselves and their families. In these circumstances, they will clutch at whatever straw offers the best hope of restoring order, whether that be a right-wing dictator (the commonest solution) or a highly organized revolutionary party (as in Petrograd in 1917 and Nicaragua in 1978). For most people faced with a climate of collapse, family survival matters more than politics.

Guerrilla and civil wars

Sometimes, however, governments hold on and the selective terrorist killings escalate into guerrilla war. This may be urban or rural or both, but killings are measured in thousands instead of dozens or hundreds. The other characteristic is that the guerrillas try to create 'no-go areas' in which the government's writ no longer runs. A first stage of this may be that police officers and local government officials 'live-and-let-live' by going through the motions of their duties by day but lying low at night, as was described on pp. 7–8 in the context of Vietnam. The next stage is for even the appearance of government to be withdrawn and the 'no-go area' becomes a 'liberated area'.

When liberated areas spread and link up, the revolutionaries can openly establish their own government and reorganize their guerrilla forces into overt military units to enforce their own form of public order and mobilize the people into armies with which to drive back the government forces.

The conflict has by then become a civil war. The commonest pattern is for the remoter areas to be liberated first, sometimes including the marginal areas, and shanty towns on the fringes of big cities. From here the revolutionary government spreads into more economically active agricultural regions, provincial towns, and city suburbs until, eventually, the big cities or city centres are isolated and, with the growth of internal disorder, can be picked one by one like ripe plums. A number of examples of past and contemporary guerrilla warfare, and civil wars, and trends for the future, are discussed in Part IV.

Proxy war and invasion

Successful guerrilla movements often, though by no means always, receive support from outside. If guerrilla warfare escalates into civil war, such support habitually continues and occasionally the supporting power has finished off the conflict with an overt military invasion. The most complete example of this was the take-over of South Vietnam by North Vietnam. This began in 1955–8, when cadres from the newly independent North came clandestinely South as agit-prop teams to arouse and organize the villagers. In 1959–60 this developed into terrorism (especially intimidating local officials as described above) and guerrilla warfare. In response to the deployment of US military advisers in the South, soldiers from North Vietnam came South to reinforce the Vietcong, and by 1965 the North Vietnamese regular army formed the major part of the guerrilla force in the South. After the US forces withdrew from the combat role from 1970 onwards this grew into civil war, with an unsuccessful attempt at invasion in 1972, culminating in a successful invasion in 1975. The world has been kept aware of the agony of the conquered South Vietnamese by the continual flood of refugees – the boat people – out of the country ever since.

When the possibility of an invasion is contemplated, a systematic campaign may be conducted internally, with external aid and encouragement, to weaken the target country's ability to withstand civil war or invasion. This consists of a combination of subversion and espionage, though the sponsoring power usually keeps the two activities separate. This is, first, because they are carried out by different kinds of people with different kinds of contacts, and second, because citizens trying to undermine the organs of the state by subversion will hope to attract a modicum of popular support, which would quickly be lost if they were found to be spying or linked with others spying on behalf of a foreign country.

Countering destabilization and insurgency

Since the prime purpose of destabilization is to break the **rule of law**, the first essential in countering it is to ensure that soldiers, police, intelligence officers, and others claiming to support the government do themselves act within the law. If the law is inadequate, the remedy is not to act outside it but to get it changed. That can be done quite quickly in a democracy. The Prevention of Terrorism Act in Britain was introduced and rushed through all its stages in Parliament within a week after two IRA bombs in Birmingham had killed twenty-one people in 1974. This can be facilitated by having emergency legislation ready in draft to answer foreseeable contingencies, so that it can quickly be revised or adapted if the need for it suddenly arises. In a more compelling crisis (e.g. one in which there is a real risk of massive loss of life unless action is taken immediately) the enactment could be completed even more quickly than in 1974, though it is important that it should incorporate a specific date for early review by Parliament and for regular review thereafter (as has been done with the Prevention of Terrorism Act). The Republic of Ireland, France, Germany, and Italy have all, in recent years, had to introduce emergency legislation to meet terrorist activity (see Chapter 19).

By the same token it is important to deal firmly with vigilante groups if they take the law into their own hands in fury and frustration with the failure of their governments to contain terrorism. Any attempt, whether by vigilantes ('death squads') or over-zealous security force members, to 'fight terror with terror' must be ruthlessly suppressed.

Under this umbrella of the rule of law within the law, the tactics of countering destabilization must be built round security and intelligence.

Security is the baseline without which there will be no intelligence because, unless they fell confident that they can and will be protected, members of the public will not dare to give information about the terrorists. This security must not just be a daytime facade as described above in Vietnam; it must also provide adequate police watch and ward by night. Security and intelligence are, in fact, interdependent, since effective counter-terrorist activities depend on good information.

As with any other forms of conflict there will be ebb and flow, local set-backs, and local victories. On occasions, the ability of insurgents to concentrate strong forces in areas where they dominate the local population and have a virtual monopoly of eyes and ears, the police and army may be able to operate only by forays by powerful military formations and there will therefore be times when certain inhabited districts become 'no-go areas'. Where this arises it is urgent to re-establish a permanent security force presence to reassert the enforcement of government law (in place of coercion by terror under the name of 'people's justice') as quickly as possible. The longer the insurgents retain control, the more they will seek out and eliminate individuals likely to give information to the security forces when they return.

Where a country is in the grip of a major insurgency there may

11

be large 'liberated areas'. In that case the best strategy is to restore the government's writ first in those areas where it will be easiest to restore them, that is where popular support for the insurgents is weakest. Elimination of terrorist activity in these areas will then rebuild public confidence in neighbouring areas that the government does have the will and the ability to reassert control. This will ease the task of dealing with tougher districts and then, at the last, overwhelming strength will be available to concentrate on the hardest core areas of all.

Intelligence comes from technical and human sources. Valuable though technical intelligence can be, human intelligence is decisive. Creating an intelligence system and then building up the flow of intelligence through it are, however, long and arduous processes. To prosper, they must grow in parallel with the development of a climate of public confidence at two levels: confidence that the government will, in the end, prevail, and confidence that individuals who co-operate with the government will have their identities protected, and therefore that they and their families will not suffer. Once these basic levels of confidence have been established, it should be possible to turn the uncommitted public against the idea of change being brought about by violence. These are the bulk of ordinary people who are more concerned about family safety than about political conflict, and normally comprise more than 80 per cent of the population, even in the most strife-torn communities.

The intelligence system couples the hardware to acquire technical intelligence (e.g. by interception and electronic surveillance) with a network of handlers, safe houses, and so on for acquiring human intelligence. To collate, analyse, and evaluate this can be greatly facilitated by electronic data storage and processing, and some of the possible developments of this are examined later in the book. Computers, however, can as yet only assist and extend the capacity of human brains, not replace them, and ultimately the quality of intelligence will depend on people – the staffs, agents, and informers who comprise an intelligence organization.

Intelligence can be divided into background information and contact information. Background information comes from a mass of largely overt sources – studying facts and statistics, monitoring publications and broadcasts, briefing police officers and soldiers on what to look for and report in the course of normal duties, and providing a safe channel for casual information from the public. Contact information is what enables the security forces to find their enemies by knowing their intentions or likely actions *in advance*, and is more delicate. It normally comes either from technical sources (e.g. intercepts) or from covert informers in contact with or living in the environment of the insurgents, guer-rillas, or terrorist cells, or of those who support them.

While spies have sometimes been infiltrated into revolutionary or terrorist cells, it is far more common to achieve success by 'turning' someone who is already in the cell system or is an auxili-ary who has contact with them (e.g. the couriers, cut-outs, or suppliers, who are the links between clandestine cells and their supporters amongst the public). 'Turning' is the intelligence jargon for persuading such a person to become an informer. This may be best achieved by spotting a participant whose heart is not in it or who, for personal or family reasons, wants to 'get off the hook'. Pressure to turn may be exercised by arousing fear of prosecution or by offering rewards, perhaps large enough to enable the informer to go far away, with his family, to start a new life with a new identity. An essential feature is that the informer is made confident that he and his family will be protected against retri-bution. Examples of successful recruitment and subsequent hand-ling of such informers are given in Parts IV and V of this book, including the sometimes spectacular cases of the 'super SEPs' in Malaya, the 'supergrasses' in Northern Ireland, and the *pentiti* in Italy.

There is nothing more demoralizing to hard-core revolutionaries or terrorists than the fear that people inside their movement or trusted supporters amongst the public are giving information. They will try to stifle it by ruthless exemplary punishments, but this increases the desire of the waverers to get off the hook: to avoid being caught between the Scylla of government surveillance and the Charybdis of terrorist reprisal. As sympathizers are detected and terrorists arrested, they are increasingly ready to be turned if this offers the best hope of escape from intolerable insecurity.

As this leads to further arrests, and to more districts' being freed from the scourge of violence, this same urge spreads to other districts still afflicted, where the people look with envy at neighbourhoods no longer subject to the cross-fire of terrorists and soldiers and, as it becomes clearer that the terrorists are not going to win, there is a growing incentive to get rid of them. Demoralization of the terrorists and their supporters yields more defectors, the flow of information becomes a flood, and the whole movement begins to crumble. Even though a residue of violence and defiance may persist, if there is no hope of victory or popular support it declines into a fringe of violent criminals; the threat of destabilization, insurgency, and civil war has been removed.

Part two

Technological development

Chapter three

Terrorist targets in the 1990s

The microelectronics revolution

The microelectronics boom, the fifth industrial revolution, will continue to be the fastest industrial revolution of all time, especially in the fields of robotics and information technology. In 1970, 40 per cent of the working population in industrial countries were employed in productive industries, that is manufacturing or extractive (e.g. mining, agriculture, etc). By the early 1980s this had fallen to 30 per cent, with 60 per cent in service industries, and 10 per cent unemployed. By the year 2000 we may well see only about 10 per cent in productive industries and 80–90 per cent in service industries, the biggest growth being in the leisure industries. Moreover, the proper harnessing of robotics and information technology should not only eliminate the drudgery of the assembly line and paper-pushing, but also enable us to reduce the standard working week to about thirty hours if we wish. Many more people will be able to work at home.

With so much more time and energy saved by shorter hours and freedom from rush-hour travel, there will be a growth not only in DIY (do it yourself) but also in moonlighting: mainly by bartering useful services within the neighbourhood, for example, 'I'll repair your computer terminal if you'll baby-sit for us'. This will raise the standard of living but leave still more money to be spent on travel and leisure. However, this can all be poisoned through the malign influences of drugs, violence, and lust for money and power, which are the interlocking themes running through this book.

The flood of information already pouring into every household will further explode with access to up to fifty television channels, by cable and satellite, mostly in pictorial form which gives greater ability to manipulate the emotions. Authoritarian governments will take control of these sources to exercise a tighter grip on the minds of their people. Pluralist societies, maintaining the principle of freedom of speech and communication, will allow all sources to use this access to people's minds with only the loosest restraints on flagrant pornography and incitement to violence and crime. These restrictions will be easily overcome, and there will be a bonanza for mind-benders, including foreign mind-benders through the satellite aerials, all of whom will dress up their messages in appetizing and entertaining programmes. The opportunities for propaganda by official sources, commercial interests, determined minorities, and foreign governments will be immense. Unlike the authoritarian societies, the pluralist societies will be much more vulnerable to destabilization; though if this over-reaches itself to the extent of alarming the mainstream of the public, it may lead pluralist governments to ride on a tide of populism to become more authoritarian themselves.

Vulnerability of the sinews of the new society

The sinews of the post-industrial society are already taking shape – the network of electronic data-processing and communications – and these sinews are already becoming more vulnerable to disruption and terrorism. The service industries, in particular, are increasingly inter-independent, and ripe for attack by fraudsters, hackers, eavesdroppers, disrupters, and extortionists.

Economies of scale have now concentrated vast amounts of data-processing into huge main computer centres, sometimes at the heart of a giant multinational corporation, and sometimes in a communal centre run by the big computer firms, with a mass of hardware serving corporations all over a large city. The data come in, are automatically processed, and go out, untouched by human operators and totally secure – except against the hacker and the electronic eavesdropper. The computer centre itself is vulnerable to sabotage, and to extortion by the threat to damage or disrupt it. Software is especially vulnerable to malicious disruption or espionage, and the volume of business is now so great that many cannot afford the expense of software duplication. Cable communications can be tapped and radio communications intercepted – subject to a constant battle between defence (e.g. by encryption and burst transmission) and interception (by code-breaking or unscrambling). Fibre-optics currently offer the best security against interception but here too the technological battle between attack and defence will continue.

Cash, electronic transfer, and extortion

Cash is needed less and less. As well as credit cards, there are debit cards which can transfer money direct from a buyer's to a seller's bank account, with no more than the tapping of numbers on the keyboard. The principle of the green phone-card, bought anywhere (with a credit card instead of cash), where residual value is electronically recorded on the card for each minute on the telephone, could be extended to almost every day-to-day transaction, from paying a bus fare to buying a cup of coffee. The tills of the supermarket check-out will steadily be replaced by electronic diodes and debit cards. The last surviving Edwardian pay-days in cash through a window will surely be phased out by the early 1990s. Electronic transfer will dominate the market-place so there will be less and less cash in the pocket, in the tills, in the safes, in the bank vaults, and (most vulnerable of all) in the bags of money in the security vans plying the streets of the city centres and suburban shopping areas. Opportunities for theft and robbery will decline and they will largely be replaced by fraud and extortion.

Fraud involves criminal abuse of this electronic system. Extortion involves applying pressure to induce a person who has a legitimate key to it to transfer or release the money. This pressure may be exerted by kidnap, or the threat of murder, maiming, product contamination, bombing, arson, sabotage, or disruption (e.g. of the computer system).

A new and developing art form is the disposal and laundering of this money. One way is through conversion into drugs, which have become an international currency with a huge circulation and, after a few transactions, almost impossible to trace. Another way is through multiple transfers between international banks.

An extortionist may make the acceptance of a ransom or black-mail payment conditional on its being electronically transferred to a named bank in a foreign country, or perhaps split between many different banks in different countries. This can now be done within a few seconds. In most civilized industrial countries (including Switzerland, despite a myth to the contrary) bank accounts can be made available, if ordered by the Courts, to government or police inspection if a case can be made out that money in the account was acquired by criminal means. This, however, takes time, and a sophisticated international criminal or terrorist group will have installed accomplices with legal access to these accounts to transfer it quickly to others in other countries. Moreover, there are many Third World banks which do not permit official inspection of suspect accounts, and certainly not at the request of the authorities outside the country. The criminal or terrorist has only to process the money through one, or better still two, of these banks to ensure that it cannot be traced; $12 million acquired by the Colombian M19 movement in the early 1980s and transferred in this way have never been traced and probably never will be. It can be (and some no doubt has been) transferred piecemeal by these means back to a perfectly respectable bank in Colombia, held by an apparently respectable pillar of the establishment who collaborates with M19, for use as required. Where drugs are involved, the amounts of money available are ample for the rewarding of such collaborators world-wide. These problems, and possible answers to them, are discussed further in Part III and Chapter 19.

As will be illustrated in some case studies in later chapters, there is a great overlap in these fields, and between both of them and corrupt officials, politicians, and businessmen, not only in Third World countries but also in some of the advanced countries.

The Military Industrial Complex (MIK)

In western Europe (and especially Germany) there has for ten years been a growing movement to attack the so-called Military Industrial Complex (MIK is the German acronym, now widely used elsewhere). This was largely initiated by anti-NATO and 'Peace' movements, not necessary pro-Russian, but anti-capitalist, and partly motivated by frustration with inability to attract any mass response from the lumpenproletariat. They have attracted a large number of collaborators, including environmentalists, animal rights activists, and fringe movements of all kinds seeking the strength and security of membership of a bigger grouping.

These groups also embrace both overt pressure groups (which rely on demonstrations coupled with disruption and sabotage) and clandestine terrorist groups such as the German Revolutionary Cells (RZ), the Red Army Faction (RAF), and the French *Action Directe* (AD). By far the commonest means of disruption and sabotage are bombing and arson.

Targets have obviously included military installations and defence industries, but the MIK is also more widely interpreted to embrace all high-tech industries, telecommunications, construction, transport (especially air transport and airfields because of their environmental overtones), energy of all kinds, and especially nuclear power stations. Most of these targets are highly dependent on computer networks, as described above.

Human targets

People, however, remain the most effective targets for terrorists. Though the damage done by bombing and arson in Germany is enormous, its impact on the decision-maker in the MIK targets is relatively small, because it is generally covered by insurance or government compensation. The prospect of death, injury, or kidnap (including kidnap of families), however, causes him far greater concern.

This applies also to the public at large because, if the price of giving information to the police may be death or loss of a member of the family, many people will keep their mouths shut. This, as described elsewhere in the book, is particularly effective in making the law unworkable by intimidating witnesses and juries, and also in deterring 'opinion formers' from speaking out – journalists, teachers, civil servants, and politicians.

As in many quite lawful human activities, the aim of the political terrorist and criminals is power, measured in terms of keeping options open and exercising influence or control over other people, and the acquisition of money which provides this power and influence.

Chapter four

Personal weapons

A mature market

Personal weapons fired at short ranges are the primary weapons of the guerrilla and terrorist and of the policeman and soldier fighting them, and the first impression gained from comparing personal weapons is that they have changed a lot less in the last fifty years than other weapons (such as missiles, artillery, and aircraft). They have been little affected by the great technological revolutions in nuclear, electronic, and aerodynamic guidance and control systems. And metal has clung tenaciously to its predominance over plastics in small arms and ammunition. As a result, the changes in such things as weight, range, and rates of fire have not been dramatic (see Table 1).

The most significant change in personal weapons is probably the controlled burst: this comprises a setting between single shot and sustained automatic fire whereby the gun fires a short controlled burst of three rounds (or other choices). In some cases, e.g. the Heckler & Koch 4.7 G11 assault rifle, the three rounds leave the barrel before the gun has time to kick and this can give a very tight grouping. Even without the G11's facility, three-round bursts conserve ammunition and give more effective fire for normal use. Another development, which may well go further, is the use of caseless ammunition, obviating the need to eject a cartridge. Plastic ammunition has thus far been designed primarily for training but could be effective at short ranges where the use of metal rounds could be undesirable, e.g. in executing or countering a hijack. An attempt has been made to develop a gun in which everything, including bullets, screws, springs, and firing mechanisms, is non-metallic. If developed and proved, these will not only be lighter but also be more likely to evade detection at airport hand-baggage checks (as will be discussed in chapter 7).

Most experts, however, are sceptical about its being a working proposition.

Closely linked with weapons are the sights: the laser sight, in particular, may enable terrorists to fire accurately from a briefcase without appearing to be carrying a gun or taking aim, as described later. And the development of night vision equipment – infra-red (IR), image intensification (II), and thermal imagery (TI) – will also have an increasing effect on the options available for the use of weapons in attack and defence. But sophisticated night vision sights can cost ten times as much as the weapon itself.

This chapter looks at developments in ammunition, then at the most revolutionary of weapons under trial, the German G11 assault rifle, then briefly at other rifles and sights and finally at sub-machine-guns and machine pistols.

Ammunition

There are three main areas of contemporary debate about small arms ammunition: calibre, stopping power, and the use of caseless ammunition.

The great majority of sub-machine-guns, pistols, and machine pistols fire 9mm short, blunt bullets, with low muzzle velocity, designed for use at ranges of 100 m at most (usually much less) but with good stopping power. Some use 7.62 and even 5.45 mm ammunition, e.g. the very small Soviet PSM police pistol, designed for concealed carrying, whose bullet is probably designed to be unstable so that it tumbles as it hits the target and stops rather than penetrates.

Calibres around 7.62 remain the commonest ammunition for machine-guns, combining long range with stability and good ballistic qualities. For infantry personal weapons, however, most armies have now switched over to smaller calibres to save weight, with higher muzzle velocities, such as the 5.56 Armalite or M16. These have a shorter effective range (450 rather than 600 m) but infantry weapons (other than snipers' rifles) are very seldom fired at more than 300 m in any case. The revolutionary Heckler and Koch G11 fires 4.7 mm caseless ammunition at a very high cyclic rate (discussed on pp. 27–30)

The weight of 4.7 ammunition is about half that of 5.56 mm, and the weight of 5.56 mm is about half that of 7.62 mm, but many experienced combat soldiers have doubts about the stopping power of the 5.56 bullet in close-quarter combat. With its high muzzle velocity and stable flight, it is likely to penetrate a soft target at short range and tumbles only when it hits at longer range.

Table 1 Examples of small arms development

Period	Weapon	Origin	Weight (loaded) (kg)	Length (mm)	Muzzle velocity (mps)	Cyclic* rate of fire (rds/min)	Remarks
Rifles (including assault rifles)							
1930s (WW2)	.303 Lee Enfield No 4 Rifle	UK	4.10	1,130	751	20	manual
1950s (current)	7.62 L1A1	UK	4.30	1,143	838	40	semi-automatic single shot
Late 1960s (current)	5.56 Armalite M16 A2	USA	3.58	940	1,000	800	fully automatic three-round burst
Late 1970s (current)	5.45 AK74/AKS/74	USSR	4.70(?)	930 (690 AKS)	900	650	bullet nose distorts to cause tumble
Late 1980s	5.56 L85 A1 (IW)	UK	4.98	785	940	600–850	optical or II sight with grenade launcher
Late 1980s (user trials)	4.7 G11 Heckler & Koch	FRG	4.30	750	930	600 2,000	automatic three-round burst
Light machine-guns							
1930s (WW2)	.303 Bren Mk III	UK	8.76	1,080	744	480	
Late 1980s	5.56 L86 A1 (LSW)	UK	6.88	900	970	700 (to 850)	same system as 5.56 L85A1 rifle

Period	Weapon	Origin	Weight loaded (kg)	Length with stock (mm)	Length without stock (mm)	Muzzle velocity (mps)	Cyclic rate of fire (rds/min)	Remarks
	Sub-machine-guns							
1920s	Thompson .45	USA	5.37	810	NA	282	700	
1941 (WW2)	9 mm Sten, Mark II	UK	3.44	762	NA	366	550	
1950s	9 mm Ingram Model 11	USA	2.10	460	222	293	1,200	
1960s	9 mm MP5 Heckler & Koch	FRG	2.73	660	490	400	800	
1970s	9 mm MP5 KA1 Heckler & Koch	FRG	2.52	NA	325	375	900	with three-round burst
1983	9 mm Spectre	Italy	3.10	580	350	400	900	double action

Sources: Jane's Infantry Weapons 1987–88, London, Jane's, 1987, and manufacturers' specifications

Note: * Manufacturers' specifications and textbooks usually quote the 'cyclic rate', i.e. the number of rounds the gun would fire in a sustained burst of one minute. This, of course, is purely theoretical, and it is easier for the non-expert to visualize the performance of the gun in rounds per second by dividing by 60, e.g. a gun with a cyclic rate of 600 fires 10 rounds per second.

A Royal Marine in the Falklands campaign complained that he fired his Armalite four times at an oncoming enemy soldier at 20 metres and he still kept on coming.

The Soviet 5.45 bullet fired by the AK 74 Kalashnikov rifle is tapered at the base (boat-tailed – see Figure 1). Inside the streamlined jacket it has a steel core with a small lead plug in front; in front of this again is a 3 mm air gap inside the nose of the bullet. This not only brings the centre of gravity back but also causes the nose to bend over on hitting even soft targets at short range so that is has quite good stopping power. The bullet does not fragment, however, and it is fragmentation which causes the most serious wounds.

Figure 1   The Soviet 5.45 bullet

Caseless ammunition is also a recent innovation which is likely to develop in one or more of several current designs. The principal idea is to dispense with the cartridge in order to save weight and avoid the propensity for jamming involved in its ejection. In the German G11 ammunition (4.7 mm) the propellant is a hard block in which the bullet is embedded and which burns up completely in the breech, so there is nothing to eject. Among other things, this allows a very high·cyclic rate of fire for the three-round controlled burst and will be described more fully in the next section dealing with the G11. Another method is typified in the 9 mm Benelli CBM2 sub-machine-gun, whose ammunition is semi-caseless, the propellant being held in a case-like skirt with no base. The skirt is part of the bullet and goes out with it, leaving only gas in the chamber, so again there is nothing to eject (see pp. 36–7) The means of ejecting a complete round in the event of a misfire is also discussed later, for both the Benelli and the G11.

Plastic ammunition is useful not only for training but also for use in operations at very short ranges in circumstances where there is a desire to limit the area in which casualties or damage may be inflicted, for example in an area crowded with bystanders or in an aircraft during a hijack. Heckler & Koch make a 9 mm plastic round for use in their MP5PT training sub-machine-gun and P7PT8 training pistol. The maximum trajectory is 125 metres and, though the safety area for training is 170 metres, the projectile energy drops to about one-twentieth of its muzzle energy within about 25 metres. The MP5PT can fire single shot, sustained automatic fire or three-round controlled bursts.

Finally there is a range of shot-gun ammunition from armour-piercing solid shot through various sizes of buckshot and pellets to flechettes (miniature steel arrows fired at very high velocity). Being peculiar to shot-guns these are described with that type of weapon on pp. 39–40.

The G11 assault rifle

The German Heckler & Koch G11 assault rifle and its ammunition are of a revolutionary design which provides a combination of characteristics, especially for three-round bursts, which seem quite outstanding. The weapon is currently undergoing troop trials in the German army and, if these prove successful, it is likely to lead to the biggest single change in small arms design this century.

The 4.7 mm caseless ammunition is extremely light; 100 rounds in two magazines weigh only 0.6 kg, half the weight of 5.56 mm and a quarter that of 7.62 mm. The bullet is embedded in a solid square-sided block of propellant in the base of which the priming charge is also embedded. Everything burns up in the chamber when the round is fired. The magazine, which is the full length of the barrel and slides into the gun above it, contains fifty rounds, side by side in a single row, nose down, as they are fed by a spring downwards into the chamber.

There are two revolutionary features about the gun as a whole. First, it consists of an outer casing which includes the butt, the optical sight, the trigger, and the selector; all the other moving parts, the barrel, the chamber, the firing pin, and the magazine, are in one piece and recoil and return together when the gun is fired. Second the chamber is in a cylinder, rotating about an axis at right angles to the barrel, which receives a round in a vertical position and rotates to come into line with the barrel for the round to be fired (see Figure 2).

To load, the chamber is rotated by turning a cocking handle 360°, in the course of which it receives a round and presents it in line with the barrel. (Should there be a misfire, this same 360° motion allows the faulty round to fall out base first from the underside of the gun.)

If the selector is set for single shot, the barrel/chamber/magazine assembly recoils, picks up a new round and returns, ready immediately to be fired again. If it is set for sustained fire, it operates in the same way except that it repeats the cycle automatically and continues firing so long as the trigger remains depressed or until the ammunition runs out. Each round causes a full recoil and recovery before the next is fired – as in most other guns, giving a cyclic rate of 600 rounds a minute or 10 rounds a second – about the same rate as light machine-guns at the end of the Second World War and considered ideal for covering fire at 300 metres range.

When the selector is set for a three-round controlled burst, however, the process is entirely different. The first round is loaded by rotating the cocking lever as before, but when it is fired, a second round and then a third are all loaded, fired, and out of the barrel, fed by a counter within the recoiling mass, before the barrel assembly has even reached the buffer on completion of its recoil. It then returns, automatically loading another round, and is ready to fire another three-round burst.

This cycle has two main effects. Since it has to cope neither with ejecting cartridges nor a reciprocating action to reload, it produces a very high cyclic rate of 2,000 rounds per minute for the three-round burst, meaning that the three rounds are all out in less than one-tenth of a second. Since the barrel assembly, with the added inertia of the magazine and the chamber and firing mechanisms moving with it, is still absorbing the three shocks and has not even reached the buffer at the end of the recoil, the firer has felt no more than a steadily increasing pressure on his shoulder. All three rounds are on their way before he feels the kick when this recoiling mass hits the buffer. It is this kick which produces the reflex action causing ordinary guns to deflect up and to the right during sustained bursts, but in this case all three bullets are out of the barrel before that happens. The result is that the three rounds will fall in a much tighter grouping on the target than if there had been a full recoil between each of them, as there is when the selector is set to automatic. This is significant both at long ranges (100 m to 300 m), where there will be a

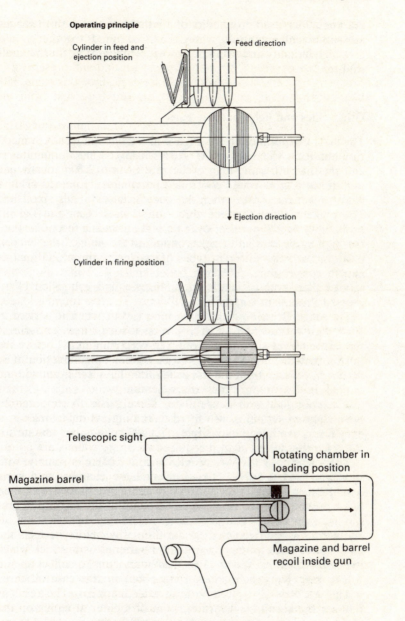

Figure 2   The 4.7 mm G11 rifle

Source: Heckler & Koch specification

markedly increased probability of a lethal hit, and at short ranges in a sub-machine-gun role, where the three rounds together should give high lethality and stopping power, compensating for the small calibre.

Other rifles and light machine-guns

The AAI Corporation in the USA is also developing an Advanced Combat Rifle (5.56 mm AAI ACR) using caseless ammunition and this has the same high cyclic rate of fire (2,000 rounds per minute) in a three-round controlled burst mode. Like the G11, it has a slower rate of fire when the selector is set for sustained fire. The makers claim that the three-round burst increases the hit probability by 100 per cent over normal automatic fire because of the high cyclic rate and tight grouping of the shots. Trials are in progress with two different types of caseless ammunition for this gun: a conventional 5.56 mm bullet and a 4.32 mm discarding sabot bullet, both of which are embedded in a cylindrical Compressed Propellant Charge.

The latest British individual weapon (IW) came into service in 1987. This is the 5.56 L 85 A1. A version with a heavier barrel is the current light support weapon (LSW) 5.56 L86 A1. Both are fully automatic and can be fitted with a grenade launcher but they do not have a controlled burst capability. They are fitted with an optical sight with four times' magnification, which enhances their use in poor light and is useful for surveillance. An emergency open sighting system is also fitted to the optical sight for emergency firing. An image intensifying (II) sight can quickly be substituted for the optical sight if required.

The Soviet 5.45 AK74 (and AKS74 with folding butt) came into service in the late 1970s. There is also a light machine-gun version – the RPK74. All are fully automatic, but do not have a controlled burst capability. Like other Soviet weapons they are robust and simple, with a foresight post and U-notch backsight. Their most interesting characteristic is the design of their bullets (described more fully above in the 'Ammunition' section) with an air gap in the nose which causes them to distort and tumble on striking a soft target, giving them a better stopping power at short ranges.

The AK74 is also fitted with an effective muzzle brake. This reduces the recoil by diverting some of the thrust forward, and also compensates for the usual upward movement of the barrel during firing by imposing a simultaneous downward thrust. These, obviously, should help the firer to hold his aim on the target during a long burst, but they make the weapon unpleasantly noisy for the firer and his immediate neighbours.

One other trend which may be developed is the greater use of plastics to save weight. Thus far, plastics have been used only in such parts as the butt, hand-guard, and magazine, as in the Swiss 5.6 SG 550/551 SIG assault rifle, and weight savings have so far been marginal (5 to 10 per cent). There is constant development in plastics so it is worth watching this trend, but there is no technological breakthrough yet in sight for substituting anything for metal in the barrels or other machine-moving parts of accurate or long-range weapons. If there is any development it is more likely to have its first effects on sub-machine-guns and pistols with their shorter ranges, reliance on a spread of burst rather than precision, and lower muzzle velocities. These are, in any case, the kinds of guns which terrorists are most likely to want to smuggle on to aircraft through magnetometers and X-ray searches at the boarding gates.

Snipers' rifles have now reached a degree of maturity in which the excellence of manufacture of barrels, ammunition, and telescopic sights already matches the capability of the most skilled and experienced sniper. The accepted NATO standard of accuracy for 5.56 or 7.62 weapons is 1½ minutes of arc, that is every round should fall within 40 cm (16 inches) of a point of aim at 500 m range. The 7.62 Model 85 Parker Hale sniping rifle is designed to give a guaranteed first-round hit *capability* on man-sized targets at ranges up to 600 metres and about 85 per cent from 600 to 900 metres. Few humans will do justice to this specification even under ideal meteorological conditions. Sterling Armaments claim that their sniper rifle with telescopic sight gives a trained person a 99 per cent capability of a hit on a point target at 400 metres in daylight. This rifle can also be fitted with an II for night use. In theory, microelectronics might enable a small projectile to be made responsive to external guidance and this could provide some new capabilities, particularly in conjunction with TI equipment, but in practice the advantages, if any, over current skills and accuracy of equipment seem unlikely to justify the expense of development and manufacture. Many experts are sceptical.

Armour-piercing bullets, though some can be fired by personal weapons, are more relevant to the discussion of other anti-vehicle weapons. (see Chapter 6).

Sights and night vision equipment

The design of sights for personal weapons has been mentioned, in passing, in discussing some of the weapons above. Passionate arguments will continue over the pros and cons of open U-notch, aperture, optical and telescopic sights, each of which has its own advantages for certain conditions.

Night vision and night-aiming equipment are likely to be areas of continuing development. Traditional IR surveillance equipment transmits invisible infra-red rays which bounce back from a foreign body (as radar does). Its advantages are that a high level of power can be transmitted, giving it long range. The main disadvantage is that it is 'active' – its transmissions can be detected by an enemy with the equipment to do so. This is less likely to be a disadvantage in fighting guerrillas and terrorists than in fighting sophisticated armies.

II is passive, that is nothing is transmitted. It receives the smallest trace of daylight, moonlight, or starlight and amplifies it to ten or twenty times its natural intensity. Its effectiveness may, however, be reduced or even eliminated by heavy fog or rain.

TI is also passive. It receives infra-red rays – heat rather than light – and converts them to an image on a screen; it can penetrate any weather.

There are now many II sights which can be fitted to standard rifles. For some it is claimed that accurate fire is possible at 500 metres in starlight. They are also valuable for surveillance, up to 5,000 metres.

There are two other types of sights which work on a quite different principle. One is an aiming point projector which projects a narrow beam of light like a torch to illuminate the target, with a small dark spot in the centre, zeroed to the gun. A typical example is the one which can be fitted to almost all Heckler & Koch rifles and sub-machine-guns. This has a 10-watt Halogen lamp which illuminates a target for surveillance up to 120 metres and firing up to 100 metres. At this range, the illuminated circle is 4 metres in diameter, with a 60 cm black aiming spot. More practical ranges would be 50 m (giving a 2 m circle with 30 cm spot) or, for sub-machine-guns, 25 m with a 1 m circle and a 15 cm aiming spot.

The other type, likely to develop a lot further, is the laser sight, which projects a small bright orange spot marker on to the target, by day or by night, and is zeroed to the gun. As an example, the US R100 laser gun sight can be fitted to an M16 (Armalite) rifle or to a sub-machine-gun and, in normal daylight in a building, the dot may be visible at up to 100 metres. If is not, of course, much use in bright sunlight out of doors. Ranges would be longer at night but the limit would lie in the effective range of the gun. A possible application of this sight for terrorist use is discussed on p. 36.

An alternative laser sight is available in which the spot marker is invisible to the naked eye and can be used only by a person wearing night vision goggles or a weapon with a night vision (II) sight. It is totally invisible to the target and very effective for night use.

Sub-machine-guns

A serviceable and effective sub-machine-gun, albeit of a half-century-old design but unused and well maintained, can be bought for $35. There are literally millions of them in warehouses, of thousands of different models. (The latest edition of *Jane's Infantry Weapons* describes over 150 models still found in regular use.) 'Tommy-guns' from the 1920s and Stens from the 1940s are still used in large numbers by militias, irregular 'paramilitaries', and guerrillas. As is shown in Table 2, development over this half century has been of degree rather than of kind. Nevertheless many of the more significant developments have been in the past ten years, particularly in the field of caseless or semi-caseless ammunition, controlled burst capability, and 'double-action'. Any or all of these could burgeon into more radical development in the future.

Because they are so cheap, and in such profusion, terrorists tend to use the older designs of weapon. Of those listed in Table 2, the Uzi, Mini-Uzi, and Ingram are particularly popular, along with the 7.65 mm Czech Skorpion, which is really a machine pistol but is included in the table as it has a retractable stock and is used by terrorists as a sub-machine-gun. The Ingram Model 11 is no longer manufactured but a lot remain in use by terrorist groups. It is probably still the lightest (1.59 kg empty or 2.1 kg with loaded 32-round magazine) and the shortest (222 mm) sub-machine-gun available. It has the same unloaded weight (1.59 kg), is shorter than the Skorpion machine pistol, and has a very high cyclic rate of fire. The Skorpion can be fitted with a silencer and this, with the butt extended, gives it a total length of 716 mm, as long as some rifles. The Ingram can be fitted with a suppressor, which differs from a silencer in that it allows the bullet to reach its full supersonic velocity but is less silent.

Most popular with police forces and soldiers in an anti-terrorist

Table 2 Development of sub-machine-guns

Period	Weapon	Origin	Calibre (mm)	Weight loaded (kg)	Shortest length (mm)	Muzzle velocity (mps)	Cyclic rate of fire (rds/min)	Remarks
1920s	Thompson .45	USA	11.4	5.37	810*	282	700	* cannot be retracted
1941 (WW2)	Sten, Mark II	UK	9	3.44	762*	366	550	
1949	Czechoslovak Model 23	Czech.	9	3.27	445	381	650	
1949	Uzi	Israel	9	4.10	470	400	600	
1950s	Mini-Uzi	Israel	9	3.30	360	350	950	
1956	Sterling L2A3	UK	9	3.47	483	390	550	
1950s	Ingram Model 11	USA	9	2.10	222	293	1,200	
Late 1950s	Skorpion	Czech.	7.65	2.00	269	317	840	
1960s	MP5 A5E Heckler & Koch	FRG	9	2.73	490	400	800	three-, four-, or five-round burst
1970s	MP5 KA1 Heckler & Koch	FRG	9	2.52	325	375	900	three-round controlled burst
Late 1970s	Benelli CBM2	Italy	9	3.50	450	390	800–1,000	semi-caseless ammunition
1983	Spectre	Italy	9	3.10	350	400	900	double action

Rifles used as or adapted as sub-machine-guns

1980s	5.56 HK53	FRG	5.56	3.65	563	750	700	
Late 1980s	4.7 G11 Heckler & Koch	FRG	4.70	4.30	750	930	600 2,000	automatic three-round burst
1980s	5.56 Ruger AC556F	USA	5.56	3.50	584	885	750	three-round burst
1980s	AKSU–74	USSR	5.45	3.50	420	800	800	version of AK74

Sources: Jane's Infantry Weapons 1987–88, London, Jane's, 1987, and manufacturers' specifications

Note: * Manufacturers' specifications and textbooks usually quote the 'cyclic rate', i.e. the number of rounds the gun would fire in a sustained burst of one minute. This, of course, is purely theoretical, and it is easier for the non-expert to visualize the performance of the gun in rounds per second by dividing by 60, e.g. a gun with a cyclic rate of 600 fires 10 rounds per second.

role are the various weapons of the Heckler & Koch MP5 series. The MP5 A5E was one of the first guns to have a controlled burst facility, but this of a totally different character from that described earlier for the G11. The control is exercised simply by a ratchet on the trigger mechanism which is set during manufacture for three, four or five rounds: this ratchet holds the sear off the hammer for the indicated number of rounds. The trigger can then be released and pressed again to fire another similar burst; thus the fire is neither more nor less accurate than normal sustained firing. The firer is simply restrained from wasting ammunition by restricting each burst after which he aims and fires again. The close grouping of the burst achieved by the G11 is, however, less important for a sub-machine-gun where a degree of dispersal may be an advantage; the values of the three-round burst are mainly in conserving ammunition (to avoid having to change the magazine at the height of the engagement) and the lethal and stopping power of three rounds is better than that of one.

The MP5K series (MP5K, KA1, KA4, and KA5) were specially designed for police and military anti-terrorist squads as they are short enough for concealment under clothing, in the glove compartment of a car, or in a briefcase. Heckler & Koch sell two specially designed briefcases from which the MP5K series guns can be fired.

Several of the shorter sub-machine-guns can be fitted with a laser sight (see pp. 32–3). The whole assembly could then be fitted inside a slightly larger than usual briefcase, with a porthole through which the laser beam could be directed, and triggers both for the laser sight and the gun on the handle of the briefcase.

A number of assault rifles have been adapted to produce a weapon suitable for a dual role as a sub-machine-gun. The 5.56 HK 53 (adapted from the German G3 rifle) and the 5.56 Ruger AC556F (from the US AC556 selective fire weapon) are examples of this. Being of smaller calibre, however, they are thought by some to have an inferior stopping power to that of 9 mm sub-machine-guns at short range. The 4.7 G11 assault rifle is of even smaller calibre and is short enough for reasonably easy handling as a sub-machine-gun. Both the G11 and the Ruger compensate for the small calibre ammunition by having a three-round burst – the G11 at a very high rate of fire. The AKSU–74 is a short-barrel version of the AK74 assault rifle and is fitted with a flash-reducer.

The Italian Benelli CBM2 sub-machine-gun, uses semi-caseless ammunition (mentioned earlier in this chapter), which gives it a high rate of fire; the risk of a jam is reduced by there being no cartridge to be ejected. The 9 mm AUPO (autopropellant) bullet has a case-like skirt, like a cartridge with no base, attached to the bullet and it goes out of the barrel with it. The gun fires from an open bolt position: the resting place of the bolt is fully retracted so that when the trigger is pressed the bolt carries a round forward with it into the chamber. An unusual feature is that the hammer strikes the side and not the base of the round, for which purpose there is an annular ring of primer at the appropriate position fused into the propellant. This gun completed trials in the early 1980s, but did not go into production due to lack of orders. The patents have been taken over by another Italian armaments company so some of its original features may reappear in different form.

More original still is the Italian 9 mm Spectre, which was first publicly displayed in 1983. It fires from a closed bolt position but has a separate hammer unit which pushes the firing pin through the bolt from behind. It has no safety catch but, once the gun has been cocked and the bolt comes forward to its closed position, there are two alternative positions for the hammer unit: forward and back. It can be fired from either – by a strong pressure from the back (ready for quick action) position.

The process (see Figure 3) is as follows:

1 With the gun empty, all working parts forward, a magazine is inserted.
2 The cocking handle (A) is drawn back.
3 The cocking handle is released, allowing the bolt (B) to push the first round into the chamber, but the hammer unit remains back full cock: this is the quick action position, e.g. for entering a room in which there is an adversary who is believed to be ready to fire; a light pressure on the trigger will release the hammer unit to fire the firing pin through the bolt.
4 If, having cocked the gun, there is no immediate expectation of firing, pressing a de-cocking lever (C) allows the hammer unit (D) to move forward under control behind the bolt; the gun is now in the 'safe' position but can be fired with a stronger pressure on the trigger, which takes the hammer unit (not the block) back and immediately releases it to fire.

Thus the gun offers a similar alternative to the traditional 0.38 revolver (see below), which can also be fired from the cocked (light pressure) or uncocked (deliberate pressure) positions.

Pistols

Pistols (revolvers and self-loading) are still much used, both by terrorists and by police officers, because of their ease of conceal-

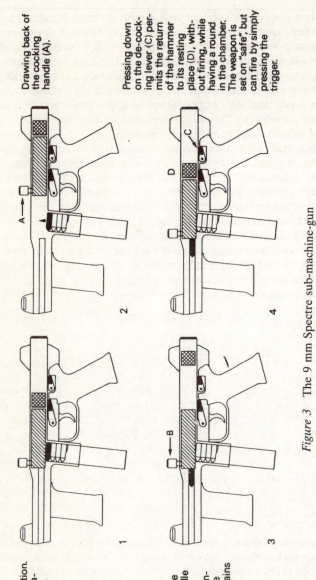

Drawing back of the cocking handle (A).

Pressing down on the de-cocking lever (C) permits the return of the hammer to its resting place (D), without firing, while having a round in the chamber. The weapon is set on "safe", but can fire by simply pressing the trigger.

Starting position. Loaded magazine inserted.

Release of the cocking handle (B): the first round is chambered and the hammer remains at full cock.

Figure 3 The 9 mm Spectre sub-machine-gun

Source: Manufacturer's specification

ment in a pocket, or carriage in a hip or shoulder holster, leaving both hands free until it becomes necessary to draw the gun.

Ironically one of the oldest revolvers still in regular use, the British .38 dating from the 1930s, shares the same advantages and disadvantages of double action firing with one of the latest sub-machine-guns just described, the Spectre, though it uses a totally different system. The .38 revolver can be carried cocked, with or without a round in the chamber aligned with the barrel. When cocked, a very light pressure will fire it if there is a round in that chamber and this could lead to accidents in moments of stress. For this reason, the hammer comb has been removed in most models. Uncocked, the pistol is safe and stable, especially if the chamber aligned with the barrel is empty. A double action is used to fire it, first to rotate the chamber and cock the action and then a second pressure to shoot. In emergency a single strong pressure will carry through both of these without significantly affecting speed of reaction or accuracy. A similar Smith and Wesson .38 revolver is still the standard weapon for Personal Protection Officers in the British police service, who regard it as the most reliable weapon on the market, with none of the propensities for stoppages inherent in automatic pistols, and provided that it is never carried cocked, there is virtually no risk of accidental discharge.

Most pistols are self-loading or semi-automatic, that is the short recoil from a single shot loads the next one. Some pistols, however, are fully automatic machine pistols, that is they can fire sustained bursts. These are generally not very successful, as it is too difficult to maintain the aim of a small pistol during a burst. One of these, the Skorpion, was described under 'Sub-machine-guns' (p. 33) because it is much used in that role, as it has a folding butt and can be conveniently held in two hands. There is, in fact, no clear division between sub-machine-guns and machine pistols.

The recently developed 9 mm Beretta 93 R is probably the most advanced of the currently available machine pistols. It has a choice of self-loading single rounds or controlled three-round bursts. The magazine holds twenty rounds, and still fits into a normal-sized pistol grip as the rounds are staggered. As well as a folding stock, the gun has a folding forehand grip which greatly improves the steadiness of aim in the sub-machine-gun role.

Shotguns

Shotguns are useful both to terrorists and to police officers and soldiers, because they offer a wide choice of ammunition, some of which (with small pellets) can be fired within a small safety area.

One of the best is the SPAS (Special Purpose Automatic Shotgun) specially designed by Luigi Franchi in Italy as a riot weapon. Ammunition varies from armour-piercing solid shot (which can penetrate an 8 mm steel plate) to small pellets. Being a smooth bore weapon it spreads its pellets over nearly 1 metre diameter at 40 metres. It has an automatic action, firing about four rounds per second and, loaded with buckshot, it can put 48 pellets per second on to a 1 metre square target at 40 metres' range – each buckshot pellet having greater residual energy than a 7.65 mm pistol bullet at the same range. With seven 12-bore rounds in the magazine this gives it formidable killing power at short ranges. The gun can also project a CS gas canister 150 yards.

The CAWS (Close Assault Weapon System), jointly developed in the early 1980s by Olin in the USA and Heckler & Koch in Germany, is also a 12-bore weapon and offers two new choices of cartridge. One fires eight '000 Buck' pellets each weighing 4.5 g and ejected with a muzzle velocity of 488 metres per second (more than most sub-machine-guns). The other fires twenty flechettes each weighing 0.376 grams, with the very high muzzle velocity of 900 metres per second. Both the buckshot and the flechettes are effective at ranges up to 150 metres.

There is great potential for development of shotguns and shotgun ammunition for use at the short ranges at which most guerrilla and terrorist actions are usually fought.

Chapter five

Missiles, longer range weapons, and bombs

Free flight armour-piercing missiles (hand held)

Terrorists make increasing use of armour-piercing weapons to attack both armoured vehicles (including VIP limousines) and the walls of buildings. Thus far they have had little success against vehicles, because they have generally failed to achieve the clean hit at the right angle in the right place on which hollow charge missiles depend for their effect. The attack on the armoured limousine of the US Army General Kroesen in Germany in September 1981, for example, was made with an RPG 7 at short range while the car was stopped at traffic lights but it bounced off the boot and inflicted only superficial injuries.

The Soviet **RPG 7** is the hand-held surface-to-surface missile (SSM) most commonly used by terrorists, as they have been lavishly provided for Arab governments, some of whom pass them on to Arab terrorists or to the IRA and other European terrorists. Though first issued in 1962, it remains an effective weapon, able to penetrate 320 mm of armour, with its hollow charge projectile of 85 mm calibre weighing 2.25 kg. It is, however, thrown off course by cross-winds and defeated by wire mesh protection outside buildings (as at police stations in Northern Ireland), because the hollow charge relies for its penetration on detonating at right angles and the right distance from its target. It is also unsafe to fire it in confined spaces, or with a wall within 2 metres of the back of the launch tube (a fault overcome in the Armbrust – see p. 42. More modern versions such as the **RPG 16** and **RPG 18** are more convenient in use but generally have the same shortcomings.

The US **M 72. 750 LAW** (light anti-tank weapon) now completing development, fires a similar projectile (66 mm, weight about 1 kg) but it has higher penetration (380 mm of armour). The makers claim that the high muzzle velocity (230 mps) and good aerodynamics give a 65 per cent probability of a hit at 250 metres, the projectile having a flight time of 1.2 seconds at this range. For moving targets, the optical sight has a series of crosses each side of the central range line, each giving the correct aim-off for a target crossing at 15 mph (24 kph). The major advantage of this weapon is its lightness: the missile and launcher together weigh only 3 kg.

The British **LAW 80** (light anti-tank weapon) which went into production in 1987, fires a bigger missile (94 mm) with very high penetration (over 600 mm – precise figure not published). The missile and launcher together weigh 9.6 kg. It is a one-shot low-cost disposable weapon and contains a spotting rifle integrated with the outer tube. This is pre-loaded with five rounds of tracer ammunition designed with the same ballistic characteristics as the missile, so that operators can get their weapon aimed accurately on to the target without giving away their position. The bullet has a flash head which indicates when it has hit a hard target, upon which the operator fires the missile. With a range of up to 500 metres, this greatly increases the probability of a hit. It can also be fired at ranges as short as 20 m.

The West German **Armbrust**, recently adopted by NATO and by several armies in Latin America, Africa, and the Middle and Far East, incorporates two major improvements: it is free of flash, smoke, and blast, and makes a noise no louder than a pistol shot, and it can safely be fired from inside a room with a wall close behind it. Both of these things are achieved by the fact that the missile is projected forward and the counterweight projected backwards by pistons which effectively lock in the flash, smoke, blast, and noise. The counterweight consists of some 5,000 small plastic flakes which fan out as they leave the launch tube, and fall harmlessly to the ground within 15 metres; they do not rebound from a wall as close as 80 cm behind the weapon. The launch tube, though hot and under high pressure from the gas trapped inside, can safely be discarded without risk of its exploding.

The **AC 300 Jupiter** is a joint Franco-German product incorporating the same flash and blast-free system (pistons and flakes) as the Armbrust. It is ejected at a lower muzzle velocity (180 mps compared with 210 for the Armbrust) but, once stabilized in its flight, is assisted by a booster rocket to 275 mps.

Heavy machine-guns

As an alternative to the shoulder-fired hollow charge weapons described above, there are signs that the medium and heavy machine-gun (HMG) with armour-piercing ammunition may be regaining popularity. A Soviet **12.7 mm Degtyaref** was found in an IRA arms cache in July 1988. This is an old model first produced in 1946, but improved versions with similar essential characteristics are still under active development. The US **0.50 inch (12.7 mm) GPHMG** (general purpose heavy machine-gun) using Saboted Light Armour Penetration (SLAP) ammunition is completing trials; it weighs 25 kg, fires 400 rounds per minute, and has a maximum theoretical range of 6,650 m (over four miles) though its effective range is probably not more than 4,000 m. Also under development is the Belgian **15 mm FN BRG–15** heavy machine-gun, which fires 700 rounds a minute with an armour-piercing bullet weighing 70 grams (compared with 46 grams for the 0.50 inch SLAP ammunition), but the gun weighs more than twice as much (55 kg) and is twice as long (2,000 mm compared with 914 mm) as GPHMG. Both will penetrate the kind of armour used on VIP limousines at the longest ranges likely to be used by terrorists and the chances of a hit are high; they can also be used effectively against aircraft. The guns are, however, much heavier and more awkward to manhandle then either the free flight projectors above or the guided missile projectors below.

Guided armour-piercing missiles (hand held)

The earlier anti-tank guided missile projectors used the manual command to line of sight (MCLOS) system of guidance. The Soviet **3M6 (Snapper)** was issued to the Arab armies in the 1960s, and used in the 1967 war, but has now been replaced by the **AT3 (Sagger)**. The MCLOS missile is wire-guided, that is it feeds out a multicore cable from spools in its base, through which the operator's instructions are transmitted to two jetavator nozzles which swivel to correct its course. There is a flare on the base to enable the operator to see it. At ranges up to 1,000 metres this done by eye. At longer ranges (3,000 metres maximum but more practically up to 2,000 metres) The operator steers it on a line above the target and guides its final approach through a ten-times magnification periscopic sight.

More modern weapons use the SACLOS (semi-automatic command to line of sight) system. The Soviet version is the **AT4 (Spigot)**, also known as Fagot. The NATO equivalent is the joint Franco-German **MILAN** (a French acronym) which came into service in 1985. The missile weighs 11.3 kg and the launching and guidance system 16.4 kg. The SACLOS missile is again wire-guided, but the operator has only the task of keeping the cross hairs of the optical sight on the (presumably moving) target. The guidance system follows the missile from an infra-red signature emitted from its base and corrects its flight to the line of sight. The makers claim a 98 per cent hit probability between 250 and 2,000 metres (the maximum practical range). The flight time for 2,000 metres is 13 seconds. The terrorist attacking an armoured limousine (or tank) has only to select a stretch of road long enough for it to be in view for, say, 15 seconds (250 metres at 60 kph or 500 metres at 120kph). The weapon system will comfortably go into the boot of a car (missile 1,260 mm long and launching/guidance system 900 × 650 × 420 mm – combined weight about 30 kg). The chances of a hit are much greater than with a free flight missile at ranges over 250 metres (though at ranges less than that the advantage falls away sharply as there is insufficient time for the guidance system to be fully effective).

Mortars

Improvised mortars are very easy to make but are usually inaccurate and unreliable. The IRA regularly use home-made multi-barrelled mortars mounted on trucks to attack police and army posts in Northern Ireland, but many of the bombs fall far from the target and accidents are commonplace.

Most suitable for terrorist use are light mortars (51 mm to 61 mm). The British **51 mm Mortar** weighs 6.25 kg and its bomb weighs 0.9 kg. It has a range of 800 m and a probable error of 2 per cent in range and 3 mils (about one-sixth of a degree of angle) in line. This means that about half the rounds should fall within 15–20 metres of the point aimed at. The British **81L16 ML Mortar** is much heavier (35 kg with a 4.5 kg bomb) but has a much longer range – up to 6,000 metres. Its choice of ammunition includes the **Merlin 81 mm terminally guided mortar projectile**, which incorporates a radar seeker in the nose which commands a guidance system directing the bomb on to any large armoured vehicle in the immediate target area; it has a hollow charge filling which will penetrate the top armour of any known tank.

Anti-aircraft missiles (hand held)

The use by guerrillas of surface-to-air missiles to shoot down helicopters and other an aircraft is increasing. One was found under the flight path of aircraft taking off from Rome Airport in 1973, with intelligence that Palestinian terrorists were targeting a civil airliner carrying a particular passenger. In 1978 and 1979 guerrillas in Zimbabwe (then Rhodesia) shot down two civil airliners, killing forty-eight and fifty-nine passengers respectively. And the use of American Stinger missiles by Afghan guerrillas to shoot down helicopter gunships probably accelerated the Soviet decision to withdraw from Afghanistan in 1988.

The soviet **SAM 7 (Grail)** was first seen in action in Egypt in 1967 and was used against US piston-engined aircraft and helicopters in Vietnam. It incorporates an infra-red seeker in the nose, which, launched into the vicinity of an aircraft, pursues the heat from its exhaust tube. More modern versions incorporate an IFF (Identification Friend or Foe) system. The launcher weighs 10.6 kg and the missile 9.2 kg (total 19.8 kg or 44 lbs) and is 1,346 mm long. A first-stage motor launches the missile from the tube and burns out before the tail of the missile has left the tube, so as not to injure the operator. At a safe distance out a booster rocket is initiated from within the missile. The latest version, SAM 7 B, can fly 5 km at a maximum altitude of 2,000 m before it self-destructs. It is believed to cost less than $1,000 and a large number are in use by guerrillas all over the world.

The British **Blowpipe** is of similar overall weight (20 kg) and length (1,390 mm) and has two-stage firing, but its guidance system is quite different. The missile and its launching tube are contained in a single canister weighing 14 kg to which the operator attaches a 6-kg aiming unit. After firing, the empty canister is removed and a fresh one attached to the aiming unit. The guidance is by optical tracking and radio command. The missile has a flare in the back so that the operator can follow the path. The operator then has a choice: either thumb control can be used to keep the missile on the line of sight, or the automatic control can be switched off and the missile guided manually. In either case, the steering signals are transmitted by radio to a steering unit in the missile.

The British **Javelin** is an advanced version of Blowpipe. The guidance principle is similar but the operator does not have to watch the flare on the tail of the missile; this is tracked by a television camera linked to a microprocessor and the operator has only to concentrate on keeping the sights accurately on the line of sight. The television camera and microprocessor then send the necessary radio signals to operate the missile's steering system to keep it on the line of sight. (Compare the SACLOS system for wire-guided armour-piercing missiles described on pp. 43–4.) The range is in excess of 4 km. Blowpipe and Javelin are both manufactured by Short Brothers in Belfast.

The British **Marconi close air defence weapon** (currently under development) again used a different guidance system, on the fire-

and-forget principle. The missile incorporates its own active radar seeker. Once the operator has acquired a target visually in the aiming unit and, if necessary, identified it by IFF interrogation, he presses the trigger and this automatically locks the missile's active seeker on to the target, correcting any error in his aim. From the moment of launch, therefore, no further action is required by the operator. The system can track fast-moving targets advancing, crossing, or receding.

The US **Stinger**, introduced into service in 1976 by General Dynamics, is also a fire-and-forget weapon, using a passive infra-red seeker and a proportional navigation system. The operator visually spots the target, finds it in the optical sight, initiates the missile functions, performs the IFF interrogation and, if it is identified as hostile, launches the missile which is by then locked on to the target and guides itself automatically to hit it.

Stinger POST has an improved sensing and control system which guards against infra-red countermeasures. It has a rosette-scan seeker, combined infra-red and ultra-violet detectors, and a micro-processor-controlled guidance system. The production contract was awarded to General Dynamics in 1983 and the first weapons were delivered in 1986.

Grenades

Terrorists usually use improvised grenades, for example a bunch of sticks of plastic explosive with a short time fuse, often surrounded by six-inch nails bound round the outside for fragmentation (the **nail bomb**).

The more sophisticated **drogue grenade** developed by the IRA in 1987 is a hollow charge grenade designed for use against armoured Land Rovers and troop carriers in Northern Ireland. It is shaped like the familiar stick grenade and comprises an ordinary food can with a ten-inch plastic tube emerging from a wooden block wedged into the top. The can contains a hollow charge of Semtex plastic explosive, shaped between the wooden block and a copper cone in the bottom of the can. The tube contains the firing mechanism. The initiator is housed in a wooden plug at the bottom of the tube, comprising a detonator protruding into the Semtex, its open end inserted in place of the bullet in a rimfire-type small arms cartridge above it, its rim resting on the hole through the plug. The rimfire cartridge has its priming composition packed into the extraction rim, not held in a central cap. The cartridge is fired by a chisel-edged bolt in a wooden slide, which slides down the tube against a light creep spring which collapses under the momentum of the bolt and slide on the impact of the grenade on its target. In its safe position, the bolt is held back by a detent (a transverse bar through the tube) held in position by a ring and pin. When the pin is removed, the detent is still held in by a lever, and when the thrower releases this lever, the detent is ejected by a spring and the bolt is free to compress the creep spring and strike the cartridge when the grenade hits the target.

The release of the lever also releases a polythene drogue which streams out from the top of the tube like the tail of a kite and is supposed to make the grenade strike with the base of the can square to the armoured surface of the target so that the hollow charge is properly directed. In practice, it seldom strikes squarely when thrown from the side, but it has been effective when thrown from upper windows on to the top armour of passing police and army vehicles.

Bombs and mines

By far the largest number of terrorist attacks are by bombs and mines of various kinds, almost always improvised except for standard anti-tank mines, usually of Soviet or east European manufacture, which are delivered to Arab armies and passed on by their governments.

Improvised road mines are usually either fougasses (large charges with metal fragments in them concealed by the roadside) or bulk explosive under culverts fired by remote wire or radio control. Anti-personnel mines to catch survivors or rescuers may be fired either by military booby-trap switches (pull, press, or release) or improvised switches using electrical contacts or crushable phials of acid. Improvised bulk explosives can be made by mixing certain types of fertilizer and diesel, or various other combinations of individually harmless and easily obtainable materials. Only the detonators and priming charges need to be factory-made, and these may be obtained either from sympathetic governments or by theft from mines or quarries. All of these techniques are well known and do not change very much.

Road mines, usually buried in dirt roads or verges and set off by pressure of a passing vehicle's wheels, have also changed little in the past fifty years. To defeat the metal detector, plastic and wooden mines (with only the detonator made of metal) were used from 1942 onwards; so were booby traps to catch the sapper lifting them.

Improvised bombs to wound or kill are concealed in letters (normally at least ¼ inch thick), parcels, packages of goods, shopping bags, suitcases or vehicles, and may again be combined with booby traps to catch bomb disposal officers or people rescuing casualties. Again, most of them have been regularly described in the press, and ingenuity rather than technological development accounts for most of the new techniques.

Just as the radio control for toy aeroplanes was developed to fire remote-controlled bombs, so the development of timing devices for home video recorders was applied to precise delay fuses for bombs. One of these was used to blow up the Grand Hotel in Brighton in October 1984. The bomb was planted in a suitcase inserted behind the bath in a room on the fifth floor (the VIP rooms being on the first and second floors) by an IRA man booking in as a hotel guest three weeks before the Conservative Party Conference. Mrs Thatcher and most of her Cabinet were sleeping in rooms below. Five people were killed (though none of the Cabinet). The IRA's expert bomb-maker tried to plant twelve more such bombs in holiday hotels (aimed to terrorize ordinary holiday-makers in the summer of 1985) but the first of these was discovered, with the plans for the rest, in time to prevent them, and the bomber was caught and convicted. This technique will be used again, and other types of electronic development will be adapted and exploited by bombers as they arise.

It is in the field of car or truck bombs that most of the current development is taking place, especially in Ireland and the Middle East. These are broadly of three types: those parked in advance beside a target building or on the road where a target vehicle is expected to pass (like fougasses or culvert mines) and fired by remote control; those driven into the heart of a target area by 'suicide drivers' and also usually blown up (with the driver) by remote control; and those placed underneath cars to kill the driver or passengers when they start up or drive away.

Remote firing of static car bombs can be done in many ways. An electric detonator fired by an observer through field telephone cables is the simplest. Radio initiation using the control systems for model aircraft, cars, or boats is now freely available in the shops. And a new system devised by the IRA – named by the army as the Projectile Controlled Improvised Explosive Device (PCIED) – has proved cheap and effective: the bomb is in a truck or van, and a pair of metal sheets separated by an insulating layer (e.g. chipboard) are connected one to each side of an electric circuit incorporating a battery and detonator. The triple layer assembly is then set up on the side of the vehicle (e.g. casually loaded or disguised as a board carrying a company name or advertisement), so as to be clearly visible as a target visible from, say, a distant building or hillside. If it is about one metre square, any reasonable marksman should be sure of a hit from several hundred metres away. The metal bullet penetrates the three layers simultaneously, and thereby closes the circuit.

Road bombs may also be fired by the electromagnetic field from a passing metal vehicle – in the way that magnetic mines are detonated by passing ships. These, however, are not selective, though they can be made more so by reacting only to metal above a certain weight (e.g. on an armoured vehicle) but even these may be prematurely detonated by a passing truck. They can also be designed to react only to the presence of a radio transmitter or possibly to a combination of heavy metal and a radio. There is scope for inventiveness in other ways of improving selectivity by finding characteristics peculiar to the target vehicles, but complexity and uncertainty are likely to mean that remote control is more likely to remain the normal method.

Suicide bombs are almost invariably fired by radio control. It may soon be possible to obviate the need for the suicide driver as a means of remotely controlled locomotion is developed. This is already well developed for 'Goliath' and other remotely controlled bomb investigation vehicles. The advance may come with a combination of radio guidance with sensors on the vehicle itself, which enable it to 'see' and divert from obstacles such as bollards or concrete blocks in the zig-zag check point at the entrance to protected premises. Prototypes of such AGV's (Autonomous Guided Vehicles) are already under development for the robotization of certain factory operations. An AGV linked to an operator with radio control observing from a window or hillside may be able to guide the vehicle to 'bounce' a barrier or roadblock and drive fast into the heart of the target (e.g. under an arch to an inner courtyard) with a dummy in the driving seat. If the control equipment is cleverly sited with armoured protection, it will be less vulnerable to shots from the guards than if it were relying on even the most suicidal of drivers.

Car bombs designed to kill the driver or passengers are now most commonly made of metal pipes with powerful magnets to fix them under the car, or under the wheel arch closest to where the target is likely to sit. They are usually operated by a mercury tilt fuse, that is a small tube of mercury which can be rotated to vary the slope. At one end of the tube is a pair of electrical contacts linked to a battery and detonator. For normal carriage the tube is vertical with these contacts at the top. When the bomb is set, the tube is rotated to the required slope so that, when the car accelerates or climbs a hill the inertia of the mercury will carry it up the slope to close the contact; the gentler the slope of the tube the more sensitive it is.

Mercury tilt fuses may be fitted with one or both of two types of safety device (in addition to the removal of the wire or pin which sets them). There may be a test circuit in parallel with the firing circuit incorporating a torch bulb. Before the bomb is made live by removing the arming pin, the electric circuit is closed to test it and the bulb will light *unless* there is a short circuit in the parallel firing circuit: that is if the bulb failed to light in the test, the bomber would not remove the arming pin. There may also be a built-in delay of, say, twenty minutes or an hour between the time the bomber pulls the activating pin and the time the circuit becomes live. This will give him time to get clear, in case the owner of the car comes to drive away earlier than expected, as well as ensuring that the bomber is far away in the event of the circuit being faulty and firing prematurely as soon as the circuit is live.

Nuclear, biological, and chemical weapons

It has been feasible for at least ten years for terrorists to obtain the components of or even to manufacture a crude nuclear bomb in a university laboratory and workshop without any access to unpublished material. A public-spirited American graduate student carried out and documented each one of the processes required, to show that it could be done, though he did them separately to ensure that nothing like an actual bomb came into existence. Frederick Forsyth's *The Fourth Protocol* also describes a convincing scenario for the smuggling in and assembly of the components for a nuclear bomb.

Such a bomb could be concealed in, say, a crate of machinery or spare parts substituted for a similar crate in a stack awaiting shipment. The bomb would be tracked by radio and fitted to be fired by radio. When it had reached a port in the target country, the terrorists' accomplice would telephone an ultimatum to the government: 'There is a nuclear bomb in one of your ports. Unless our comrades are released by 12 noon it will be fired.' Would the government stand firm? Probably, because it would know that the terrorists would be reluctant to carry out the threat because of the political price they would pay. (They are all aware of the damage done to the IRA and Palestinian cause even by the massacre of ten or twenty people at Enniskillen or Rome Airport.) The terrorists themselves realize this, which is presumably why, despite its being quite feasible, none has tried it. Moreover, the operation is far more complex than a shooting, kidnap, or hijack, and more likely to lead to failure or arrest – as well as being far less credible and less effective as a bargaining counter.

The argument applies even more strongly to chemical and biological weapons. It has been feasible for at least 100 years to release poison gas in suitable wind conditions, or to contaminate an entire city water supply, or to unleash a plague. Although the Iraqis used poison gas in the Gulf War, neither poison gas nor biological agents has been used by terrorists, presumably for the same reasons – even by the illusory 'mad anarchist' so regularly cited in nightmare scenarios.

Clearly we should not be complacent about nuclear, biological, and chemical weapons, both because of the need to evaluate hoax calls (there have been quite a lot of these, but none credible) and because all of them would be feasible for a group which was both desperate and suicidal. But the threat is far less, and would in many ways be easier to handle because of its lack of credibility, then the terrorist actions to which we are accustomed.

Incapacitating weapons

There are as yet no really effective non-lethal incapacitating weapons, that is weapons which render everyone in the target area, friend or foe, temporarily unconscious without inflicting permanent injury. To be effective they must be instantaneous. There are incapacitating gases and darts (used for disabling and capturing wild animals), but they do not take effect quickly enough to prevent a terrorist from shooting or throwing a grenade. Nor do low-frequency electromagnetic pulses, nor the 'sub-sound' waves which after a time have the effect of disorienting people without their realizing it. The high-voltage electric shock weapon (with a metal missile on the end of a wire fired from a generator producing an instantaneous non-lethal shock) has too short a range and its results are not sufficiently reliable for it to be effective against rioters. If, however, a non-lethal incapacitating weapon with an instantaneous effect is ever developed, it could be a very valuable anti-terrorist weapon especially to counter ambush or hijack attempts.

It may be that an instantaneous blast weapon will be developed. This at present is limited to the stun grenade, as used by the SAS, which stuns and disorients everyone in a confined space (e.g. terrorists and hostages) for a few seconds but does no permanent damage. A similar blast effect, from a sudden pulse of compressed air from emission points down the full length of an aircraft cabin, might be able to stun all those in it (both passengers and hijackers) for the few seconds needed for a simultaneous emission of a more lasting incapacitating gas to take effect.

Chapter six

Detecting explosives, bombs, and guns

The developing challenges for detection

Thus far, detection of guns and bombs has largely been by detection of metal, though dogs and chemical sniffers are also now increasingly used for detecting explosives. A great deal of further development, however, is needed in the detection of plastic and other materials and of explosives by various kinds of penetrating ray or radiation, the most promising being by neutron bombardment and the detection of dielectric properties of materials. Trends and prospects will be examined in this chapter.

The wholly **plastic gun** has already been produced, including firing mechanism, screws, springs, and bullets; many experts are sceptical, but if it does prove to be a practical and reliable weapon it would have many applications for terrorists in a hijacking, assassination, or kidnap operation. There are also ways of detonating bombs, especially with rough (though not precise) delay fuses without the use of any metal. X-rays and other forms of radiation can already be adjusted to screen tell-tale shapes of plastic but, as with metal, these shapes can be concealed in metal or other containers so the various means of detection of explosives probably offer a more promising area of development.

Improvised explosives present a particular problem because there are so many pairs of innocent materials which become explosive when brought together. Well-known mixtures include fertilizer and fuel oil, and the so-called 'Co-op' mixture of nitrobenzine and sodium chlorate. Most such mixtures do, however, contain considerable quantities of nitrogen compounds and it is these which currently provide the commonest characteristics for detection either by vapour or by neutron bombardment. If sufficient effort is devoted to research, however, other detectable characteristics are likely to be discovered. Detection of regular characteristics in other components – eg. initiating or firing mechanisms and detonating or priming materials – may well provide the best answers.

Improvised explosive devices (IED) can be fired by many different methods – mechanically, chemically, electrically or electronically – using delay or remote control systems or by booby-trap mechanisms (press, pull, release, photoelectric, etc.). Areas in which IED may be concealed (e.g. behind walls, under cars) may therefore have to be subjected to several different forms of search before they can be declared safe.

Other methods of triggering which are likely to be developed include infra-red, microwave, and ultrasound. Infra-red can be jammed by electronic counter-measures (ECM) and methods of detecting the others are being developed, such as the microwave 'fuzz-buster' used to detect police speed traps in the USA.

The **precise delay fuse**, as used in the attempt to kill Mrs Thatcher and her Cabinet with a bomb in the Grand Hotel, Brighton (described in Chapter 5) may be detected by counter-bugging techniques or by vapour sniffing.

Bombs to attack cars can be quickly slipped underneath or in the wheel arch, held in position by magnets. They can be fired in several ways, for example by a simple pull switch operated by a wire attached to the wheel, by a pressure switch under the front of the tyre, by a pull or release switch operated by the car door or boot, by an electric detonator linked to the ignition or lighting circuits (or by a tilt-fuse – see pp. 49–50). Sharp eyes aided by mirrors, and vapour detection offer the best means of detecting car bombs.

The **range of search capability required** is almost unlimited. Weapons, plastic grenades, or components for IED may be concealed in personal clothing or in inaccessible parts of the body (terrorists have long recognized the reluctance of searchers to probe into the private parts of the female body, especially if the woman is pregnant or carrying a small child). Weapons can be hidden in hand baggage or baggage for check-in at airports. Bombs may be inserted behind walls or easily removable panels (as in the Brighton hotel room), under floors, in cupboards, chimneys, bookshelves, piles of junk (including especially metal junk,) and so on.

The two biggest **limitations of detection** are fatigue of the searcher and exasperation of the public, especially the travelling public. Operators can concentrate on an X-ray screen only for a limited time and even then only with difficulty if they do it every day. Few air travellers will object if they or their hand baggage have to pass the screen a second time, but they will object strongly if a false alarm reading of one their pieces of hold baggage results in their being prevented from boarding the aircraft: for this reason the US Federal Aviation Authority (FAA) has set its specifications for search equipment at a 95 per cent detection probability (DP) and a false alarm rate (FAR) not exceeding 1 per cent.

Aids to the senses

Eyes, ears, noses, fingers, and experience leading to suspicions and hunches remain the most effective of all the armoury at the disposal of anyone searching for guns, bombs, mines, or explosives. Every army sapper who has cleared mines or searched for and disposed of bombs knows this, and his first lines of hardware are those which reinforce those senses, such as **stethoscopes** to help him detect the tiny sounds of timing mechanisms inside a device, and **mirrors**.

In recent years **fibre optics** have also come to be used when looking round corners, down holes, or inside sensitive boxes or packages. Fibre optics comprise a relatively new physical science whereby light is reflected along a bundle of transparent threads of glass or plastic by bouncing between the outer walls of the thread. The threads are of minute diameter (usually between 5 and 100-thousandths of a millimetre) so they can bend round corners without interfering with the reflection of light along them. The bundle of threads has an optical screen which resolves the images into a picture of the scene at the far end with a resolution of up to 100 lines per millimetre, that is, depending on the intensity of the illumination, a well-nigh perfect photographic image. The bundle of micro threads is encased in a larger flexible tube, the bottom of which contains a rotatable light source and lens which can be inserted into the package or bomb, enabling the operator to view it through an image intensifier and eye-piece at the other end of the tube. This technique is already much used in microsurgery in which, instead of making an incision, the surgeon injects a very small flexible tube into the patient. Because of this obvious and widespread surgical benefit, research and development in the science of fibre optics is extremely active and well-funded and some scientists see the applications as so widespread that they believe it to be potentially one of the most dramatic areas of scientific development in the coming years. The detection, assessment, and neutralization of IEDs will be amongst its beneficiaries to an extent as yet unpredictable.

Tagging of explosives

Tagging of explosives can achieve two aims: to enable the presence of concealed explosive to be detected and to enable the source of the explosive to be recognized and proved.

For either form of tagging to be effective, it would be necessary for a substantial number of countries (ideally all, of course, but there is little hope of that) to subscribe to the tagging system and enforce severe penalties on anyone manufacturing, distributing, or smuggling untagged explosive. So long as manufacturing countries subscribed, however, it would be possible to narrow down the source of an untagged explosive to one of the few non-co-operating countries (presumably those like Libya and Cuba which support international terrorism as a tool of foreign policy). This would improve the chances of success in detecting the individuals involved and, because of the retaliatory action thereby justified, it might make it worthwhile for more of the non-co-operators to subscribe to the system, eventually narrowing the field of those who opt out to a handful.

In view of the many forms of bulk explosive which can be improvised by combining otherwise innocent materials (as described earlier in this chapter) the most essential tagging would be of the detonators, detonating cord, and priming explosives which thus far have proved more difficult to improvise effectively.

Tagging for detecting explosives would consist of incorporation during manufacture of constituents which would react to an internationally agreed form of penetrating ray (Röntgen rays, neutron bombardment, gamma rays, etc. – see pp. 58–60).

Tagging for identification can be achieved by techniques tested as long ago as 1979 by the US Government Bureau of Alcohol, Tobacco, and firearms (ATF), but not pursued – allegedly due to opposition from within the explosives trade and firearms lobbies. The method – developed by 3M in Minnesota and manufactured by the Microtrace Corporation – comprised the incorporation of 'microtaggants' in explosives during manufacture, consisting of particles of colour-coded melamine plastic. A large number of colours can be used and these are easily changed, so the number of permutations and combinations is almost infinite. This would enable the manufacturer to use a different combination of colour codes for every batch of explosives manufactured and the system would require this coding to be recorded each time any of this batch is sold to a wholesaler, retailer, and user, anywhere in the world. Thus when a bomb containing tagged explosive was discovered and defused, its origin and channels of distribution could quickly be traced, greatly facilitating the process of police investigation. If – as would often happen – the explosive was found to have passed through the jurisdiction of one of a relatively small number of non-co-operating countries, the finger of guilt would be pointed firmly at that country and appropriate international action could be taken, ranging from diplomatic pressure to cutting off air traffic under an extended Bonn Convention (see p. 77), economic sanctions or, in flagrant cases, military action to apprehend individuals suspected of complicity in the crime.

Vapour detection

Currently the most widely used method of detecting explosives is by detection of vapour or dust particles (aromic detection) by dogs and chemical sniffers. These are also effective in detecting drugs and other illicit materials, and are in regular and successful use at sea and airports.

Dogs can recognize astoundingly small percentages of certain vapours, especially those associated with the human body, in which their responsiveness is at least a million times more sensitive than that of the human nose. Bloodhounds, for example, have followed trails up to four days old for one hundred miles and can identify the hand which has touched an object from the briefest of contacts. The value of this lies mainly in helping the police to detect and identify a subject, though corroborative evidence would be needed to persuade a jury to convict. Explosives, cocaine, heroin, amphetamines, and marijuana also have characteristic odours and the dog is not fooled by deliberately-placed masking smells such as spices, perfumes, onions, or mothballs.

The limitations of dogs are that their senses become fatigued and that, if they are hungry or thirsty, they may switch to searching for scents of food or water. Though these can be largely overcome by good training and good handling, it is not easy to tell when a dog's senses or concentration have lapsed. At their best, however, they can detect vapours better than any of the machines.

Mass spectrographic analysis is the method of vapour detection and analysis of minute dust particles mainly used by customs and security services in seaports and airports. The process involves sucking in samples of air which are then analysed in a computerized mass spectrometer. The plant is quite large and is normally housed in a building of up to 1,000 square feet, alternatively in a semi-articulated pantechnicon some 40 feet long. Samples of air from trucks, cars or containers are drawn directly into the machine through a long hose; alternatively the samples can be drawn into a separate hand-held remote sampler which sucks the air through an adsorber cartridge, which is then taken to the main plant for analysis. The maximum throughput of the system is twenty vehicles per hour and it can be combined with an X-ray plant which simultaneously maintains the same throughput.

A smaller sniffer, manpackable with a hand-held probe, is the **Computerized Organic Tracer (COT)** developed by Thorn EMI and manufactured by Jasmine, which detects nitrobenzine vapour but this, like mass spectrographic analysis, takes minutes rather than seconds.

There are **instant hand-held sniffers** such as the PD4, though these are inevitably not as sensitive as the heavier equipment. At Changi Airport, Singapore, every piece of hand and hold baggage is hand-sniffed *before* check-in and, if there is any doubt about the reading, the bag is opened and searched in the presence of the owner.

Semtex explosive, manufactured in Czechoslovakia and shipped in large quantities to Libya to the IRA in 1987, emits virtually no vapour. Even with normal explosives it is possible to defeat the sniffer by multiple wrapping, that is three or four layers of sealed impermeable plastic added successively in a sterile environment. It is therefore essential to have supplementary means of detection, such as X-rays and neutron bombardment (see below), so that one at least will find the bomb.

X-rays

X-rays (Röntgen rays) are familiarly used to detect metal. X-ray machines can, however, be calibrated to present images of plastic of various densities, though they will not effectively record plastic and metal shapes at the same setting. The plastic images are thus far rather faint, though research will no doubt improve this. The problem is that both metal and plastic shapes can be masked, e.g. by placing parts of a gun in square boxes, or by disguising them as some other apparently innocent shapes (e.g. of a statuette or metal brush). Though an alert operator may be suspicious and demand to see inside, there is a risk of the deception succeeding.

Neutron bombardment and other methods

Various forms of neutron bombardment are being developed which may supplement or eventually supplant X-rays in the detection of plastic and other materials or vapour detection as the most effective means of detecting explosives. Some problems remain to be solved, in that innocent materials may give rise to false alarms, but if sufficient priority and funds are given to research it is hard to believe that these will not be overcome. Another problem is the many pairs of innocent materials which provide bulk explosive when brought together. As was mentioned in the case of tagging (pp. 56–7) the solution probably lies in concentrating on detonators, detonating cord, and priming explosives.

Most of the research is financed by private firms and potential customers are reluctant to place advance orders or provide money until they are confident that the system is going to succeed; the manufacturers will continue research or launch production only if they are confident that they can sell the product. In view of the urgency of the need to find new means of detecting explosives there is a strong case for governments to finance the research and possibly also to provide incentives in the form of guaranteed orders dependent on the system's achieving certain defined levels of performance.

Hydrogenous explosive detection (HED) is one of the most promising methods. This picks up water-based materials (which includes most explosives) and also detects differences in density of materials. The technology depends on neutron bombardment from a cobalt source and therefore requires careful use and a well-trained operator. Different materials cause measurable differences in neutron scatter. This equipment is already in use and further development is likely.

Prompt neutron thermal activation offers a promising means of searching baggage. A source emitting prompt neutrons is positioned above the package with a gamma ray detector underneath. If the package contains materials with a high nitrogen content, the detector will record a high emission of gamma rays which will, above a certain level, trigger an indicator or alarm. Some other materials with a high nitrogen content – notably some kinds of cheese – will at present also trigger the alarm and this needs to be overcome.

There is also a **portable contraband and explosives gamma detector** which can search behind seats, panels, and so on. Attempts are being made to find an imaging system but the technology is still in its early stages.

Materials differ in their **dielectric properties**, that is in their ability to store an electric charge. There is reason to believe that every material has a unique and measurable 'dielectric fingerprint'. Dr William Gregory developed such a system for use in detecting letter and parcel bombs in the US mail in 1977. It was tested for a year in the US post office in Washington DC and a very high detection rate was claimed but the method was not further pursued.

Various other forms of **sniffers** and **chemical sensors** were the subject of experiments during and after the Vietnam War in the 1970s, but none was considered viable. This does not mean, however, that these avenues are necessarily closed.

More promising is the development of **sensitive infra-red detection** of minute variations in temperature. One possible application is the detection of guns and other high-density items concealed in the clothing. These may mask the emission of body heat to the extent of lowering the temperature by an amount well within the capacity of sensitive infra-red detectors to measure. The problem is to convert these measurements into a recognizable image. Currently the images are too blurred to be of any use, but the development of image enhancement may in time solve this. Again this technology is still in its infancy.

Detection and jamming of radio-controlled bombs

Using a similar principle to that used for detecting bugging, Miriad International are marketing a remote receiver detector designed to locate a radio receiver at a range of about 100 metres, and to measure its frequency; it is used in conjunction with an 'inhibitor' which can jam the receiver and so prevent a radio-controlled bomb from being fired. The whole assembly can be comfortably carried in a backpack by one person. An alternative is being developed for use in the leading vehicle of a convoy to detect and jam a radio-fired roadside bomb.

The multiple approach

No existing or potential method of searching is ever likely to give 100 per cent certainty of detection. The best security will therefore be achieved by developing as many methods as possible. Where the need for reliable detection is vital because of the price of failure (e.g. hazarding the passengers and crew of a large aircraft) it will be worth using all the methods which are effective in the hope that one at least will pick up the required object. This is, in fact, the principle behind security of large premises and many other forms of security, and the prospect of facing a minefield of different means of detection may often deter criminals or terrorists from attempting their operation at all.

Chapter seven

Intelligence and the microelectronics revolution

The magnitude of the change

The English word 'intelligence' has at least two distinct meanings: information (about adversaries or likely events), and the faculty of understanding. This chapter is about the first of these, that is, operational intelligence for police, military, or political purposes; about how the microlectronics revolution can create the second, the faculty of understanding; and about how artificial intelligence (AI) can contribute to operational intelligence. Unless otherwise indicated by the context the word 'intelligence' can be taken to mean operational intelligence rather than the faculty of understanding.

The scale of the changes and potential changes brought into view by the microelectronics revolution can best be illustrated by taking examples of intelligence handling in the past ten years and looking at prospects as we move into the 1990s.

In 1977 Dr Hanns-Martin Schleyer, President of Mercedes Benz, was kidnapped in Cologne by terrorists of the Red Army Faction (RAF), who were regarded with disgust by the German public. The police were bombarded with information – 3,826 messages within a few days from members of the public anxious to help. Two of these concerned a small apartment in a nondescript suburb of Cologne, neither of which in itself seemed to have any particular significance. One of them was from a neighbour who reported that this apartment had been rented three weeks earlier by a young couple who paid a month's rent in advance in cash but had only just now moved in; the neighbour rightly thought it unusual for young people to pay cash for a place which they were not going to use for three weeks. The second message, about the same apartment, was that a furniture van had delivered a single large box to it. The police intelligence records were at that time kept in card index and filing systems and, although Schleyer was probably held in that apartment for a week or more, by the time the police had spotted the significance of these reports and the link between them, he had been moved. They missed him by a day.

As a result of this and other terrorist incidents at that time, the German police installed a sophisticated computer system which would have drawn attention to those reports – and especially to the link between them – immediately.

This computerized system led to a series of successes over the next seven years which resulted in numerous arrests and such pressure on the RAF that they were unable to achieve any success-ful operations (other than stealing enough money to keep alive) until 1985. One of these successes occurred in Frankfurt in 1979. The police had information that an RAF safe house was operating in the city. They deduced that semi-clandestine terrorists would not risk paying bills using cheques or credit card transactions which could be traced; they therefore asked the electricity auth-ority to provide a list of names of all those who had paid their electricity bills in cash. There were 18,000 names. They then approached other organizations (e.g. hire purchase companies) and ran all the names of people paying bills in cash through the computer. Only two of the 18,000 fitted the criterion in every case, and both were clearly paying their bills in false names, so their apartments were raided. One was occupied by a drug-dealer, the other by Rolf Heissler, an RAF terrorist on the wanted list. Heissler obliged by drawing a gun and was arrested.

The traumatic experience in the case of Britain was that of the 'Yorkshire Ripper', Peter Sutcliffe, who brutally murdered thirteen young women in Leeds and neighbouring areas. There was a clear connection between these crimes. Large numbers of police officers obtained vast amounts of information from wit-nesses and from door-to-door enquiries. During the case, the weight of information on paper reached twenty-four tons, far beyond the ability of any human being to sift and correlate. Eventually Sutcliffe was caught, largely by by luck, in a neighbour-ing police force area by two quick-witted traffic policemen whose suspicions were aroused when checking his car on some quite unconnected matter.

As a result of public disquiet over this case, the British equival-ent of the German system was developed: the Home Office Large and Major Enquiry System (HOLMES), which can within thirty seconds correlate facts whose links would otherwise not be immediately apparent. It has proved particularly useful in solving 'serial crimes' like sequences of rapes or child murders.

In both HOLMES and the German system, however, the decisions are still human. The computer simply makes binary 'yes-or-no' decisions. By taking about 4 million binary decisions in a second, it helps the humans to make their decisions by tirelessly sifting data faster than people could do it, so contributes in efficiency, speed, convenience, and economics.

Other systems have been developed for assisting in identification from photographs, for example the Facial Analysis Comparison and Elimination System (FACES). This is based on forty-nine characteristics, each categorized on a 1 to 5 scale. This can be enriched by the 'Photo Retrieval from Optical Disc' (PROD), in which the data are held in digital form and characteristics can be projected pictorially on a screen. As witnesses describe a person they have seen, the picture can be amended – 'No, his mouth was a bit smaller – until gradually the synthesis from several witnesses takes shape. In due course, this can be compared, both digitally and pictorially, with a small number of pictures of known criminals or terrorists. Positive identification is far more likely to be achieved by these means than by bemusing the witness with a continuous succession of photographs, which experience has shown results in positive identification in only 5 per cent of cases and in an even smaller percentage of convictions.

FACES proved particularly successful in trials in a group of towns around Blackburn in Lancashire, with a population of 250,000, where 82 per cent of the reported crimes in 1986–7 were committed by local criminals. The number of photographs held in police records pictorially or on the computer is of manageable size and can be quickly narrowed down as witnesses eliminate certain characteristics in turn. In due course only a handful remain, from which a positive identification by several witnesses can be made.

These systems are in an early stage of user trials and new applications and new horizons will come into view as the 1990s unfold.

Similar developments can be expected in the matching of fingerprints. Currently these are matched better by human beings than by computers, but a new Automatic Fingerprint Recognition (AFR) system is undergoing trials which could link every police force in Britain to a central fingerprint collection. Police records contain some 40 million individual fingerprints and palmprints from 3.5 million people with criminal records. The hope is that it will become possible for detectives at the scene of a crime to feed in a fingerprint on their terminal from which the central AFR system can match it to a shortlist of three or four candidates, after which more detailed analysis and other evidence will in due course provide enough material for an arrest and conviction.

The successors to HOLMES, FACES, AFR, etc. will be built round parallel computer systems currently coming into effective use. In these systems there may be, say six computers, each one doing a number of things simultaneously. Such a system can make about 25 million decisions per second and can also make logical inferences (of which more to follow). In the laboratories, and in sight, are massively parallel computers which may be able to handle 25,000 million decisions per second. These will add a qualitative element as well as a quantitative one. They will be thinking machines and certain scientists do believe (and have believed for nearly fifty years) that they may, within the foreseeable future, be able to rival the human brain in their capabilities – though others doubt if they will ever quite do that.

The computer and the brain

Alan Turing, who invented the computer which broke the apparently impregnable German 'Enigma' code system in 1940–1, forecast that 'within fifty years a machine may be able to fool people that they are talking to a human being', that is by the early 1990s. We are not quite there yet but Turing may not have been far out.

The human brain, which the computer hopes to match, comprises a huge number of brain cells (neurones) and cell junctions (synapses). There are about 1,000 billion such junctions in each brain. With Turing's computer in the 1940s, relying on thermionic valves and metal grids, a system with 1,000 billion electrical contact points capable of taking binary decisions would have required premises as large as Greater London. The transistor which replaced the valve in the 1960s would have reduced this to the size of the Albert Hall. By 1980 the microchip could have assembled these 1,000 billion within a small room. Microprocessors now in the laboratories should be able in the 1990s to fit them at last into something the size of a human brain.

This does not necessarily mean, however, that they will be able to make all the logical, qualitative, intuitive, and emotional judgements that the brain can make – though some believe that one day they may (perhaps in another thirty years?).

The way in which a brain does these things is through its ability to learn by experience. Some of its qualitative powers are built into a brain at birth: a human baby and a kitten both know instinctively that their food comes from a nipple to which they are guided by scent. They are then taught certain skills and judgements by their mothers; others they may teach themselves without knowing precisely why; and others they learn from experience, such as that some things are prickly or taste nasty so that they give them a wide berth.

Environment and artificially imposed experiences can distort the learning process: kittens denied access to their mother and brought up from infancy with a certain species of rodent will never hunt that particular species, though their mother would have taught them to do so if she had been with them.

These learning processes, whether induced by instruction or by experience, seem to come about from the ability of the brain to strengthen the relevant cell junctions (synapses) when a number of experiences pass a certain threshold. In laboratory tests, animals with much simpler brains, e.g. slugs, have been given access to a plant which has an unpleasant effect. Eating it once does not noticeably change their behaviour but, when the experience has been repeated a number of times, they learn to avoid that plant 'instinctively'. This 'instinct' has in fact been programmed into the electrical contacts in its brain – its memory – by experience. A computer memory can be similarly programmed to learn by experience to an increasing degree each time that experience is repeated. This is the beginning of the process of instructing it to make 'logical inferences'.

The nature and development of the computer

Turing's computer – and indeed every computer – was based, like the brain, on a number of electrical points of contact, each capable of taking a binary decision, that is to close or not to close the circuit. The development of digital computers has been in terms of speed (number of decisions per second) and reduction in size from the conductor grid to the microchip.

The digital principle of selection has been used for more than two centuries, in the form of the punched card machine. The machine is asked, say, to select a person fitting a specific profile. A personnel manager may specify fifteen ideal qualifications for a job, such as (1) under 25, (2) unmarried, (3) in good health, (4) holds a driving licence, (5) speaks fluent French, and so on. Only if the candidates' cards have holes punched to indicate 'Yes' to every one of these fifteen qualifications will the machine put their names forward for consideration. Experience shows that a potential terrorist or criminal may also have a similarly quantifiable profile from which a short list of suspects can be distilled.

The limitation of the card system depended on the number of

holes it was possible to punch in a card – the number of bits of information the card could hold. Today a common silicon chip, a few millimetres square, can hold 250,000 bits of information (250 K-bit) and those under development can hold 1 million (1 M-bit).

In essence, the binary decision is made by currents passing along an intersecting grid of conductors and it has only one possible route, when the circuit is closed at one particular intersection, which thus holds one bit of information, like the hole in a punched card. The early computers did comprise a large stack of such grids, until the ever-shrinking microchip took their place.

The principle of this kind of decision is familiar to anyone accustomed to finding a grid reference on a map. A normal map sheet at 100,000 scale, say 50 cm × 100 cm, contains 5,000 squares each 1 cm × 1 cm. A four-figure reference, say 47–23, indicates square number 47 along and 23 up. The eye can then subdivide each square into 10 each way, estimating, say, 6 out of 10 along and 9 out of 10 up – a six-figure reference of 476–239. This fixes a point within 1 millimetre on the map or 100 metres on the ground. On one such sheet there are 500,000 – half a million – different six-figure references, and the limitation is that the eye perusing the map cannot in practice judge differences smaller than one-tenth of the square (1 mm) each way. Experienced map-readers can find a six-figure reference on the map in about two seconds and, in so doing, they are choosing one intersection out of half a million.

This is what a computer does and it does it a good deal faster than the human eye, picking out co-ordinates on the way. It can also be programmed, depending on its 'yes-no' choice from the quarter million on the first 250 K chip, to ask another question and make a choice from the next quarter-million chip, then another, then another. Whether it makes a choice from 4 million (16 x 250 K) or 25,000 million alternatives in a second, the basic nature of its decisions is binary – yes or no – and is made by the intersection of conductors, whether on an old tangible metal grid or a modern microchip, or a linked series of such grids. It is very fast and (provided it is programmed to answer the right question) very reliable; but, as so far described, it is still strictly 'data-based', rather than 'knowledge-based'.

The human brain, even if a little slower and less reliable over automatic data-based decisions, can go a very great deal further than the computer. Reverting to the map squares, human map-readers may not know the exact map reference but they may remember that the place they wanted was, say, just outside a village, after crossing a bridge over a stream, by a road junction;

a quick sweep of the eye and – 'Ah, here it is!' People can also judge quality from the map – 'That hill-top should give a fine view of the village. I should be able to pick out the house'.

Taking another example, instead of looking at a map, some people might be looking at a painting on which, without any grid references, they can instantaneously pick out a fieldmouse nibbling at some seeds on the ground; then they can see a cat about to spring out of the bushes at the mouse; then there is a dog coming round the corner and experience tells them that, when the cat jumps out, the dog will be jerked into action and chase the cat. They need no conscious 'yes-no' decisions; they spot the three animals and instantly judge their relationship; in a single glance at the picture as a whole they can predict what is likely to happen, not for certain, but in all probability. An immediate logical inference has been made from a picture which in fact consists of millions of blobs and pinpoints of pigment, each contributing its bit to the story.

Teaching a computer to make logical inferences

The purely data-based computer can be programmed to make a whole series of specific one-in–250,000 binary choices, each depending on the answer to the last one. To approach the human brain, however, it has to become knowledge-based, that is, to make logical inference based on experience. (For the non-professional, the most understandable book on the subject is Yazdani and Narayanan 1984.) Each logical inference is a series of choices, each based on an 'if-then' rule, which lead to a *probable* conclusion, just as a child learns to recognize, say, a duck: 'If it looks like a duck, waddles like a duck, and quacks like a duck then it probably is a duck'; if, however, there are other non-duck-like characteristics – too big, wrong colours, long neck – then on balance the child learns that it is probably not a duck after all, but maybe some kind of a goose. Unlike the simple binary decision this is a muzzy one – a balance of evidence and a probable conclusion. Children of 3 or 4 years old, long before they can explain why in words, can tell the difference between a duck and a goose or between a horse and a cow, or between an Austin Maestro, a Vauxhall Astra, and a Volkswagen Golf – even if some mischievous hand has switched over the names, because children can tell the difference before they can read the words.

A computer can similarly be trained to make logical inferences. Each inference may be based on 100 or 1,000 individual machine instructions or binary decisions, some of them grouped into key words or concepts. Current knowledge-based computers can work through 30,000 'LIPS' (logical inferences per second) each one involving (at 100 to 1,000 each) 3 million to 30 million binary decisions. Coming on stream now are parallel computer systems capable of 200,000 LIPS (that is making 20 to 200 million binary decisions per second). This is what the human brain is doing, albeit unconsciously.

Such systems are already in use to assist certain commercial processes and medical diagnoses. A diagnosis can often be made from fewer than 500 sequential rules ('Is the pain in your chest?', 'Is it a steady pain?', 'Is it a stabbing pain?') provided that the questions were selected by an expert doctor. A preliminary questionnaire on these lines leading to a conclusion before a consultation can save the doctor a lot of time. A similar set of rules could be applied to a computer interrogation before clients talk to their lawyers. But the idea that a computer system could become a chess grand master is not yet in sight: it is estimated that grand masters have some 50,000 rules in their brain – a far cry from 500 or 1,000.

A computer can be trained to try every possible solution – every permutation and combination in turn – until it finds the best. This can be useful to, for example, tour operators who wish to include thirty places in their itinerary and to pick the route which involves the minimum travelling time. Throughout the process, the computer retains the best so far. If the next is worse, it is rejected; if better, it supplants the reigning champion. For a complicated itinerary the computer can do this far more quickly than a human brain. A computer can also be programmed so that, when it tries something which fails and is rejected, it propagates the error backwards into its programme so that it is avoided next time – as the slug does with the nasty plant.

To supplement the 'if-then' rules, a number of other schemes can be used to assist computers to make logical inferences. Two in particular are worth mentioning: semantic networks (with key words) and frames. Key words have long been an aid used on normal computers: of millions of words recorded on floppy discs by a word processor, a computer can call up every page containing, say, the word 'bomb'. This can be carried further by programming it to link synonyms or associated words – e.g. pub, bar, inn, hotel – or to link concepts or relationships – e.g. Bogota (as capital of) Colombia.

'Frames' are what psychologists call 'schemata' to represent stereotyped situations. A house, for example, almost always includes certain rooms – kitchen, bathroom, bedrooms, living-rooms. Someone who owns a car will normally have bought a driving licence and an insurance policy, and will buy petrol and tyres from time to time. If one of these is missing, the computer will draw attention to it. It can be programmed to pursue the matter further, acting on incomplete knowledge in much the same way as a person reasons. If it is equipped with a hierarchy of frames, it can do a lot of things a human cannot, or at least can do them more quickly and reliably. Looking further into the future, there is current research into the automation of 'hunches'.

Expert systems for anti-terrorist intelligence

The knowledge-based computer will be a particularly useful tool for police or military intelligence handling. The ability of a computer system to make logical inferences makes it possible for ordinary police officers, not trained in computer technology beyond knowing which keys to press, to have immediate access to an expert system which is able to provide them with judgements and knowledge far wider than they could carry in their own head; it can also prompt them on the questions they should ask. The officers can carry a simple terminal with its keyboard and visual display unit and link it either by radio or with a modem through any telephone to the mainframe computer at police headquarters; better still, they can carry a portable intelligent computer containing a large memory of its own, able to tell them most of what they want without reference to headquarters. There are now such computers, about the size of a pocket book and costing less than £100, whose memory contains information equivalent to that in a 300-page reference book, which people can call up far more quickly than if they had to hunt through an index and 300 pages. If they are equipped with a portable briefcase-sized desktop machine, they can have in their hands information equivalent to that in a thirty-volume *Encyclopaedia Britannica*. If, by any chance, the information is not there, the 'intelligent computer' will tell them so and they can still tap in to their station or force computer and thence, if needed, to the national police computer system.

This gives the police officers the option of making straightforward decisions themselves or, if they wish or in the event of the answers not being clear, to refer the question to a higher level, where there is a more complex system working to more complex rules.

When they arrive at the scene of a crime (e.g. of a murder, kidnap, or robbery), they will feed into the headquarters main-

frame computer all the evidence they see and obtain from neighbours, etc. This computer will also, however, have information
from other sources, including the past, which human beings will
not know or, if they do, the relevance may not strike them. Any
linkages such things as car registration numbers or telephone
numbers found in diaries will at once be thrown up by the computer. If it is properly programmed, however, it will also draw
attention to linkages with 'shadow events' having no apparent
connection, such as a red Ford Cortina hired in a town one
hundred miles away. It can do this because of its ability to sift
vast amounts of data automatically at lightning speed and spot
relationships. The more data which are recorded and the more
the computer is capable of logical inference, the more quickly and
surely it will build up a meaningful picture, giving clear signposts
for further investigation.

Amongst the leaders in research of the potential of Artificial
Intelligence (AI) for acquiring and handling police intelligence
against crime and terrorism in 1987 were Chief Superintendent
John Hulbert and Superintendent David Webb, the Head and
Deputy Head respectively of the Operational Research Depart-
ment of the Devon and Cornwall Constabulary. Dr Hulbert, with
degrees in computer science and psychology, must have been one
of the best qualified police officers in his field before his retirement
to the commercial world in 1988. David Webb, himself also now
working for a PhD, encapsulated some of their ideas in a presentation to a symposium on International Terrorism at the Office of
International Criminal Justice at the University of Illinois in
Chicago in August 1987. He took as his theme a quotation from
Douglas Hofstadten.

> The aim of AI is to get at what is happening when one's mind
> silently and invisibly chooses, from a myriad of alternatives,
> which one makes most sense in a very complex situation. In
> many real-life situations, deductive reasoning is inappropriate,
> not because it would give wrong answers, but because there are
> too many correct but irrelevant statements which can be made;
> there are just too many things to take into account simul-
> taneously for reasoning alone to be sufficient.

Though still far behind the human brain in other respects, parallel
computer systems can simultaneously take account of more factors
and inferences, thereby eliminating the need for consideration of
whole ranges of enquiry, more quickly and surely than the brain.
The process was described on pp. 67–9 in the already familiar
context of medical diagnosis. In the field of criminal and anti-

terrorist intelligence, this instant elimination of superfluous lines of enquiry can release the human brain from wasted time and exhaustion to concentrate on what it can still do better than the computer.

There is still no substitute in sight for the human expert who (like the diagnostic doctor) feeds into the computer the 'if-then' rules on which its inferencing depends. It is rare, however, for someone who is a leading expert in one field (medical, behavioural, psychological, economic) also to be a trained computer scientist. It is necessary to have a 'knowledge engineer' who acts in effect as an interpreter. They discuss together the line of reasoning, and the knowledge engineer programmes the computer in accordance with the expert's logical sequence of 'if-then' rules and inferences.

The greatest value of the resulting expert system is that it saves future, less expert users from wasting time in proceeding down a cul-de-sac. This has a particularly strong application to police and military intelligence organizations, in which officers' postings change fast. This is healthy in almost every other way: constant input of fresh ideas, new challenges and stimuli preventing staleness and boredom, and building up a breadth of varied experience for senior officers. The price to be paid is that an outstanding person often takes his expertise with him. Operating an expert system, with the aid of his knowledge engineer, he will now be able to revise its programming week by week as his own experience and ideas evolve and new technology develops. Thus, when he leaves, the system will have in its memory the best of his expertise on call to his successors. This should provide the best of both worlds.

This may be particularly valuable in such fields as hostage negotiation and prediction of political and security risks. The London Metropolitan police have an outstanding record in hostage negotiating, built up over some years of experience from the Spaghetti House and Balcombe Street sieges in 1975 to the Iranian Embassy siege in 1980 and some other, less spectacular cases. The number of actual cases, however, is relatively small, so every one is likely to contribute a considerable advance in at least some areas. Access to 'state of the art' advice should therefore be instantly available to all when the next emergency arises.

Parallel computer systems should in future enable past predictions of political and security risks to be exhaustively analysed against the way events actually did unfold. Analysis of the factors affecting success or failure of the predictions will be more surely identified and made conveniently available to guide (though not to direct) others in avoiding mistakes in future predictions.

This ability to amass and correlate data at a speed and scale beyond human capability will similarly place a powerful tool in the hand of those searching for a pattern and a *modus operandi* in the data from past terrorist acts and other crimes. The human expert will be able to amend the rules and frames to enable the AI system to decide when certain data and inferences cease to be relevant and to feed in new ones with appropriate weighting. As AI develops, the system will develop a growing capability of learning from its own experience to eradicate error and improve judgement.

Fine-grained parallel computers

The prospects ahead for computer-aided intelligence may be quite revolutionary as technology develops, particularly in the field of fine-grained parallel computers. They may at last begin to emulate the brain in its instant recognition capability – spotting a face or picking out a familiar voice in a crowd. The brain clearly uses quite a different system from that used by the present generation of AI systems. The author asked Dr John Hulbert – now Managing Director of a research and development firm (Cogitaire Ltd) – if he could explain this in terms comprehensible to the non-professional and his reply was so clear that it is repeated here, with his permission, unaltered.

The current AI frame and rule-based systems were extremely powerful logical analysers, but suffered from the defect that the operation was essentially sequential. This can be improved to a large extent by the application of what is termed coarse-grained parallelism. This essentially means modest numbers of parallel computers, such as the famous 'Transputer' produced by the UK firm Inmos. However, these machines are still essentially sequential (Von Newman machines in the jargon) computers, operating in some degree of co-operation: they naturally increase the power available just by the fact that there are a lot of them. It is however apparent that such an approach will not be totally successful for all aspects of information manipulation.

How does an observer recognize the face of a friend from a glimpse lasting a fraction of a second? Nobody knows for certain; however, answers are beginning to emerge. The well-known '100-step rule' is beginning to have dramatic effects on computer design in the high volume information-processing area. The 100-step rule is based upon some fairly simple arithmetic. It is well known how fast the average neurone in the brain can fire. It is also known how long it takes for complex recognition tasks to be completed by the human being. It only requires secondary school mathematics to work out that each brain computing element can have fired only a small number of times, hence the 100-step rule. This rule essentially says that the human computer cannot have taken more than 100 programming steps in order to achieve the complex recognition that we all personally experience. Recognition systems in military, police, and other areas involve programmes with millions of lines of code, large amounts of which are used for every recognition event. Obviously therefore some parts of the human brain must approach the recognition problem in a fundamentally different way. This fundamentally different approach is known as fine-grained parallel or neural computing. The essential difference here is that instead of designing parallel computers in terms of hundreds of computing devices, the design objective is to produce parallel computers numbering thousands if not millions on a single board. Each of these computers has a very reduced capability (the technical term is Risc: reduced instruction set computers). However, each of these low Risc machines can be connected to an arbitrarily large number of other computers or neurones (as the researchers in this area tend to call the ultra micro computers), and can affect the behaviour of the other computers to which they are attached. This arrangement is very reminiscent of what we know about the brain, hence the reasons why this research area is redolent with a combination of physiological as well as computer terminology.

This science fiction prospect is nearer than one might imagine. Dramatic advances in the electronics industry have made available at an economic cost facilities which can be used for these new 'neural computers'. This type of facility will be of particular value in sensory systems, systems which have to sift through vast amounts of information in large data banks, and of course within the intelligence community, both military, police, and commercial.

Dr Hulbert stressed in his future prognosis that in the next few years, intelligence systems are likely to incorporate a mixture of the current artificial intelligence paradigms using sequential and moderately parallel computers, with much of the information fed by parallel facilities using the latest neural technology. During

1987 approximately twenty start-up companies in the neural computer area sprang up in the USA, and interest in Europe and the UK began to blossom. In 1988 the International Neural Network Society was founded and it held a series of conferences in 1989. There was a dramatic increase in publications on this subject in 1988 and 1989 and it is fast gathering momentum as each month goes by.

At the International Police Exhibition and Conference (IPEC 87) in London in August 1987, New Scotland Yard announced plans for the development of their Crime Reporting Information System (CRIS). By 1991 they intend to link all the 75 divisions of the Metropolitan Police with 2,000 microcomputers linked to 8 mainframe computers. The aims will include pattern-spotting and 'fuzzy matching' of scraps of partly remembered information from witnesses, such as three of the letters on a car number plate. This again will correlate these scraps of information in a way which no human brain could do without hours of hunting through files or VDU displays. The irony is that the human brain had developed the ability to reach other conclusions in a flash from other fleeting scraps of information (like children, as described on p. 67, distinguishing between the *appearance* of two birds or animals or cars before they can read) but this is the product of millions of years of brain development in which alphabets, still less car numbers, played no part.

Few computers are yet knowledge-based. As they spread, and as the phenomenal processing speeds of fine-grained parallel computers begin to take effect, the more dramatic will be the capabilities of the computerized intelligence systems. They cannot yet rival certain of the more subtle things a human brain can do but they can process facts and make inferences more quickly and in some cases more reliably; they do not become tired or bored; and, though they are still relatively stupid, they get brighter every year.

Chapter eight

Physical security

Access control and identification

'The strongest castle walls are not proof against a traitor within.'
This ancient proverb applies more strongly each year with growing
scope for treachery as electronic technology develops. So the
control of access and the identification of moles, sleepers,
intruders, impersonators, criminals, and terrorists have become
more crucial than the efficiency of perimeters, surveillance systems, and alarms. The main risk is of entry through the front
door.

Access control requirements include vetting and selection; control of admission of staff by a guard checking identification or by
electronic locks operated by a key card; checking credentials of
visitors and contract workers and tying down responsibility for
their supervision while they are inside; detecting impersonators
(see pp. 78–80); and spotting would-be terrorists or criminals,
including hijackers, by detecting suspicious personal characteristics or weapons or explosives.

Access and parking of vehicles is equally important. Tagging is
the best way, for example with a coded tag on the windscreen,
which is read by a surveillance beam, or the tag can be under the
vehicle to be read by a coil buried in the roadway. Each tag can
be unique, enabling the vehicle's authorization and movement to
be recorded and cross checked. The tags can also be used to
operate automatic gates or to lower a robust road-blocker which
is normally kept raised from the road surface.

The traditional pass or identity card, relying on a photograph,
a signature, and sometimes a thumbprint, is no longer good
enough for sensitive premises. Watermarks, metallic strands, and
holograms make forgery more difficult, but none of these provides
a reliable guard against impersonation.

In recent years, various forms of machine-readable card have been developed, some passive and some active (i.e. with a power source, transmitting, receiving and processing signals recorded). The simplest passive cards contain a strip of electronically recorded data, as on the familiar key card and credit cards with their black strips. The 'smartcard' is better, incorporating its own microprocessor – a small computer memory activated when the card is placed in the slot of a host computer terminal, in an entrance lobby or check-point. Alternatively, authorized persons can be issued with uniquely coded tags, like those for vehicles, clipped to their lapels as an identity badge, and checked by a reading head built into the wall by the door (invisible if necessary), so that they can pass without pausing or putting down what they are carrying. If required, the system can be programmed to record each occasion and the time when someone goes in and out, which could be useful for any subsequent investigations. Active cards or tags, transmitting their own signals and processing signals received, need be no more than 4 mm thick, like the smallest pocket calculator. Passive smartcards, with a lot of data in the memory of their microprocessor, are no bigger than a credit card and some cost less than £2.

Embarkation and disembarkation

Identification and control of passengers embarking and disembarking at airports to prevent, respectively, hijacking and the entry of terrorists is at least as important as detecting weapons or explosives concealed on their persons or in their baggage (which was discussed in Chapter 6).

Existing technology is already available for much tighter control if the threat becomes more serious. The Germans introduced machine-readable passports and identity (ID) cards in 1987. These, on insertion into the computer terminal at the point of exit or entry, can directly activate the German national police intelligence computer memory, indicating at once any recorded information about the holder, prompting the checker to interrogate or to hold the person for further investigation. (Detection of the use of stolen passports or cards and of impersonation are considered below.) Other responsible governments in Europe and elsewhere may well follow suit, though there is considerable prejudice to be overcome, particularly in the UK and the USA, against the holding of personal data and the issue of ID cards.

It is obvious, however, that the countries most likely to sponsor or support hijackers and other terrorists (e.g. Iran, Iraq, Libya, and Syria) are the least likely to issue such passports or ID cards,

or to co-operate with the systems of those who do. It may therefore become necessary for target countries to issue machine-readable visa cards as a condition of entry for people originating
from certain countries, involving fairly comprehensive background
checks before issue coupled with interrogation at the points of
entry or exit. (The Israelis have found that two or more such
checks or interrogations are likely to detect dubious passengers,
because of minor discrepancies, more effectively than machines.)

Another alternative (or supplement) would be the issue of
machine-readable 'International Air Travel Permits'. These could,
in the first instance, be issued by the seven countries which meet
regularly at the economic summits and signed the Bonn Convention in 1978 (Canada, France, Germany, Italy, Japan, UK, and
USA). Between them, they operate 80 per cent of the non-Communist world's air traffic and, for this purpose, they could be
joined by other responsible countries operating large airlines (e.g.
KLM, SAS, Swiss Air). All of these countries would issue International Air Travel Permits, after full background investigation,
to the overwhelming majority of air travellers who constitute no
security risk. Permits from any one of these countries would be
acceptable (subject to an agreed right to monitor or investigate)
to any of the others. Passengers holding them would have the
privilege of rapid processing at embarkation and disembarkation.
Passengers not holding them would be subject to detailed investigation, in a different queue, possibly involving long delays, defer-
ment to later flights, or denial of entry altogether. There would
thus be a strong incentive for regular air travellers to obtain such
a permit in advance, which need be no more arduous than getting
a passport or visa in advance and could remain valid, subject to
review, for some years.

All of this would be made possible by computer science, and
would be facilitated by people being willing to have their personal
data recorded on their national computer (as they already are, to
some extent, on bank and credit company computers) for their
own protection and convenience. People not wishing to do so
usually have dubious reasons for refusal, and their number would
be narrowed down as the advantages became clear.

The development of fine-grained parallel computer systems (see
Chapter 7) will enable data to be processed up to 1,000 times
faster, and particularly to draw attention almost instantaneously
to links between apparently unconnected details amongst a mass
of irrelevant data. Because of the growing speed and falling cost
of recording and processing data, and the readiness of the majority
who have nothing to hide to participate for their own safety and

convenience, it should be possible to feed so many details of each person's background, movements, purchase of tickets, and objects carried with them by hand or in baggage that there would be every likelihood of the hijacker, terrorist, or intruder being caught in one or other of the nets built into the computer system – or at least being pinpointed for further investigation. When the computer system approaches the ability of the brain to spot, instantly and 'instinctively', anything that does not seem quite right, we will be well on the way to detecting terrorists before they have a chance to act. This will depend chiefly on the will of the majority to exploit the technical capabilities available, and on the parallel building in of safeguards against improper use of the information about them that is recorded.

David Webb, whose research was quoted in Chapter 7, has suggested that the rapid analysis of personal data of airline passengers, either from machine-readable data on cards if they have them, or from a standard pattern of questions if they do not, could be used to detect links between a group of potential hijackers. For example, it may be assumed that a team to hijack a wide-bodied aircraft would comprise at least four or five people. They would clearly have bought their tickets separately (perhaps in different countries), would check in separately, and keep well clear of each other in the departure lounge. A sophisticated, knowledge-based computer could be programmed to take note of certain aspects, such as personal, behavioural, national characteristics, possessions carried, entry to the country, and stated purpose of visit or journey, also the procedure used for buying tickets, getting to the airport, and checking in. These individually would mean nothing, but collectively could pick out the very few passengers who might conceivably be hijackers and, more important, link the four or five together. Given an expert system made up of the next generation of fine-grained parallel computers, this recognition could be almost instantaneous, in plenty of time for the four or five people to be quietly picked out in the boarding lounge and taken for additional checks. Their reaction to this might well add further reasons for suspicion. (A hypothetical example is given on page xviii.)

Impersonation

The more the system develops, the more important it will be to guard against impersonation, for example, by the use of a card or pass by an imposter who has stolen it, or who has coerced its proper holder into letting him have it. This can now be done in a number of ways, all of which depend on biometrics: the measurement and identification of some bodily characteristic unique to the authorized person. This can be a fingerprint, DNA body fluids, retina, voiceprint, signature dynamics, or vein pattern. Alternatively simpler biometric measurements can be recorded (hand measurements, face measurements) in sufficient number to make it impracticable for any imposter to match all of them.

Biometric measurements can be recorded digitally or by electronic photography. This record may be on the microprocessor of a smartcard or on the memory of a host computer linked to the interrogating terminal. Recording it on the card is simpler and more convenient but there is a danger that sophisticated criminals or terrorists with access to the technical equipment could record their own biometric data on a forged or stolen card, so it will be better to record it on a host computer memory as well or instead.

Fingerprint matching is currently the most advanced method. In one system now on the market from Identix in the USA and Ferranti in the UK, the terminal consists of a scanner and a keyboard and it is linked to the memory of the main computer of the establishment to be guarded. To enrol, the person to be authorized first asks the interrogating terminal to give him a personal identification number (PIN) which only he and the computer memory need know. He then places a chosen finger on the scanner, which records it both optically and digitally on to the memory. All this takes a minute or less. When he comes to seek entry, he taps his PIN on the keyboard, places his finger on the scanner, and the computer confirms identity (and can operate an electronic lock) within about four seconds. Alternatively if the data are recorded on a smartcard, this can be matched to his finger on the scanner in a similar time. Ideally it should be recorded on both.

It has been suggested that the system could be operated by cutting off the finger of an authorized person. It would however, be feasible to overcome this by building in a means (perhaps by thermal imagery) for the scanner to check that blood was flowing in the finger.

Another system using an analog machine, currently in use in some US prisons, records an electro-optical image of the fingerprint on the computer memory and matches it to a similar image of the actual finger when it is placed in the scanner.

The DNA genetic molecule is unique to each individual and is present in almost all body fluids, such as blood, saliva, and semen. It has been successfully used to secure convictions by positive identification in rape cases and its potential application is unlimited. At present, however, the matching requires analysis of samples taking hours or even days in the laboratory, so it is not yet suitable for access control but, if this delay factor can be overcome, it could become the most reliable of all.

The retina is as unique as a fingerprint or a DNA molecule and its blood vessel system can be scanned by a laser beam and matched to a record on the computer memory within three seconds. The makers claim that the odds against a fake acceptance are about a trillion to one. There has, however, been some understandable consumer resistance to having a laser gun pointing into the eye.

Voiceprints can be a quick and useful auxiliary check and the manufacturers of the equipment claim that it is simple and reliable but neither this nor signature dynamics (by computer analysis, not just visual comparison) have so far produced anything as promising as fingerprints or retina reading.

In early stages of development in UK is the checking of the vein pattern under the skin, which is, once again, unique. A transducer projects infra-red light, of which the blood in the vein absorbs more than the flesh around it so that a pattern of the veins is returned. This is converted into digital form on a computer memory or smartcard. In one version under development, an active card (the size of a credit card calculator) has a photo-diode array at one edge, which is drawn across the back of the user's hand, matching the vein pattern to the pattern of its microprocessor, proving immediately that the user is its rightful owner. This is as simple as drawing a scanner across the bar code on a jar of jam in a supermarket. In this, as with other biometric systems tied to a smartcard, other checks will also be needed to ensure that an imposter has not had a card made with his own biometric data on it.

In fact, in every security system, the most reliable results will come from a multiplicity of relatively cheap and simple checks, of which at least one is likely to reveal a discrepancy prompting more detailed investigation. This might include, for example, a smartcard which matches the holder's fingerprint and which can also activate the national or corporate computer, prompting questions by the official conducting the check to reveal any discrepancies or grounds for detaining the person for more detailed investigation. But perhaps in the future, even that will be done automatically.

Tagging

Tagging of explosives was described on pp. 56–7. Tags under vehicles or on windscreens to react to a coil in the road or a surveillance beam, and personal tags on the lapels of staff authorized to enter sensitive areas, were all mentioned above and are in common use.

There is, however, scope for much more widespread and sophisticated tagging, which could be introduced if the criminal or terrorist threat were to become serious enough to justify it – and if the majority of the public were prepared to support the inconvenience and restriction on civil liberties which it could involve if it were abused. The dilemma is the same as that discussed earlier regarding the recording of personal data on the national computer system.

A form of voluntary tagging successfully used in parts of the USA equips prisoners allowed out on parole with a bracelet which can indicate if they are not within a required distance of a sensor in either their home or work-place, or by which they can report their whereabouts at required intervals anywhere by placing it on the mouthpiece of a telephone. This is issued as a condition of the parole and gives prisoners much more freedom than if they had to report at the same intervals to the police station. The bracelet is, of course, as robust as a handcuff and is sealed on the prisoner's wrist or ankle. If the sensor indicates the prisoner's absence or that the seal has been broken, or if they fail to check in at the required time, the police would automatically be alerted.

There are parts of the body which could be tagged with compounds incorporating unique combinations of colour coding as described for explosives in Chapter 6 – e.g. in the hair or in the pigmentation in the skin – in such a way that they could be identified by their reaction to a scanner. It may also be possible to develop agents, which could be injected into the bloodstream or other body fluid, which would be harmless, longer lasting, and more difficult to remove. Prisoners sentenced to life imprisonment for serious criminal or terrorist offences might be released under licence with the condition that they would be permanently tagged with an agent which they could not remove and which they were required to have topped up at the necessary intervals before it became too weak to be reliably detected. This would, however, be acceptable only if research established that it could not harm the body and if public opinion demanded it in the face of a considerably more serious threat of violence than has so far been experienced. Public opinion would probably already support its use for convicted rapists or child abusers.

Perimeter security, surveillance, and alarm systems

No barrier, surveillance, or alarm system can provide 100 per cent security. The best that a security system can offer is concentric rings of protection, each of which detects and delays intruders and which, collectively, may present enough visible and perceived hurdles to deter them from attempting to break the system at all.

The outer concentric rings are procedural, including selection and vetting of staff, location, and design of buildings (security advice at that stage can avoid expensive and often insoluble problems later), training of staff, and active liaison with the police. Access control at authorized points of entry, aided by reliable means of identification and technical aids, have been discussed earlier in the chapter: they are the most important of all security measures.

The biggest problem in perimeter security, in both outer and inner concentric rings, is the false alarm rate (FAR). Police records show that 98 per cent of automatic burglar alarm calls have been false. As well as wasting time and money, a high FAR dulls the alertness and response of staff and produces dangerous complacency. The astounding story of the intruder who got into the Queen's bedroom at Buckingham Palace early one morning gave an awesome warning. A passing policeman happened to see him jumping from the wall and reported it, but his report was ignored. The intruder jumped over an 'impregnable' beam, triggered two other alarms (both quickly dismissed as false), and was finally seen in the corridors (staff assuming that he must be an authorized maintenance man). The Queen had to keep him talking on the edge of her bed for some time before help came. No one believed it could happen.

The outer physical concentric ring, that is the perimeter fence (barbed or razor wire, chain link, or solid wall with wire on top), will impose no more than a few minutes' delay, when the intruder may be observed by human, canine, electrical, or electronic eyes. Dogs are probably the best, but for an airfield with a ten-mile perimeter a large number would be needed. Where there are long straight lengths of fence on level ground, narrow line-of-sight radar coverage is practicable, but there may be false alarms from animals or large birds. Patrols by security guards require good lighting – effective (especially as a deterrent) but expensive. There are various alarms which rely on changes in the tension of the wires between special fence posts. The problem of tensions changing with temperature variations (very large in a hot continental climate) can be overcome by building in a system which eliminates such gradual changes and reacts only when they are abrupt.

Another method is for two of the fence wires to radiate and create a capacitance field between them. When any foreign body enters this field, the alarm is triggered. The limit of length of these wires is usually about 200 metres but the Canadian Sentrax system, for example, incorporates a controller which can read and analyse thirty-two lengths each of 150 m – a perimeter of more than three miles.

A variant of this system is for the radiating cables to be buried, up to nine inches deep and about five feet apart, arranged so that anything passing over the ground above them triggers the alarm. This, for economic and maintenance reasons, is usually more suitable for inner perimeters round key points (e.g. a pumping station, main switchboard, head office) rather than for a long outer perimeter.

The innermost ring for key points will be robust walls and doors and windows, possibly using bullet-proof glass or Kevlar screens.

Closed circuit television (CCTV) is widely used but to be effective it is expensive in manpower. No one can remain alert enough to be sure of spotting movement for more than about ten or fifteen minutes on end, and even then the boredom is such that there is a risk of its being missed. There are various means whereby the system can be made to react to movement automatically but these usually have a high FAR because, for example, strong winds may cause trees and bushes to move or, by turning up the underside of the leaves, can change the light pattern enough to trigger the alarm.

Volumetric alarm systems using radar or infra-red transmissions can detect intruders either in the open or within a designated area indoors. There are some free-standing models, each with its own power and radio link. Once successful application of this is to dispense a number of such units on the tarmac where aircraft are parked.

Pilkington have developed an alarm system based on fibre optics, which is triggered only if an optical fibre is actually broken, which should have a low FAR. They also exhibited in 1988 a covert version in which the fibres are buried and react to pressure without being broken.

Generally, however, progress in perimeter surveillance and alarm systems has been less dramatic than in, for example, computerized intelligence analysis and collation, vapour detection, neutron bombardment (discussed in earlier chapters) and seems likely to remain so. The biggest challenge is to provide an economic system with a low FAR: large rewards should come to the firm which makes the first practical and significant breakthrough in this field. Meanwhile, and still thereafter, the best security will be achieved by presenting the intruder with a succession of many hurdles to jump, some not easily recognizable as a hurdle, each one in itself cheap and simple, and with a combination of automatic and human responses. With reasonable luck and an alert staff, the intruder should trip up on at least one of them.

Travel and VIP security

The most vulnerable time for VIPs is when they are travelling, and especially on regular journeys between home and work. The most effective protection is procedural, that is making it difficult for the would-be assassin or kidnapper to predict their routes and times of travel, or to recognize their cars, that is to maintain a low and unpredictable profile. It may well be better to travel inconspicuously in a junior-level company car, frequently changed, than in an armoured VIP limousine which will be easier for terrorists to recognize. These aspects are discussed more fully in Chapter 17 (p. 191).

Vehicle armour obviously gives some protection but if terrorists know that it is armoured they can employ a big enough weapon to pierce it (see Chapter 5). Other aids will include internal and simultaneous locking of doors and windows, two-way radio, alarm and tracking systems, and smoke projectors. Robust construction and bumpers will assist escape from an ambush, given an expertly trained driver.

No major technological development is likely, however, which will defeat a well-planned attack in strength using heavy enough weapons. The equipment being developed to detect and jam radio-controlled roadside bombs (see p. 60) tackles only one of the rarer threats. The root of the danger is the stricture of being on the road.

The prime targets – presidents, ministers, and chief executives of very large corporations – can often travel by helicopter from within one defended landing zone to another, travelling by road only in well-populated areas and where heavy protection can be given for a short distance. But this can be only for very few.

The development of microlite and of short (STOL) and vertical take-off and landing (VTOL) aircraft offers a ray of hope for widening the scope for local door-to-door air travel. Eve Jackson who flew from Europe to Australia in 1987–8 will have contributed greatly to solving two problems – robustness and reliability. The real breakthrough, however, its likely to depend on the invention of a dramatically lighter engine with a powerful thrust. Experience of other quantum leaps (from horse-power to steam, from high explosive to nuclear fission, or from thermionic valves to the microchip) suggests that this is not impossible, and that if a leap does come it could revolutionize the generation of power – especially jet power for aviation – within a very few years. Coupled with automatic air traffic control emulating that of the bat, a VIP travelling like one of a flock of birds in a busy air corridor would be virtually impossible to pick out. The art lies in being ready for a quantum leap when it comes.

Part three

Drugs, political violence, and crime

Chapter nine

Cocaine

The narcotic supply chain

The cultivation, processing, transport, and distribution of narcotics is probably the greatest single generator of political violence and crime in the world. Its profits are used to finance and arm rural guerrillas, urban terrorists, and criminal gangs and to facilitate the trade by intimidation and corruption and by keeping the army and police away. In certain countries it is now a far more potent motivator of terrorism than Marxist ideology or religious fundamentalism. In some of these it dominates the national economy and governments govern by its leave. And almost all of this is ultimately financed by the money extracted from drug addicts on the streets of the western world, so this is where the problem must be tackled.

There is a small, lawful, production of narcotics for medical purposes – e.g. cocaine as an anaesthetic, morphine processed from opium – but this can be tightly controlled and is quite insignificant in relation to the quantity of drugs used illegally.

The estimated annual world profits from illegal drug-trafficking are $300 billion and there has been an estimated rise of 10–15 per cent per year and possibly a great deal more than this. Precise estimates are difficult because, if traffickers are blocked in one area, they switch to another. This could prove to be the most dangerous of all the threats to the democratic way of life in both rich and poor countries. The cocaine trail permeates and poisons the societies of the main producing countries (Bolivia, Peru, and Colombia), through the transit areas (mainly in the Caribbean and Mexico), to Florida and thence to the rest of the USA and Europe. The peasants who cultivate the coca get a price sufficiently attractive for them to resist any attempt to force them to grow other crops instead, and in this they are assisted by guerrilla movements who gain their support by protecting them from the army. The growers' price is, however, only a fraction of the pickings of the traffickers and dealers on the way, and of the street value. The whole process is organized by huge international drug 'corporations' based mainly in Colombia and the USA, where a new narcotics millionaire is created every day.

A similar situation prevails over the heroin trail in Asia, which will be discussed in Chapter 10.

Bolivia

One-third of the world's supply of cocaine comes from Bolivia, where coca production is not illegal. Its cocaine trade is officially estimated at $3.6 billion. This amounts to ten times as much as all the legal exports put together, so no one need be surprised that Bolivian governments have sometimes seemed to be half-hearted in their determination to stamp it out. Coca plants are hardy and not generally susceptible to herbicides. The only effective one is Tebuthurion, known as Spike, but environmentalists point out that it also seriously damages other plant and animal life, and might also damage human health; thus far, it has been used only for brush clearance on land not destined to grow crops in the USA. Cutting back the coca plant acts as pruning and enhances future yield. The growers deter spraying by growing alternate rows of coca and other plants. It is very time-consuming to dig out coca roots in remote areas not easily accessible to mechanical plant. Moreover, 23,000 Bolivian peasants and their families depend for their livelihood on 60,000 acres of coca cultivation. Their rural dwellings are basic so they can easily move – as they have done when soldiers have been sent in to uproot their plants – whereafter they have been that much more hostile to government and welcoming to anti-government guerrillas. Political pressure and aid from the USA to promote crop substitution has some effect but will never cure the problem. Most of the Bolivian coca goes to Colombia for processing, though an increasing amount is going out through Paraguay, Brazil, and Argentina.

Peru

Peru grows 50 per cent of the world's coca plant, the main centre being Tingo Maria in the Huallaga valley on the eastern side of the Andes Mountains, some 250 miles north-east of Lima. From here it is transported, mainly in light aircraft from about one hundred tiny airstrips, to Colombia, where the main processing plants are located. Though Peru is not as dependent on coca as Bolivia, coca still makes up about 50 per cent of Peru's exports.

As in Bolivia, coca is by far the most profitable crop which peasants can grow wherever the soil and climate are suitable. In response to the demand from addicts in the west and encouragement from the drug barons, the area under coca cultivation around Tingo Maria increased from 4,800 acres in 1970 to 40,000 in 1985. Attempts to induce Peruvian peasants to co-operate in crop substitution have, not surprisingly, met with no more success than in Bolivia. The drug barons employ armed gangs to encourage this resistance and the drug-traffickers provide money and arms for one of the most fanatical terrorist movements in the world, SL (*Sendero Luminoso* or Shining Path), which will be described more fully in Chapter 12. SL not only keeps the army and police tied up, but also reacts violently to any attempt by government forces or agencies to dig up the coca or encourage crop substitution. In November 1984, for example, SL attacked the main base of a US-sponsored crop substitution programme near Tingo Maria and killed nineteen local employees; the project was suspended indefinitely and coca production continued to expand. SL now has a stronghold which is in effect a no-go area in the Upper Huallaga Valley, which is probably the world's biggest single source of cocaine. The government declared a state of emergency in the whole area in July 1987 and strengthened the police force by 1,200. Though this to some extent disrupted the cocaine-based economy in Tingo Maria itself, it has not so far significantly reduced the coca output. To uproot the coca plants in these areas would necessitate a series of major military operations with helicopter transport and in sufficient strength to beat off a powerful SL counter-attack. It would cost a lot of time and many casualties to uproot even a tiny percentage of the coca.

The government had an encouraging success in capturing SL's senior military leader, Osman Morote Barrionuevo, in Lima on 12 June 1988 and it remains to be seen what long-term effect this will have.

Colombia

While some of the coca is processed in Bolivia and Peru, the majority goes north into Colombia for refinement into cocaine. This is very big business indeed. There are two main centres, Medellin, the biggest, about 150 miles north-west of Bogota and Cali, a similar distance to the south-west. Each has a cartel of drug rings, and there is a continuing and often violent feud between them.

The leaders of these drug cartels exercise an enormous influence on the whole fabric of Colombian government, business, journalism, and on terrorism and crime. Due in great part to the huge inflow of drug money, Colombia has amongst the healthiest balance of payments figures in the world. It has, at the same time, one of the strongest democratic traditions in Latin America and, for many of its people, a good life. On the other hand, Colombia has an appalling history of violent crime, with by far the highest kidnap rate in the world. In the long run, the power of the drug barons is such that the country *could* fall completely under their control, with government and industry subservient to them. This awesome possibility is examined as one of the 'nightmare scenarios' at the end of this book in Chapter 18.

The production of coca in Colombia itself, as in Bolivia and Peru, has been increasing – from 2,500 metric tons in 1981 to about 18,000 in 1985 – but Colombia's really big business comes from the refining and marketing of the crops from all three countries. Though the price is falling, the output is rising.

The scale of the problem was illustrated by a helicopter raid by the Colombian police on a coca-refining plant on the Yari River, 700 miles south of Bogota, in March 1984. After a two-hour battle they secured the perimeter and then repulsed a counter-attack by an estimated force of one hundred men from a jungle guerrilla base nearby. The plant consisted of forty-four buildings and other structures, ten cocaine-processing laboratories, seven aircraft with a runway equipped for night landings, and six months' supply of food for eighty people. The police seized 13.8 tons of cocaine, with a street value of $1.2 billion.

But even this, the biggest cocaine seizure in history, was a mere drop in the ocean. The street value of cocaine exported from Colombia to the USA was estimated in 1985 to be $80 billion per year.

As in Peru, the expansion of the cocaine industry in Colombia was closely linked with the growth of political terrorist movements, and of two especially, FARC and M19, whose organizations and techniques are examined more fully in Chapter 12. They were founded respectively in 1966 and 1973 and were making no great political impact until the end of the 1970s, when they began to raise a 10 per cent levy on peasants growing coca in exchange for 'protection' from the police and military. This was estimated to produce a revenue of about $40 million per year. The big drug rings saw huge profits in keeping the government out and the two movements grew rapidly under their patronage. In May 1984 (shortly after the Yari River raid described above), FARC, M19, and another movement, EPL, signed a truce with the government, but there were suspicions that this was as much a live-and-let-live agreement as a cease-fire, and drug-running seemed to continue unabated. M19 and EPL soon dropped out of the truce. FARC continued to observe it to some extent, though not at the expense of the continued flow of cocaine and the prosperity of the Medellin drug rings with whom FARC have a good working relationship for mutual benefit. Medellin is totally dominated by the drug trade and there are few of its inhabitants, policemen included, who do not have some family links with people involved in it. As in any community involved in big money crime, there are many gang murders. The homicide rate per thousand is reputed to be three times as high as anywhere else in the world: one murder every three hours in a city with a population of about 1 million.

In 1984, the drug barons offered the government $5 billion if they would grant a total amnesty for drug-dealers, but the offer was refused under pressure from the US government. The dealers then put a price of $500,000 on the head of the US Ambassador and offered $300,000 for the capture, dead or alive, of any of the 450 US agents of the Drug Enforcement Administration (DEA) operating in Colombia, some of whom had played an active part in planning the Yari River raid.

In his book, *The Financing of Terror*, James Adams states that after the Yari River raid the DEA identified two leading drug magnates, both of whom lived like robber barons, one of them breeding the finest trotting horses in Latin America and the other gaining support by donating lighting systems to the stadiums of popular soccer teams. Others have financed local hospitals and provided jobs and other welfare benefits for the people. They try to project a 'Robin Hood' image and in some cases the government would lose much local popular support if it acted too firmly against them.

As further encouragement, the drug barons offer lavish bribes to politicians, judges, police officers and other officials which only the most determined and courageous refuse because, if corruption fails, they know that the next stage is intimidation and, if that fails, murder or kidnap of the victim or his family.

Thus, as in the countryside, so in the cities, especially Bogota, Medellin, and Cali, there is a joint threat from armed criminals and political terrorists subsidized by the barons. In the cities, the predominantly urban/student-based M19 will usually oblige.

Drugs, political violence, and crime

Despite this, the governments of President Betancur and, since taking over in 1986, President Barco, have made determined efforts to fight the drug barons and the criminal and terrorist gangs, who have hit back without scruple. One of the most courageous politicians was Betancur's dynamic 38-year-old Justice Minister, Rodrigo Lara Bonilla. In 1983 a congressman suspected of links with the drug barons attempted to undermine Lara by a well-organized smear campaign. The congressman produced a photocopy of a cheque for one million pesos from one of Colombia's top drug barons, Evaristo Porras Ardila, which was proved to have been paid into Lara's election campaign fund. Lara protested that this was a frame-up and intensified his campaign against drug-trafficking, which included the successful raid on the Yari River processing complex in 1984. In May 1985 Lara was assassinated in his car by a gunman riding pillion on a motor cycle. The motor cyclist was killed and the gunman revealed that he had been paid $20,000 to shoot the minister because of his anti-drug activities. Two days later President Betancur himself received a death threat and replied by declaring a state of siege, under which drug dealers could be detained without bail and tried by military courts. The drug barons let it be known that, if their business was interfered with, they would cause 1,800 businesses to close down and arm a terrorist force of 1,800, but Betancur was not deterred.

As part of its plan, the Colombian government announced that it was implementing its dormant extradition treaty with the USA. At this, Colombia's Supreme Court justices began to receive daily threats of death and caved in by ruling that the extradition treaty was unconstitutional.

During the three years following Lara's assassination, about thirty judges, twenty journalists, and a large number of police officers were killed in drug-related violence, including Guillermo Cano Isaza, the publisher and editor of the Bogota daily newspaper *El Espectador*, which had taken a courageous line in support of the government's anti-drug campaign. He was murdered on his way home from work in December 1986.

One of the most spectacular incidents was perpetrated by M19 in November 1985, after their short-lived truce, when they took over the Palace of Justice in Bogota, killing the President of the Supreme Court, Alfonso Reyes. The army recaptured the building with heavy casualties on both sides, eighty being killed in all, of whom fifty were M19 terrorists. The building was reduced to rubble but, during the occupation, the terrorists had sought out and destroyed files of suspects wanted by the USA for drug-related offences. President Betancur said afterwards that M19 had carried out the raid on behalf of the drug-dealers, to obtain their files and to kill or intimidate the judges.

In January 1987 Porras (the drug baron involved in the smear attempt against the Justice Minister in 1983) was arrested as part of a nation-wide police operation which netted 350 suspects, 72 of whom were described as 'big fish', whose extradition had been requested by the USA.

Within a few days of these arrests a former Colombian Justice Minister, Enrique Parejo Gonzales, was shot and seriously wounded by unidentified gunmen in Budapest, where he had been appointed Colombian Ambassador in August 1986 in the belief that in Hungary he would be safely out of reach of the drug-traffickers' hit squads.

In February 1987 the Colombian authorities had a major success in arresting Carlos Lehder, the alleged leader of the drug cartel in Medellin. He was charged on twenty-nine counts of conspiracy and drug-related offences, and announced that his supporters would kill a judge each week in Colombia or the USA until he was released.

Government and police pressure supported by the US DEA has recently driven the barons to shift some of the cultivation, processing, and transport of cocaine out of Colombia into neighbouring countries. In June 1987 Venezuelan national guardsmen were destroying marijuana and coca plantations close to the border when they were attacked by about eighty-five Colombian guerrillas acting on behalf of the drug barons: ten guardsmen were killed. Brazil is also being brought in, but it is in Colombia and (as will be discussed next) in Florida that the heart of the cocaine business is based.

Central America, the Caribbean, and Florida

Across the Caribbean and the Gulf of Mexico the cocaine has traditionally gone mainly to Florida, though DEA activities are forcing more of it to go directly to other distribution points stretching from New Mexico to Maryland. The primary market-place is unquestionably Miami.

The Panama-Colombia border is only 150 miles from Medellin, and Panama is an important staging post both for drugs and for laundering money. As long ago as 1983, a light aircraft about to take off from Miami for Panama was found to contain $5 million in cash. Further investigation revealed that this one aircraft had carried over $150 million to Panama over an eight-month period.

Corruption in Panama, at government level, in the army, and in the financial world, is notorious, and the army chief, General Noriega, was named by a Grand Jury in Florida in November 1987 as having links with the drug trade. He replied by seizing power as President. US attempts to strangle his economy by various sanctions, including freezing the supply of US dollars (which are Panama's currency too), caused some irritation to the public over wages and shopping, but it seemed to have little effect on Noriega, leaving the strong impression that he had other, far more important sources of currency for running the country. The US government looked stupid and Noriega's personal position in the country was probably strengthened.

Mexico is the home of large-scale wholesale brokers for cocaine from Colombia, and the business brings about $1.25 billion a year into the Mexican economy. Most of this is illegal money, which provides ample means of corrupting government officials, fuels inflation, and destabilizes the economy. Yet Mexico, like Bolivia and Colombia, is now so addicted to this money that there would probably be even greater disruption if the flow were suddenly cut off. Mexico is also heavily involved in producing and smuggling heroin into the USA (see Chapter 10).

Cuba, under a 1979 agreement negotiated with a Colombian emissary from M19, has sometimes provided transhipment facilities for cocaine at a charge of $500,000 per ship. Ships from Colombia would hoist the Cuban flag in international waters and on reaching Cuban waters would tranship their loads to small fast motorboats from Florida or the Bahamas, which would quickly transport the loads to any one of numerous beaches and inlets on the Florida coast, a mere ninety miles away. Geographically, Cuba is ideally placed for this, and was happy both to gain hard currency and to help to destablize US society but, probably for political reasons (i.e. the image she wishes to present to the world) she had never played more than a minor and discreet role in the gigantic capitalist enterprise of drug-trafficking.

Jamaica, however, provides a major transit route, with forty registered and thirty unregistered airstrips. The traffickers have become adept at filing legitimate flight plans and then diverting en route. After clearing US customs in Puerto Rico, for example, an aircraft diverts to an unregistered airstrip on one of the many other Caribbean islands to load drugs and continue its journey to the USA.

The administration of the tiny Turks and Caicos Islands has in the past succumbed to the bribes of the traffickers and in 1985 the Chief Minister, Norman Saunders, and two senior officials were arrested in Miami and convicted of participating in drug-smuggling through its airstrips to the USA. Within a year, the British government removed his successor and took over direct rule of the Islands.

The Bahamas are even closer to Florida and, with a mass of islands and numerous harbours and airstrips, provide another ideal transhipment area, particularly from light aircraft to speed-boats for the final dash to the Florida coast. The US DEA estimated in 1986 that the value of drugs shipped through the Bahamas was $10 billion a year.

The DEA admits that only about 1 per cent of the 18,000 illegal flights in the USA each year are stopped and a similar percentage probably applies to speedboats and other means of smuggling. This traffic probably comprises Florida's largest single industry, with a turnover estimated at $15 billion a year. One Colombian businessman now serving a six-year sentence in Florida took a commission of 2 per cent for delivering US dollars in Miami and writing cheques in pesos, which could be cashed with little risk in Colombia. During the eight months before he was caught $242 million had passed through his bank account in Miami. With banking regulations only loosely enforced, and a huge Caribbean and Latin American immigrant population, laundering of money is big business in Florida.

Chapter ten

Heroin and hashish

Opium and heroin

Heroin is more addictive and more damaging than cocaine. It is
produced by processing opium poppies – ten tons of opium produces one ton of heroin. There have at last been a few encouraging
developments. In Britain, for example, the number of new addicts
registering with the authorities declined by 18 per cent in 1985–6
and by a further 14 per cent in 1986–7. Furthermore, heroin
seizures fell by 46 per cent from 317 kg in 1985–6 to 17.1 kg in
1986–7. Nevertheless, not too much weight should be given to
these figures as not all addicts register and the seizures are only
a small percentage of the drugs actually smuggled into the country.

There are two main areas of opium production: the Golden
Triangle (Burma, Laos, and Thailand) and the Golden Crescent
(Iran, Afghanistan, and Pakistan). As was described for cocaine
in Chapter 9, there is a well-developed chain for processing, trafficking, and marketing, leading primarily to the affluent streets of
the West, in which Hong Kong and Lebanon both play key roles.
In 1987 the Golden Triangle produced an estimated 1,500 tonnes
of opium and the Golden Crescent 1,300 tonnes.

The Golden Triangle

Burma is the world's largest single source of opium, producing 80
per cent of the Golden Triangle's output. This is grown mainly in
areas outside government control, because a large part of the
country, especially that in the north and east occupied by the
Kachin and Shan peoples, is controlled by large insurgent armies
or warlords. The Burmese Communist Party (BCP), 10,000
strong, operates in the north-east of the country along the Chinese
border, having strong links with China. Another ten insurgent
organizations, of which the largest is the Kachin Independence

Army, form the National Democratic Front (NDF) with a total strength of 17,000. Burma's most powerful warlord, Khun Sa, has a private army of 2,000 (he says it is 8,000) and controls a large part of the border with Thailand, including the drug traffic across it. He claimed in a press interview that he makes $8 million a year from this.

The drug business was originally built up to finance these armies, particularly those of the BCP and Khun Sa. None of the hill tribes has ever accepted Rangoon's authority since Burma's independence in 1948. Now opium cultivation and trading has become the main purpose for some of them, and they have become extremely wealthy and well armed – much more so than the government army of 170,000, which is very unlikely to gain control of the insurgent areas other than the main towns and the roads between them.

The government has attempted to curb opium production by military operations and by aerial spraying, but this has had only limited success, and has naturally had a very hostile reception from the inhabitants. So long as the demand for opium and heroin persists, the Burmese opium growers will meet it.

In **Laos** the cultivation of opium poppies was officially banned in 1975 but government control of the rural areas is tenuous; the country is so poor that the government is suspected of quietly encouraging opium production in order to help the economy. Laos produced about 150 tonnes of opium per year.

In **Thailand** the government has welcomed international assistance in cutting opium cultivation, and production was down to 15 tonnes in 1988, most of this being produced in inaccessible country along the Burmese border, which is virtually outside government control. In February 1988 the Thais reported the seizure of 1.3 tonnes of high-quality heroin consigned from Bangkok to the USA, with a street value of about $2 billion. This was hailed as one of the largest heroin seizures ever, but it amounted to only about 1 per cent of the heroin produced each year in the Golden Triangle, of which about 75 per cent probably passes through Thailand.

From the Golden Triangle, the drugs are transported through China, Vietnam, Malaysia, Indonesia, and Hong Kong. Addiction in all of these countries takes some of it on the way, but most of it is destined for Europe and the USA. In February 1988 seven small statues sent from Thailand to Chicago were found to contain heroin to the value of $1.8 billion and another $1.8 billion consignment was found by Chinese customs officials in Shanghai en route from Hong Kong to San Francisco. **Malaysia** has some 180,000 addicts of its own, consuming between 4 and 5 tonnes of heroin a year. Another 4 tonnes are smuggled through the country. Mandatory death sentences (so far carried out sixty-one times) have been a deterrent to drug-smugglers, but this tends to catch only the couriers, not the big dealers.

Hong Kong has 45,000 addicts, but it is also a major transit route to the western World. Hong Kong has some fifty triad secret societies with a membership of 300,000; their tentacles extend to Europe, where they control a large part of the heroin trade. Because of pressure by the Royal Hong Kong Police, some of the big drug-dealers and traffickers have moved to Thailand and northern Europe and this drift can be expected to continue as the return of Chinese sovereignty over Hong Kong approaches in 1997. There are also well-established contacts between the triad societies and international criminal networks, including the US Mafia and the Yakusa gangs in Japan.

Today, however, Hong Kong still provides an ideal transit area for heroin. Most of it comes in fishing boats and small coasters from Thailand. On an average day there are about 5,000 boats in Hong Kong harbour, and many are turned round in a few hours. The triad network is adept at altering shipping manifestos so that goods concealing heroin do not appear to have come from suspect countries. It has been estimated that the triads collect protection money from 80 per cent of Chinese businessmen in Hong Kong. They also monopolize gambling, and a common technique is to trap a gambler into debts which he cannot repay except – under threat to his life – by serving them as a heroin smuggler. The triad societies probably now provide about 50 per cent of the heroin consumed in the USA and an even higher proportion in Europe, where Amsterdam is a major distribution centre through its Chinese community of 20,000. As an illustration of the scale of the problem in the USA, 838 lb of heroin (90 per cent pure) was seized in Queens, a suburb of New York City, in February 1989, concealed in a consignment of wheelbarrow tyres. It was valued at $1,000 million and would have supplied 200,000 addicts for six months. There were simultaneous arrests of seventeen people in New York and nine in Hong Kong.

Hong Kong is also a major centre for laundering money: some of the banks are reluctant to co-operate in enforcing the British and US laws enacted in 1987 for seizing assets and authorizing police access to bank accounts where there is a prima-facie case that they may contain money acquired by criminal means. Hong Kong is a huge financial centre, handling some 40 per cent of the flow of foreign exchange into China, so it abounds with international banks and trading, shipping and insurance agents, giving enormous opportunities to conceal unlawful transactions. China is likely to maintain Hong Kong as an international financial and trading centre in its own interests, so these opportunities may remain after 1997.

The Golden Crescent

The Golden Crescent produces less opium than the Golden Triangle, but less of it is consumed locally than in the Far East. Most of its exports are shipped through Pakistan.

Afghanistan produces about 300 tonnes of opium per year. Most of this is grown in areas outside the control of the Kabul government, and the proceeds help to maintain the many rival guerrilla armies operating in these areas. So far from improving this situation, the Soviet withdrawal is likely to exacerbate it, because there is every prospect of continued guerrilla activity, whatever kind of government eventually emerges in Kabul; it may well become a civil war. This is going to increase the demand for money for purchase of arms by the guerrilla armies. No Kabul government of any complexion has ever exerted effective control over the mountainous areas, so the cultivation and export of opium through Pakistan and the USSR is likely to increase rather than decline, and to continue to finance guerrilla insurgency. Western drug enforcement agents are not likely to be given access or protection.

Opium production in **Iran** is also centred on the traditional insurgent areas of Kurdistan and Azerbaijan, bordering Turkey, Iraq, and the USSR.

Pakistan plays a role in the heroin trade similar to that of Colombia with cocaine. Again, the cultivation of opium is mainly in the remote areas of the North-west Frontier bordering Afghanistan, where no government, including that of the British Viceroys, has ever maintained permanent control. Tribal leaders have a great deal of autonomy, and government incursions can only take the form of strong military columns, which seldom venture far from the roads. The growing of opium and, more important, its processing to produce morphine and heroin have always produced a large slice of local income and made it possible for the tribesmen to be well armed. The increasing use of helicopters by government forces will result in their needing ever more money to buy expensive surface-to-air missiles.

Opium production in Pakistan was 800 tonnes in 1979. A government ban on opium cultivation coupled with a severe drought in 1980 reduced this to 60 tonnes in 1983 but by 1986 it had risen again to between 100 and 160 tonnes. In October 1986 the government enacted harsher laws, imposing sentences of from seven years to death for cultivation of opium and life imprisonment for the use, sale, or smuggling of narcotics. The government is also co-operating fully with the UN Fund for Drug Abuse Control (UNFDAC) in crop-substitution programmes. As elsewhere, aerial spraying arouses intense hostility amongst the tribesmen and, as they are heavily armed, this can be extremely hazardous. Up till now, both the opium-heroin business and the tribal insurgencies have been supported by the Kabul government because of the Pakistanis' harbouring of Mujahideen bases amongst the millions of Afghan refugees. The effect of the Soviet withdrawal and the treaties covering it remains to be seen.

Despite the Pakistani government's determined efforts to combat opium and heroin production, the demand at the two ends of the chain – for heroin by the addicts of the USA and Europe and for money for arms by the dissident tribesmen in the Northwest Frontier Province – is going to be difficult to eradicate.

The **USSR** has been involved in drug-trafficking from the Golden Crescent, through the Soviet Central Asian republics. Some Soviet soldiers in Afghanistan became addicts and, like many addicts the world over, were drawn into becoming dealers to finance their addiction. There are allegations that the KGB recruited intelligence agents amongst the Afghan drug-traffickers, inducing them (presumably under the threat of the death penalty) to try to extract weapons from the Mujahideen – especially US Redeye and Stinger surface-to-air missiles – in exchange for drugs, with the added bonus of undermining the health of the guerrilla fighters; and that they used parallel methods to try to destabilize Pakistan.

To whatever extent these allegations may have been true, there is little doubt that, overall, the Soviet government regarded the drug traffic on and across the Afghan border, and particularly the involvement of some of their soldiers, as a menace, and this may have been one of many factors inducing their decision to withdraw. In July 1987 the KGB launched a major anti-drug programme, with publicity to ensure wide coverage in the western press. They later claimed to have destroyed 2,000 illicit opium poppy fields in the Republic of Uzbekistan and to have arrested hundreds of Soviet drug dealers. They announced a ban on the cultivation of opium in January 1988, stating that in future any opium needed for medicinal purposes would be imported.

In 1987 the Soviet government established closer co-operation

with the USA and Britain, and their police seized two large consignments of drugs concealed in sealed freight containers bound
from Pakistan and Afghanistan to Amsterdam and Hamburg.
Though the USSR is not a member of Interpol, it is the intention
to link their narcotics police to the computer network for exchange
of information, and there is now active co-operation between the
Soviet and British police and customs and a continuing exchange
of ideas on technology and procedures.

There are, of course, cynics in the west who claim that all this
is aimed to give the KGB access to details about the security of
western seaports and airports for their own nefarious purposes.
There is, however, every evidence of genuine Soviet concern over
their own increasing drug problem and, while spoons for supping
with the KGB should still be long ones, the west will have far more
to gain by co-operating with them in this field than otherwise.

Lebanon, Syria, and West Africa

Lebanon had now become a major transit route for Asian opium
and heroin, for refining heroin and cocaine and for producing
both hashish (cannabis) and opium in its own right. The drug
trade now accounts for about 30 per cent of Lebanon's GNP. As
in Peru, Colombia, Burma, Afghanistan, Kurdistan, and Pakistan,
the reason for this is the pressing need for insurgent armies and
terrorist movements to raise money.

In Lebanon the central government controls virtually none of
the country other than small parts of eastern Beirut and a few of
the Christian areas in the north. All the remainder of Lebanon is
split into areas controlled by warlords with their rival militias –
the Sunni, the Shia, the Druze, and the various Christian militias
– under loose control of the occupying Syrian army. They are
very heavily armed, with many modern weapons, and, since they
compete, there is a kind of arms race. The militias are financed by
powerful Lebanese families, some of whom are also drug barons.

The drug trade in Lebanon is not new. Soon after the Second
World War the Italian Mafia set up heroin-refining laboratories
in the Beka'a Valley to process opium from Iran and Turkey. The
start of the civil war in 1975, with Christian and Muslim militias
fighting each other and the Palestinians, set in motion the drugs-
money-arms cycle.

Syria has thus far made only half-hearted efforts to deal with
the widespread and blatant cultivation of opium and hashish since
her army moved into the Beka'a Valley in force in response to
the Israeli invasion in 1982; they have done very little better since

extending their military control over much of the remainder of Lebanon in 1987. About 80 per cent of land in the Beka'a Valley is now believed to be under cultivation of opium and hashish. Hashish production is at least 700 tonnes, valued at $100 million, and may be as high as 2,000 tonnes. There is virtually no interference with its cultivation and export.

The Islamic fundamentalist Hezbollah was sponsored and trained by the 1,000 Iranian Revolutionary Guards who have been based with the Syrian Army in the Beka'a Valley since 1982. Hezbollah justify their participation in the drug trade as a means, not only of financing their terrorism, but also of furthering the advance of Islam by fostering the weakening of western societies through drug addiction.

From time to time the Syrians have felt the need to co-operate with the west, like Iran for pragmatic reasons – e.g. to mitigate the adverse world publicity after they were caught red-handed using the Syrian Embassy in London to mount a terrorist attempt (see pp. 173–4) to blow up an Israeli aircraft taking off from London in 1986. If future world events demand more such pragmatism, Syria may try to curb the drug trade which, in theory, they should easily be able to do in a country without inaccessible cultivation areas but, with Lebanon's drug barons maintaining their large heavily armed militias, the Syrian army would have to expect a tough battle.

As pressure has grown elsewhere, the international drug rings have recently developed increased traffic along the West African coast, mostly coming from Pakistan and Lagos, Abidjan, and Accra, and thence to Europe and the USA. The three governments concerned, of Nigeria, Ghana, and the Côte d'Ivoire, are generally co-operating with the west to stamp this out but, if they succeed, the traffic may simply switch to other routes. There are people everywhere willing to make big money quickly, and the international drug rings have plenty to offer. This is a problem the world can tackle only as a whole.

Mexico – and black tar

In 1975, 87 per cent of the heroin smuggled into the USA came from Mexico; by 1981 this percentage had fallen to 36 per cent as a result of determined action by the Mexican government, with US financial aid. They eradicated more than 20,000 acres of poppy fields using the herbicide paraquat. Cultivators responded by growing poppies in small patches and interspersing them between rows of other crops. The battle continues and overall the quantity of heroin crossing from Mexico into the USA is probably increasing again. There have been disturbing increases in heroin overdose deaths and hospital admissions. These figures are more convincing than mere estimates of tonnages seized or of new addicts. And these increases have been particularly high in areas where a new form of Mexican heroin – 'black tar' – is available.

Black tar is so called because it is like coal tar in colour and consistency. Being almost solid, it is more difficult to dilute than the conventional heroin, which is a white powder, often heavily diluted with other powders by the dealers. Black tar is usually sold at 60 per cent purity or more, and is therefore extremely potent – hence the hospital admissions and deaths. It is also cheap, because the farmers can process it and smuggle it across the 950-mile border themselves or with the minimum of middlemen and couriers. So black tar can be bought for one-tenth of the price: about $2.50 for a 10 mg dose, compared with $24 for a dose of conventional heroin.

Chapter eleven

The consumers

The multinational narcotic corporations

The two previous chapters have dealt with the influence of drugs on guerrilla warfare, terrorism, and crime on the upstream or supply side; on the corruption by the cocaine trade of government and business in Bolivia, Peru, and Colombia and the nurturing, financing, and arming of terrorist groups like SL, FARC, and M19 causing tens of thousands of violent deaths each year; and the corruption and intimidation of politicians, officials, and businessmen across the Caribbean and Central America. In the same way, the heroin trade finances the continuing insurgency by warlords and guerrilla armies which have helped to make Burma one of the poorest countries in the world; the financing of dissident tribesmen in Pakistan, Kurdistan, and Afghanistan is likely to dog the efforts to restore stability after the Soviet withdrawal. The drug traffic also finances the horror of Lebanon, where warring militias have maintained chaos in the country for fourteen years.

This chapter examines the downstream side, handled by the main broking centres in Miami, Mexico, Lebanon, Pakistan, and Hong Kong, with their offshoots elsewhere in the USA and Europe. They organize the distribution of the drugs through traffickers, couriers, and pushers to the addicts on the streets, mainly of the USA and Europe, but increasingly in other countries as well, especially in Asia; and they organize the contraflow of money, partly to the distributors and traffickers, but mainly to the drug barons themselves, with only a small proportion reaching the peasant farmers who grow the narcotic plants in Latin America and Asia.

The big headquarters in Miami (now increasingly dispersing to other parts of the USA) are organized like any other giant multinational corporation, with departments for purchasing, transport, marketing, finance, international political risk analysis, and public relations. Like the multinationals, some run the equivalents of charitable foundations, to finance 'good works' to retain the goodwill of the people in the areas where that is important to deter government interference with their operations. And few multinationals could match them for 'slush money'.

The drug multinationals run large 'subsidiary companies', each with their own operating, finance, and public relations departments as appropriate; for purchasing, refining, and transportation in Colombia; and for smuggling, distribution, and retailing in Los Angeles, New York, London, and Amsterdam.

At every level they have loads of money, both upstream and downstream, to finance political terrorists or criminal gangs to protect and further their business. If at any time there is a temporary cash-flow problem, they can rectify this with a lucrative kidnap and ransom, or a demand for protection money from a businessman whom they have ways to persuade that it will be cheaper to pay.

The distribution chain

The downstream distribution is by a mixture of large consignments and small amounts concealed on the bodies or baggage or cars of individuals. Refined drugs have a huge dollar-to-weight ratio. As was quoted in Chapter 10 (p. 99), seven small statues consigned from Bangkok to Chicago contained heroin with a street value of $1.8 billion. At $24 for a few milligrams of heroin, couriers can carry a thousand dollars' worth in the soles of their shoes, tens of thousands of dollars' worth sewn into their clothing, or millions of dollars' worth in a false bottom in their suitcase or in the seat of their car. Sniffers, and especially dogs (see Chapter 6), are excellent for detecting any of these, but not every car, every bag, or every person can be sniffed. Even this risk has been overcome by 'body-packing', whereby the courier swallows one or more strongly sealed capsules of high-grade cocaine on a Caribbean island and excretes them a few hours later in the USA. Risky but, with several thousand dollars in one piece of excrement, the courier is no doubt well paid for it.

Addicts

In the USA there are about 4.5 million cocaine and heroin addicts and over 20 million more have tried one or the other. Malaysia, despite the death penalty, has 200,000 heroin addicts, with another

200,000 using opium. Pakistan has 300,000 and Italy 350,000 hard drug addicts. Italy had 517 drug overdose deaths in 1988.

As described in Chapter 10, there is an alternative version of heroin – black tar – which costs only one-tenth of the price of Mexican heroin. There is also an alternative version of cocaine – 'crack' – which first appeared in the USA in 1981 and its use is spreading rapidly in Britain. It is more powerfully and instantly addictive than cocaine. It is made by heating cocaine powder with water and baking powder, which removes the impurities put in by dealers to dilute it and the result is a hard rock, easily split into chips, which contains 70 to 90 per cent pure cocaine. Local dealers can do this and its popularity is such that, with cocaine costing them £1,000, they can produce crack with a street value of about £3,000.

In Europe and the USA the average addict has to find at least £100 ($160) per week to finance hard drug addiction. Some spend three or four times as much as this. Some of the addicts are the unspeakable playboy sons and daughters of millionaires and the yuppies who find that drugs help them to relax after a day in the exchange market. The majority, however, are people who, if they ever could earn that much money, certainly cannot do so now. If they cannot or will not seek help to break the addiction they have only two alternatives: crime or pushing drugs themselves. Most of them do it by continuous shoplifting until they are caught, whereafter they face two problems instead of one. If they have been caught and served time (and, to the disgrace of the prison service, prison spreads addiction rather than suppressing it), they may fear re-arrest and probably turn to the second alternative – to recruit new addicts and sell drugs to them to buy their own. Thus drug addicts, like animals and plants, have a powerful urge to reproduce the species. So this is where the tackling of this global problem must begin – at the level of the pusher and the addict on the street.

The cure at the demand end

Of course the drug chain must be fought all along the line from the producers through the barons and the traffickers to the addicts, but ultimately the battle can be won only if the source of all the hundreds of billion dollars can be cut off – the payments by addicts to pushers on the streets.

One frequently mooted suggestion is that all drugs, hard and soft, should be legalized and made cheaply available, to make it unnecessary for the addicts to steal or to recruit more addicts, and to cut the profits to the barons and the traffickers. There may be a case for doing this with soft drugs such as cannabis and amphetamines, though there is evidence that taking these does often lead the victims on to hard drugs. 'Decriminalizing' hard drugs, however, would be disastrous, because addiction does irreparable damage to the health, personality, and performance of the victims. It would enormously increase the number of hard drug addicts. Though the price per gram would fall, the total flow of money for the constantly expanding supply of drugs would remain high, and the producing countries would become even more dependent on drug cultivation and processing than they are now.

It has also been proposed at various times in the US Congress that aid should be cut off from Third World countries which fail to prevent the export of drugs to the USA. This would be equally disastrous, because most of their governments are doing their best, bearing in mind the constant threat to the lives of the politicians, officials, judges, police officers, journalists, and people who work loyally with them (e.g. see pp. 93–5); also the financial power of the barons and the consequent strength of the guerrillas and terrorists they support. Cutting off aid would merely ensure that these governments would either face collapse or have to live-and-let-live with the barons and the terrorists. Aid to the hard-pressed governments should continue, so that they can fight and defeat the terrorists. It is the far, far more lavish 'aid' to the barons and the terrorists, flowing from the evil fringe of addicted citizens on affluent western streets, which must be cut.

The suffering inflicted on the ordinary people in the producing countries, as well as on those who try to govern, administer, and protect them is intolerable. The heroism of the Colombian Justice Minister, Rodrigo Lara, and the many others who have died resisting the drug barons, should shame the west. The flow of 'evil aid' from their streets has financed and prolonged the terrorism in Peru and Colombia; the corruption in Central America, the Caribbean, and Hong Kong; the fourteen-year agony of Lebanon; and the insurgencies in Burma and Pakistan; it also looks set to destroy any attempt to restore stability to Afghanistan. It is hypocritical of the western powers to preach sermons to these countries, who are their victims. They must attack the real villains, their own traffickers, pushers, and addicts.

Malaysia, a major consumer country, has attempted this by hanging sixty-one couriers and distributors to deter others, but these people produce neither the drugs not the contraflow of money; they merely batten on them. Moreover, the death penalty is in practice counter-productive because it scares potential informants and witnesses away; it leaves the big fish and the addicts who provide the money untouched.

The US and British laws to freeze assets of people arrested for drug offences and confiscate them if convicted (including any which their colleagues and families cannot prove were obtained by legitimate means) will help, provided that the bigger fish can be detected and convicted. But are ten-year and twenty-year sentences enough? The middleman who laundered $242 million of drug money, taking $4.8 million himself, got only six years; yet he must have known that he was contributing to the ruin of millions of lives of previously innocent people all over the world.

Any person who knowingly contributes to ruining a substantial number of other people's lives may or may not be morally entitled to stay alive, but he certainly has no moral right ever to be free again. One way of shutting them out is the Malaysian death penalty for anyone found in possession of more than 15 grams of hard drugs. A better alternative would be perpetual imprisonment for drug-traffickers, couriers, and pushers found in possession of or proven to have distributed more than, say, 50 grams (which is 5,000 shots of heroin) – and it should be known that there will be no remission. The same penalty should be imposed on those proven to have carried out organizational or ancilliary tasks (e.g. laundering money), knowing that this was for the purpose of distributing drugs. For them too, the sentence must be for ever and they must know it. The only possible candidates for remission might be those prepared to give direct information leading to arrests, which would more than compensate for the total damage to which they had been a party.

The strongest opposition to 'life-meaning-life' sentences would come from the prison officers, wondering how they could ever control prisoners to whom they could offer no incentives. The answer would be for the prisons concerned to provide a range of three regimes. First, a really harsh regime, with solitary confinement, which they already need for recalcitrant prisoners; second, the normal punitive regime, with prisoners in cell blocks but allowed out for a number of hours each day to associate, play games, work for money, or learn a trade; third, a relaxed regime within a totally secure building inside the prison, as has been successfully tried at Barlinnie in Scotland and Bullwood Hall in Essex. In the relaxed regime, six to twelve prisoners would be allowed to live a relatively normal life, with open dormitories, each with three or four beds, within the secure building, with access to a central recreation area and, if possible, an open-air sports area (netted) on the roof. They would have almost unlimited scope for association, and facilities for studying, writing, or other activities as nearly as possible according to their choice. Regular visits (without physical contact) would be allowed. All of these privileges would be dependent on continued good behaviour, and there must be no hope whatever of escape or release.

A 'life-meaning-life' prisoner in the second – normal – section would be threatened with the harsh regime if he were recalcitrant or rewarded with the relaxed regime if he earned it: but any abuse of the privileges would at once mean transfer to the harsh regime.

What of the addicts? So long as they are free on the streets they will be a menace, being certain to commit crimes or still worse to recruit more addicts, thus ruining other people's lives. They must therefore immediately be detained for custodial medical treatment in special hospitals until the doctors consider that they have broken the addiction. Then, after release, they should have to report at stated intervals for medical tests so that, if there were any sign of reversion to drugs, they would immediately be returned to the custodial hospital until they were considered safe to be let out into the community again. No person known to be addicted should ever be at large on the streets.

It is urgent to arouse public opinion to the implications of our tolerance of drug-pushers and addiction. Most people in the west would agree that drug barons, traffickers, and pushers are amongst the most loathsome of all criminals in the ruin they inflict on other people; we must also accept the corollary that, having done it, they should never be free again. We are more compassionate about addicts; but they are not so much pitiable as despicable; more important, so long as they remain addicts, their urgent need to steal or recruit more addicts means that they carry a virulent contagious disease and must be kept in quarantine until cured.

Two countries have bucked the trend, in very different ways. First, **Turkey**, which used to supply 80 per cent of the heroin reaching the USA and had itself a major opium and heroin addiction problem, broke both production and addiction by a degree of ruthlessness which would not be acceptable in the west, but a positive feature of the government's success was that it did mobilize a massive public revulsion against drug abuse to support its campaign. Second, **Japan**, despite its affluence and its proximity to the opium trails, has succeeded in preventing any substantial addiction to hard drugs, again by mobilizing the public behind the judiciary and the police and convincing them of the dire consequences – for individuals, their country, and the world – of failure to stem the tide which they have observed flowing into

Europe and the USA. Even the Yakusa, the Japanese Mafia, have failed to overcome the power of the eyes and ears of the people and their readiness to report what they see and hear.

If the USA and Europe, by tolerating a dangerous form of individual greed, lust, and libertarianism, allow the growth of drug abuse on their streets to continue, the consequences will be dire not only for them, but even more so for the poorer countries in which their illegal money finances large-scale criminal and political violence.

By 1989 cocaine consumption was growing rapidly in Europe, especially in Italy, where the drug trade is a major activity of the international Mafia. One cause for this was the saturation of the cocaine market in the USA, where the bulk price of cocaine had fallen from $60,000 to about $15,000 per kg, while it still attracted $55,000 in Europe. The Mafia and their partners in crime therefore launched an intensive marketing drive in European countries. Particularly alarming was the growth in consumption of the highly addictive cocaine derivative crack.

A glimpse of what could lie ahead is one of the nightmare scenarios in Chapter 18.

Part four

Rural guerrilla warfare

Chapter twelve

Rural guerrillas – Latin America

Rural guerrilla conflict, though largely driven off the front pages of western newspapers by the spectacular fashions of urban terrorism (see Part V), is still very much alive and probably accounts for many more deaths, though these are in the less developed parts of the world and are usually of local people.

Chapters 9, 10 and 11 examined the involvement of the cocaine traffickers in maintaining rural guerrilla movements in Peru and Colombia and of the heroin and hashish traffickers in Burma, Pakistan, Afghanistan, Kurdistan, and Lebanon.

Chapters 12 and 13 look at how some of these guerrilla movements are organized and how they operate. Those selected are the ones which seem to teach the most useful lessons, and which cover a wide range of terrain and political background. There is no attempt to chronicle every rural guerrilla movement – nor every terrorist movement – in the world.

Peru

As was described in Chapter 9, *Sendero Luminoso*, the Shining Path (SL) has many of its strongest rural bases in the areas where coca is grown. Having a somewhat puritanical ideology, it does not get directly involved in the drug trade, but this does not stop it from extorting a levy on the cultivation and movement of coca, or from accepting substantial contributions of money and arms from the drug-traffickers to prevent or deter the army, police, and DEA from interfering.

Potentially SL's rural guerrilla organization and techniques may prove to be the most significant in the world in the 1980s. It is the first revolutionary movement which has aroused any enthusiastic response from Amerindian peasants so, if it is successful, it could be copied in other Latin American countries with a high Indian population. It has no external or internal political allies, scorning

115

all other Peruvian left-wing movements (such as the MRTA, a predominantly urban movement like the M19 in Colombia) and all the other Communist countries, including the USSR, China, and Cuba. Having begun as a rural movement, SL has in recent years begun to operate equally effectively in Lima and other cities.

It is extremely violent and vicious, terrorizing the villages with public mutilation and executions. At least 12,000 and possibly as many as 15,000 people have died, many of them innocent civilians, since the terrorist phase began in 1980.

Peru has a population of 20 million, 65 per cent of them now urban, of whom 5.6 million are in Lima and its shanty towns; 12 per cent are white Europeans, 39 per cent Mestiso or Mulatto, and 49 per cent Amerindian – one of the highest percentages of Indians in any Latin American country. Wealth distribution is very uneven, with the poorest 60 per cent receiving only 8 per cent of the national income. Only about 30 per cent of the population have full-time employment, millions of peasants being under-employed, tilling inadequate land for bare subsistence except where they can grow coca plants. Most of the 2 million in Lima's shanty towns have no regular work and the crime rate is, as a result, one of the highest in the world.

In 1968 a group of radical younger army officers seized power and ran what can best be described as an authoritarian socialist state, with disastrous results for the economy. An elected presidency was restored in 1980, under a highly respected but ageing President (Belaunde), and during his ineffective rule SL became established. He was replaced in 1985 by a dynamic left-of-centre populist President, Alan Garcia Perez, who achieved much in his first two years but the economy is under heavy strain and he is not in sight of victory yet. With inflation at about 40 per cent and the GNP expected to fall by 14 per cent in 1989, the best hope lies in the recent discovery of large oil reserves by Occidental Petroleum and of natural gas by Shell. If satisfactory contracts can be negotiated these could begin to affect the economy quite dramatically by about 1993. President Garcia, whose public approval rating has fallen from 96 per cent to 9 per cent since 1985, is barred by the Constitution from standing for re-election in 1990, but he may have his eyes on returning to power in 1995 with an oil bonanza to help him. Much, however, will depend on progress in containing the SL challenge to the democratic system.

SL was founded in 1970 by Dr Abimael Guzman, a revolutionary professor at the University in Ayacucho, an almost wholly Indian state. His philosophy was to take Peru back to the co-operative agricultural system of the Incas – the kind of primitive communism expounded by Pol Pot in Cambodia. Ayacucho is steeped in the Inca tradition, the imperial Inca capital having been in Cuzco, about 200 miles from Ayacucho city. Unlike most white revolutionaries, Professor Guzman struck a powerful chord amongst the Indians. He has been in hiding since 1978 but is still very active. In July 1988 he gave his first press interview for ten years with *El Diario*, a Lima newspaper sympathetic to SL, which ran to forty-one tabloid size pages. He analysed the ideology, organization, and tactics of the movement and declared that 'revolutionary violence is a universal law without exceptions in resolving the fundamental contradictions through the people's war to overthrow the bourgeois society'.

Guzman in 1970 had launched what was in essence a Maoist plan in which he envisaged revolution starting in the remote areas, spreading through the more prosperous districts until the cities could be surrounded and picked like ripe plums. He originally saw the process taking up to fifty years in five phases:

1 Mobilization, agitation, and propaganda
2 Sabotage and rural guerrilla activity
3 Generalization of violence into guerrilla war
4 Establishment and expansion of bases and liberated zones
5 The blockading of towns and cities by peasant armies, leading to the collapse of government.

In his 1988 interview, he spoke of a much faster timetable, indicating that the revolution should now (after eighteen years) be approaching its final stage, and criticized the movement for being too slow in its progress in urban areas.

The first 'agit-prop' phase did, however, indeed take ten years, from 1970 to 1980. Cadres of attractive young men and women were trained to secure the affection and respect of the Indian peasants by helping them in the hardships of village life and subsistence agriculture. Then, in conversation, they would discuss the shortcomings and oppressiveness of the government and all its works, and what could be done about it. Those who responded would be asked to help in building up the movement as 'pre-militants', that is as sympathizers and probationers. At that stage they would not be party to the secret organization of the party. Gradually, as they proved their commitment and discretion, they would be drawn into the secret cells as 'militants' or 'military personnel'.

The cell members are semi-clandestine – in other words they continue to live normal lives, earning their subsistence, doing secret work part time. Standard cell security – only one person

117

having any contact with the cell above or the cell below – is strictly enforced. Each cell normally has five to nine members, including a leader, two explosives experts, a physical training instructor, and a political ideologue. Their operations are normally conducted outside their own immediate districts so that they are less likely to be recognized. Above the cells is a hierarchical structure of sub-zones, zonal directors, and regions, leading to regional committees responsible to the political bureau. This structure is not easy to quantify because of the part-time nature of it, but probably now involves up to 20,000 people, with women playing a big role in the leadership.

At all levels there is dual command – political and military – with the military subordinate except during actual armed actions. Bombing is the prime technique, because Peru's mining industry ensures easy availability of stolen explosives and of people trained to use them.

By May 1980 SL was ready to carry out its first armed attack – the destruction of ballot boxes to show contempt for the restoration of elective democracy. By the end of 1982 there had been 2,900 attacks, all in the adjacent Andean departments of Ayacucho, Huancavelica, and Apurimac. The typical pattern in this – the rural guerrilla or terror phase – was reminiscent of the early days in Vietnam or the terror of the Khmer Rouge in Cambodia. The aim was initially to attract support by eliminating unpopular local officials and others described as 'social undesirables'. A strong SL column would occupy a village and assemble the villagers to witness a 'people's trial'. The people would be consulted on the punishment, which could range from public flogging and head-shaving to mutilation or execution. The postmaster of Concepción in the Cangallo Province of Ayacucho, for example, was publicly castrated and had his tongue cut out.

From 1983 these operations spread into other provinces, especially around Tingo Maria in Huánuco, the heart of Peru's drug trade, and the biggest coca-growing area in the Upper Huallaga Valley, as described in Chapter 9. It was this development, especially the support with money and arms from the drug-traffickers, which has led to the acceleration of Guzman's plan from its 1970 estimate of 'up to fifty years'. In particular, the successful destruction of the US-sponsored crop substitution project near Tingo Mario in 1984 (see p. 91) increased its support from both the drug-traffickers and the peasants.

From 1984 onwards, as SL's strength grew, there was a rapid growth of urban terrorism in Lima and other cities, and the war could be said to have moved into Guzman's third phase 'Generalization of violence into guerrilla war'. The aim, both in the countryside and the cities, was to do maximum damage to the economy by disrupting communications, mines, and factories, cutting power supplies, and driving away the tourist trade. By the end of 1986, economic sabotage was estimated to have amounted to at least $2.5 billion.

The army, however, is now at least containing the violence, which has decreased from its peak in 1983–4. The Peruvian army is by tradition an enlightened one by Latin American standards, and is getting some response from the population, even in Indian areas, where there is some resentment of the constant attacks on farms, mines, and roads affecting their livelihood. Thus far, however, it has proved difficult to convert this resentment into intelligence information. The police have been regarded as inefficient and corrupt and were generally despised but their successful arrest of the SL military commander, Osman Morote Barrioneuvo, on 12 June 1988 will have enormously increased both their prestige and their morale. The fact that this was achieved in a raid on a house in Lima suggests that it was also an intelligence coup.

Following the arrest of Osman Morote, there was a bomb attack on the home of the public prosecutor, who was leading the case against him and, on 30 June, the abduction (briefly) of the son of a senior Supreme Court judge; there were daily killings of government officials, including a provincial governor. On 20 July Morote was acquitted of some of the charges in one court but still faced charges in nine other courts. On 28 July a new right wing movement, the Rodrigo Franco Democratic Commando (CDRF), abducted, tortured, and killed the lawyer who had defended him and later vowed to kill an SL guerrilla for every soldier and policeman killed.

Equally disturbing was the arrest in Lima on 16 July 1988 of three of the Palestinian Abu Nidal group, carrying lists and plans of Belgian, British, Colombian, Israeli, and US targets in Lima. This, and the attempted murder of the manager of the Lima branch of the Bank of Tokyo, suggests that links between Peruvian and foreign terrorists may be developing.

In June 1988 an independent Legal Defence Institute reported that only 6 per cent of terrorist cases brought to Court in 1987 had resulted in convictions, 75 per cent being dismissed on grounds of the use of torture to extract confessions. Also in June 1988 government reports were leaked to the press, recording over 9,000 deaths by violence since May 1980, including 4,435 guerrillas, 3,875 civilians, 180 government officials, 131 armed forces personnel, and 395 policemen. There were a total of 12,278 guerrilla attacks, of which 11,720 were by SL and the remainder by MRTA. The actual death toll, however, is probably over 12,000.

If President Garcia can build on the arrest of Morote to improve the confidence of the intelligence organization and the police and develop the already constructive efforts of the army to attract a tacit, if not yet overt, yearning for security and order, the corner may be turned. There are, however, two main dangers, both of which are exacerbated by the actions of the drug-traffickers: a collapse of the democratic administration (especially if the President were assassinated); and one or both of these leading to another military coup led by the relatively small repressive element amongst army officers – which there is reason to believe that SL are trying to provoke, in the knowledge that in the long run a repressive military government is more brittle than a democratic one.

Colombia

Colombia has one of the most politically stable democratic systems in Latin America, with one of the strongest economies, but has been constantly plagued by violence. It is only in recent years that Colombia has largely been financed by the international drug trade, as described in Chapter 9. The $80 billion coming into the Colombian economy each year (albeit much of it clandestine, untaxed, and therefore inflationary) probably accounts for the fact that Colombia is the only country in the area which has not had to reschedule her foreign debt. Despite this alluring bonus to her balance of payments, however, and despite the constant threat to the lives of politicians, judges, and others, the governments of President Betancur and Barco have courageously fought both the drug barons and the terrorists they support.

The murder and kidnap rate, both by terrorists and criminals, is horrific. The homicide rate in the drug capital, Medellin, was mentioned in Chapter 9 – three times the highest rate anywhere else in the world. There were over 1,200 kidnaps in the eleven years 1977–87, nearly three times those in Italy, which is second in the world league. There were about 200 in 1987 alone (mainly of local people for ransom but with a sprinkling of expatriates, especially in the oil industry). On 29 May 1988 the M19 movement kidnapped the former presidential candidate, Alvaro Gomez Hurtado, the first distinguished political figure kidnapped in Colombia. He was released on 19 July 1988.

The biggest and oldest terrorist movement is FARC (Armed

Revolutionary Forces of Colombia). This is a nation-wide rural group operating in thirty-nine 'fronts'; its politics are orthodox Communist. Founded in 1966, it remained only a few hundred strong until 1980 but, since receiving support from the drug trade, it has grown to several thousand active guerrillas with many more thousands of supporters. There is no firm demarcation between guerrillas and supporters, as the movement acts more openly than any of the others and has an open political front (Patriotic Front – UP), which stands in elections.

FARC goes to considerable lengths to enlist local popular support in rural areas by applying pressure on the multinational companies. Typically when a foreign company's planning team moves into an area to prepare for a project, the local authorities, such as the mayor and the police, will approach them (with FARC approval) and ask them to employ local people to the maximum possible extent (e.g. junior management, staff, labour, and sub-contracting locally for construction, transport, etc.). It is made clear that if they do this, they will have no trouble from FARC, and this promise is honoured.

If the company declines to accept this proposal, its next callers will be from FARC members, stating themselves to be 'representatives of the people' but leaving no doubt, from their guerrilla-style dress and demeanour, who they really are. They issue a warning, and if the company then fails to fill every possible post with a Colombian, it will be attacked. Most foreign companies do comply, and integrate well with the local population. If the people say that they are happy with the company because it is bringing them work, FARC know that any attacks would be unwelcome, which is why the number of expatriate victims of murder and kidnap is relatively small.

ELN (National Liberation Army) is a Castroite rural guerrilla movement operating in the main oil-producing areas in north-east Colombia up to the Venezuelan border. Their aim is mainly to drive out the foreign oil companies. These companies, however, have largely Colombianized both management and labour, and expatriates maintain a very low profile, keeping their movements unpredictable, when they do visit the oil fields. Most of the attacks are therefore on their installations, not people.

EPL (People's Liberation Army) is a movement with roughly Maoist ideology, which operates both in the countryside and the cities (notably Bogota and Medellin).

M19 (April 19 Movement) is primarily an urban, intellectually-based movement, having rural fronts mainly in the south, with links to sympathetic movements in Peru and Ecuador. M19 operates mainly in Bogota and Medellin and, as described in Chapter 9, has conducted some spectacular operations on behalf of the drug barons, no doubt receiving its due rewards.

Only FARC now continues even to pay lip service to the truce begun in 1984, and continues to attack army posts and other government targets. Some of these attacks are in co-operation with the other three movements which, since September 1987, have all been allied with it in the CGSB (Simon Bolivar Guerrilla Co-ordination). The very active participation by FARC in protecting the drug business – cultivation, processing, and trafficking, including running a number of cocaine laboratories themselves – brings them into constant conflict with the army and the police: the level of violence and kidnap is such that a great deal of protection money is paid to the guerrilla movements. The government will be hard put to do more than contain the guerrilla activity until the western countries cut off the flow of drug money to the drug-traffickers who finance them.

As an indication of the scale of the killing, an independent church study estimated in August 1988 that there had been 1,500 political murders in the first six months of 1988, of which only 212 could at that stage be specifically attributed: 46 by ELN, 92 by FARC, 52 by EPL, 22 by CGSB, and 9 by M19; in the same period there had been 256 army guerrilla clashes, in which 208 security force personnel, 234 guerrillas, and 55 civilians had been killed. The infrastructure and the oil industry are the main targets.

Though President Barco's government is fighting back and looks likely to be re-elected in 1990, there is the constant threat of an authoritarian *coup d'état*, possibly under populist and 'progressive' labels but in fact dominated by the drug barons. A nightmare scenario of what might emerge from this is in Chapter 18; although there remains a hope that democracy in Colombia might survive, there seems little likelihood of the violence subsiding.

El Salvador

For a tiny country of under 6 million people, El Salvador has suffered horrific casualties from a long-running insurgency: 10,000 people were killed in each of the years 1980 and 1981 and the total killed in the period 1980–8 was over 70,000.

One of the unusual factors was that the guerrillas began their campaign in 1978–80 by building up a $40 million 'launching fund' by kidnapping expatriate executives from five multinational companies based in different countries, and skilfully playing off one against the other. Since then, there has been no kidnapping of expatriates and the guerrillas have continued to finance their campaign by the more normal local kidnaps, robberies, extortion, and payment of protection money. The priming of the pump with the original $40 million, however, enabled them to build an infrastructure and maintain their initial momentum with an adequate cash reserve.

In 1980 six Marxist guerrilla groups joined forces in an umbrella 'National Liberation Front' (FMLN) which, with Cuban support, has been trying unsuccessfully to bring down the government which was formed after the overthrow of the repressive President Romero in October 1979. The guerrillas had an army of about 10,000; it was supplied from Cuba and Nicaragua. For the first two years (1980–1) the new government, seeking a broad range of support from hard-line military men and Christian Democrat politicians, was unable to control either the FMLN or right-wing death squads taking the law into their own hands. Democracy was established with painful slowness, with the election of a constituent assembly in March 1982 but, although the Christian Democrats emerged as the biggest single party, they could govern only in coalition with four other parties, including some of those suspected of collusion with the death squads. The guerrillas claimed to have killed or wounded over 7,000 soldiers and captured some 1,700 more in 1983.

Jose Napoleon Duarte, a Christian Democrat of long standing, was elected president in June 1984 with enough political strength to remove some of the more unsavoury army officers, but the FLMN rebuffed his proposals for negotiations and still held about a quarter of the country. Operating in groups of 400 or more, they aimed their attacks at disrupting communications and the economy – especially through damaging the electric power systems. Only US Aid (reputedly amounting to $2 million per day) enabled the country to survive. There is little to encourage investment and there has been a continuing flight of capital, now estimated to have reached $3 billion. The economy went into serious decline, as the FMLN intended.

In 1985 the Christian Democrats obtained a parliamentary majority but peace talks again proved abortive. Ambushes, sabotage, and road mining reduced transport in the east of the country to about 10 per cent of normal, with continuing paralysis of the economy in many of the provinces. President Duarte's prestige was further damaged in September 1985 when the guerrillas kidnapped his daughter and to secure her release (along with that of twenty-four abducted mayors) he had to agree to the release of twenty-two prisoners and safe conduct for ninety-six wounded guerrillas.

On the positive side, improved army tactics and equipment made it rare for the guerrillas to be able to operate in large units and right-wing death squads largely disappeared. The number of guerrillas had fallen to about 4,000 by 1987 but there was little prospect of their being eliminated so long as their Cuban support continued, nor of their seizing power unless the USA withdrew her support and allowed the economy to collapse.

In August 1987 the Presidents of El Salvador, Nicaragua, Honduras, Costa Rica, and Guatemala signed an agreement to cease supporting guerrillas in one another's countries and to reject military aid ('beyond what was normal and reasonable') from outside powers – notably from Cuba, the USSR and the USA. The effect of this will depend largely on what happens in Nicaragua (see next section).

In the March 1988 mid-term elections, President Duarte's Christian Democrats lost their majority to the right-wing ARENA Party. Soon afterwards, Duarte had to go to the USA for cancer treatment and the consequent uncertainty of his administration ensured a comfortable majority for the ARENA candidate, Alfredo Cristiani, in the Presidential Election in March 1989. Tougher government and the possible reappearance of the death squads may erode guerrilla strength but may also alienate much of the rural population. There is little prospect of an end to the violence.

Nicaragua

The Sandinistas in Nicaragua were an amalgam of Marxist and non-Marxist resistance movements against President Somoza, whom they ousted in 1979 with the support of almost all elements of society. This resulted from a classic rural guerrilla campaign, for which they started organizing from a base in Honduras in 1962. Working up from small-scale guerrilla attacks, they built up cadres in the villages and in the shanty towns around Managua. By 1978 they were able to organize mass demonstrations in the cities and the guerrilla units coalesced into large units which defeated the National Guard as Somoza fled the country. The present head of state, Daniel Ortega, (leader of the moderate wing of the movement) and his Marxist Interior Minister, Tomas Borge, were both amongst the leaders, so they know a lot about this kind of war.

The Sandinistas assumed power with their own junta in coalition with liberal politicians, with support from the church and the business community, both local and expatriate, who were encouraged to continue functioning. President Carter tried to help the new regime with aid but by the time President Reagan assumed office in 1981, the US had become disenchanted with the ousting of the liberal wing of the Sandinistas. A new resistance movement, the 'contras' was founded in November 1981 and gained US support. The contras were based on and across Nicaragua's northern frontier with Honduras, with some co-operation from the Miskito Indians in the under-developed Atlantic coast provinces.

The contras had a peak strength of about 18,000 in 1984–5, falling to about 12,000 in 1987. They have not been able to gain permanent control of any territory inside Nicaragua. They have conducted raids into the northern provinces in strengths of 200 or more, ambushing government troops, destroying the infrastructure, kidnapping and terrorizing villagers, as the Sandinistas used to do in the 1970s and as other guerrilla groups do in El Salvador, Colombia, and Peru. The inability of the US military advisers to restrain them from these kinds of tactics caused the US Congress to limit funds for aiding the contras.

The total numbers killed in Nicaragua between 1979 and 1987 (i.e. after the Sandinistas came to power) probably exceeded 70,000 and damage to the economy was about $4 billion. The government made a continuing offer of amnesty for contra guerrillas and claim that some 200 have surrendered since 1985.

The Sandinista government, though now opposed by the business sector and the church, still enjoys majority popular support. In November 1984 it received 67 per cent of the vote in what was, for Latin America, a relatively fair election.

The tragedy of Nicaragua is that both sides had more or less become puppets. The Sandinista government was faced in 1987 with inflation at 700 per cent and maintained an army of 75,000 – equalling those of El Salvador, Honduras, and Costa Rica combined. Over the period 1981–6 the USSR provided $500 million in direct military aid to Nicaragua and another $4 billion to Cuba, much of which was used vicariously to provide a large number of military advisers in Nicaragua and several thousand Cuban civilians (mainly teachers). And the contras would certainly not be able to survive without US support.

The agreement signed in August 1987 by Nicaragua, El Salvador, Honduras, Costa Rica, and Guatemala (see p. 124) would, if honoured, prevent cross-frontier and foreign support for guerrillas and limit foreign military assistance to governments, but the first year's experience gave little ground for hope that it would be honoured. The problem may lie with the Cubans. If Fidel Castro and his successors maintain their aim to spread their brand of revolution to other countries in Latin America, and especially in Central America, the Sandinista leaders – who spent their youth in organizing this kind of revolution and achieved it in triumph in 1979 – may not be able to resist the temptation to go along with Cuba. The best hope is that the restraint will come from Gorbachov in the Soviet Union, as part of a quid pro quo whereby the USA would forbear from interference in eastern Europe and, possibly, in Afghanistan now that the Soviet armed forces have completed their withdrawal. For without Soviet economic support, neither Cuba nor Nicaragua could survive at all, still less support foreign adventures.

The other hazard is that either the FMLN in El Salvador or the contras in Nicaragua, or both, will refuse to lay down their arms and try to go it alone. This, however, could be only temporary without respectively US and Cuban (i.e. Soviet) support. If, in fact, the USA and the USSR have the joint intention that there is to be peace in Central America, peace there will be, leaving both sides free to pursue their competition for influence by economic instead of vicarious military means.

Prognosis for Latin America

The 1980s have been a tortured decade for Latin America, with some of the bloodiest rural guerrilla conflicts in her history still in progress. While there is a slender hope of pacification in Central America, there will be none in Peru and Colombia so long as the demand for drugs continues.

Nevertheless, there have been promising political developments in Latin America. For the first time ever, the great majority of the states have democratically elected governments, with constitutions which should maintain that situation. The debt crisis could still destabilize some of them unless the western banks decide that the high interest rates of recent years have clawed back all that they are likely to get. Given a fresh start, the debtor countries may develop more prudent policies to restore confidence in investment, so that they prosper and grow, thereby maintaining social as well as economic stability. The banks and multinational corporations may then decide that there is still money to be made for mutual benefit.

Nevertheless, though conventional inter-state wars have been rare in Latin America, activists have always turned readily to the gun when they cannot get what they want either from dictatorships or from a democratic process. In the fifteen states with Spanish origin (though much less so in Brazil) this tradition seems to run in the blood, and the scale of butchery in their conflicts (though small compared with conventional wars) is horrific. Sadly, it is likely that there will be more such conflicts either in the common pattern seen in El Salvador, Nicaragua, and Colombia, or, perhaps likeliest of all, in the new pattern created by *Sendero Luminoso* in Peru.

Chapter thirteen

Rural guerrillas – Asia and Africa

The Asian rural guerrilla heritage

Whether their ideology is Marxist, nationalist, religious, or a mixture of these, most rural guerrilla movements, past and present, follow the Maoist revolutionary strategy, as was outlined in Chapter 2. First, the guerrillas deploy cadres to organize popular support in remote areas, to make them a 'friendly sea in which the fish can swim'. Thereafter they terrorize any who do not co-operate, establish liberated or 'no-go' areas, extend their influence into the more prosperous areas to isolate the cities in whose shanty towns they can develop the organization for an uprising when the time is ripe. In some cases, as in Peru and Colombia (see Chapter 12) the violence in the cities runs in parallel with the rural campaign, in close co-operation with big criminal gangs, usually those financed by drug-trafficking.

The successful defeat of rural guerrillas has almost always been founded on three pillars: village security, enlightened government so that people have more to gain by getting rid of the terrorists and – the ultimate battle-winning factor – intelligence.

One of the classic successes was in Malaya, where a guerrilla army of 8,000, with a strongly established village cadre organization built up during the Japanese occupation, was worn down and broken in 1948–60. The crucial battles were fought around 400 'New Villages' in which their 400,000 strongest supporters were resettled. None was resettled until a secure village perimeter had been built and a resident police post established *inside* the village. As confidence was restored, the decisive flow of intelligence built up, handled by a unified and highly sophisticated intelligence organization.

By contrast, in Vietnam there were no resident police or army posts in the villages so that, despite a façade of government control during daylight hours, the people were unprotected by night from the avenging cadres, who did live and sleep in the villages. As a result, no one dared give decisive information and, in any case, there were eleven rival intelligence organizations (US and Vietnamese) so they could play off one against the other to keep out of trouble.

There is a myth that the winning side always has 'the support of the people'. In practice, 80 percent of the people do not want to get involved with either side for fear of retribution by the other side against themselves or their families. They prefer to see and hear nothing. Usually 10 per cent at most will actively support the guerrillas (though more may be coerced by terror into doing so) and 10 per cent at most will actively support the police, army, and local government, often encouraged by incentives and rewards.

The real breakthrough usually comes when guerrillas or their active supporters defect and give inside information. Of the 4,000 guerrillas who surrendered or were captured in Malaya, 2,700 were willing to co-operate in this way. They were known as 'Surrendered Enemy Personnel' (SEPs) and were encouraged by generous rewards and, when they so wished, resettlement, with their families, under a new name in a new country with the resources to start a new life. At the end of the campaign, a number of 'Super SEPs' – including the second-in-command of the guerrilla organization, Hor Lung – surrendered, and co-operated in persuading others to follow suit. What had started as a trickle became a flood and the whole organization quickly crumbled away. The experience in Italy with the *pentiti* (in an urban setting – see pp. 163–4) taught the same lesson.

One other part of the rural guerrilla heritage is worth mentioning. Refugees from internal conflict or oppression have often been trained in neighbouring countries to go back as guerrillas. The Indians did this to train a guerrilla force to assist their invasion of Bangladesh in 1971; and the Pakistanis, with US support, gave sanctuary, training, and support to Afghan refugees as guerrillas (the possible effects of which are discussed later – see p. 139).

The Philippines

There have been two main guerrilla groups fighting in the Philippines for the past twenty years: the Maoist New People's Army (NPA) and the Muslim secessionist group MNLF fighting for an independent Islamic state in the Southern Islands – Mindanao and the Sulu Archipelago. When the corrupt dictatorship of President Marcos was overthrown by Mrs Cory Aquino in February 1986 amid massive public acclaim, she hoped that the guerrillas would join in the rejoicing and respond to offers of an amnesty. They, on the other hand, thought that, with her liberal policies and a weakening of the suppressive police-military-intelligence structure she would be an easier proposition than Marcos. Both were wrong. The army has generally remained loyal to Mrs Aquino despite a number of attempted coups, and she has retained the support of the great majority of the people.

The guerrillas played little part in the overthrow of Marcos, except that he had used their activities as an excuse to clamp down on free speech, demonstrations, and civil rights and this made him still more unpopular with the public. He called the 1986 presidential election in response to American insistence, tried quite brazenly to manipulate the results, and was swept from power by a massive and generally peaceful flood of public demonstrations in the streets. The Americans, along with the people, clearly wanted him to go and he went.

The NPA does still constitute a serious threat, even though its sympathizers have dwindled to about 100,000 out of a population of 58 million. There are some 23,000 guerrillas, based mainly in the northern part of the main island of Luzon, in the shanty towns which make up 2 million of the 6 million population of Manila, in the peninsula in the south of the island and in some of the other islands. The plan for their campaign – which began in 1969 as a resumption of the defeated Huk rebellion of 1950–3 – follows the traditional Maoist strategy of the protracted war: building cadres to organize support in the remote villages and working inwards to control the more prosperous areas until the cities, starved of supplies and raw materials for their industries, are ripe for an internal rising.

NPA 'sparrow squads' aim to spread terror by assassinating local officials, policemen, and soldiers (they killed 100 in 1987). They had a 1988 budget of $2.6 million, raised mainly by the extortion of protection money from local and multinational businesses, who transfer the money to banks in neighbouring Asian countries where no questions are asked. NPA propaganda is conducted both in rural and urban areas by a front organization, the National Democratic Front (NDF). They have, however, been set back by the widespread popularity of President Aquino. After she came to power they accepted a sixty day cease-fire, presumably to gather strength and lull the government, but they broke it early in February 1987. Mrs Aquino, whose power was endorsed by a landslide victory in the Senate and Congressional elections in May 1987, still hopes for regional cease-fire agreements, which the public certainly want. The NPA's cadres in rural areas, however, are well organized and exercise discipline by terror both in the villages and in the shanty towns, so their threat must still be taken seriously.

The MNLF is led by Nur Misuari, supported by Iran and Libya, and sometimes offered sanctuary, if needed, by sympathetic Muslims in the neighbouring territory of east Malaysia. Their insurgency has cost about 60,000 lives since 1972. Now facing strong resistance from the Christian majority in Mindanao, they have been more amenable to truces than the NPA but, again, the insurgency is not likely to disappear.

A further terrorist dimension came to the surface in the Philippines in the run up to the 1988 Seoul Olympics. A member of the fanatical Japanese Red Army (JRA) was arrested in Manila in June 1988 and it became clear that he was not alone. There are indications that, frustrated by effective police work in Japan and supported by North Korea, the JRA may target Japanese businessmen in the Philippines and elsewhere (see pp. 165–70).

By the middle of 1988 the NPA insurgency, still active and violent, had been held to a stalemate, largely by the mobilization of the people in vigilante organizations, coupled with determined military action. If Mrs Aquino can handle her grave economic problems (assisted by the USA) and so regain the support of the people, her government has a good chance of survival.

Sri Lanka

The Tamil insurgency in Sri Lanka has cost some 6,000 killed in 1983–7 before the government offensive in June 1987 was followed by an agreement with India and the deployment of a large Indian Peacekeeping Force (IPKF). Until then the guerrillas had relied on moral and to some extent logistic support from the southern Indian state of Tamil Nadu, with at least a blind eye, if not tacit sympathy, from the Indian government. The loss of this support probably had a greater effect on morale even than the intervention of the Indian army, but violent incidents, some amounting to massacres, have continued, by both Tamil and Sinhalese terrorists.

The insurgency was centred in the Northern Province of Jaffna, where the great majority of the population are Ceylon Tamils. Including the Eastern Province, in which they comprise 42 per cent of the provincial population, and a small proportion in Colombo and elsewhere in the south, the Ceylon Tamils amount to 1.8 million or 12.5 per cent of the total Sri Lankan population. (They should not be confused with the 'Indian Tamils,' descended from relatively recent migrants and working the Central Highlands tea plantations, who comprise another 5.5 per cent of the population but who have taken no part in the insurgency.) The Buddhist Sinhalese comprise a 74 per cent majority in the island as a whole.

The aim of the insurgents is for an independent Tamil state comprising the Northern and Eastern Provinces, though some of them would settle for devolution to an autonomous Tamil state (Eelam) within Sri Lanka.

After some years of tension the insurgency exploded in July 1983, when a bomb explosion at a Jaffna bus stop killed thirteen Sri Lankan soldiers and was followed by Sinhalese mob violence, in which some four hundred Tamils were killed. The Sri Lankan army, which had never been under fire before, initially over-reacted, further exacerbating the racial conflict. In addition to individual murders by Tamil terrorists – sectarian, factional, and aimed to intimidate half-hearted supporters – there were a lot of very large incidents, with dozens and sometimes hundreds of people killed in the ambush of country buses or large bombs in public places or in trains or aircraft.

The insurgency was on a large scale for such a small country – almost civil war. The main guerrilla group was the Tamil Tigers (LTTE) who by 1985 had total control of Jaffna town (apart from a beleaguered fort supplied only by air) and virtual control of the roads and the countryside of the Northern Province. The Tigers had a hard core of some 3,000 guerrillas who dominated the local population. There were a number of other Tamil guerrilla movements, some rivals and some allies. All subscribe to some form of Marxist philosophy, including the Tamil Tigers.

The Tamil Tigers, though generally well educated, were not very sophisticated. They were almost entirely in their 20s and 30s and many joined the guerrillas because they saw little prospect of personal success in what had, until 1983, been a thriving and competitive economy. Their own people generally referred to them as 'the boys' – with overtones of tolerance, sometimes shocked disapproval, and fear of what they might do next though, as in all such situations, deeds of derring-do against the Sinhalese soldiers made heroes of some of them.

Until Mrs Gandhi's assassination in 1984, the Tigers had unconcealed support from the mainland, by both state government and from the 55 million population of Tamil Nadu in southern India. Her son Rajiv Gandhi, however, imposed some restraint for fear that supporting secession in Sri Lanka might encourage other secessionists, such as Sikhs, in India. Nevertheless, his attempts to mediate were, until 1987, unsuccessful and caused deep suspicion amongst the majority Sinhalese population in Sri Lanka.

Sri Lankan government successes led President Jayewardene to propose in mid–1986 a political solution involving a wide measure of devolution in the Northern and Eastern Provinces, subject to a referendum in the Eastern Province where, in addition to 42 per cent Tamils, there are 33 per cent Muslims (mostly Tamil-speaking) and 25 per cent Buddhist Sinhalese. These proposals, however, did not satisfy either the guerrillas or the Sinhalese majority who saw in them the seeds of future partition of the island. Nevertheless, in April 1987 Jayewardene imposed a unilateral cease-fire and there was a moment of optimism.

This was shattered by two of the worst terrorist atrocities of the war: the massacre of 127 bus passengers, mostly Sinhalese, near Trincomalee in the Eastern Province and of another 113 on 21 April by a car bomb in the main bus station in Colombo.

The government reacted with a military offensive in the Northern Province at the end of May. By mid-June they had reoccupied the whole of the coastal area (cutting off supplies from Tamil Nadu) and most of the rest of the Province other than Jaffna town and its hinterland, where reoccupation would have caused massive civilian casualties.

At the end of July, Rajiv Gandhi persuaded the Tamil Tigers' leader, Vellupillai Prabhakaran, to accept an agreement for devolution to the Northern and Eastern Province, to be administered autonomously by a single elected council pending a referendum in the Eastern Province. Rajiv Gandhi then went to Colombo to sign this agreement with President Jayewardene, subject to endorsement by the Sri Lankan Parliament. There were reservations amongst leading Sinhalese politicians, particularly the Prime Minister, Ranasinghe Premadasa, and Sinhalese rioting had to be put down by the army. However, the parliamentary majority, not wishing to force a general election on the issue, did endorse the agreement.

As part of the agreement, India sent in a 7,000-man Peacekeeping Force (IPKF) to disarm the guerrillas. The Tamil Tigers began to hand in some weapons but it was soon clear that this was only a token gesture. The Tigers were quickly driven out of Jaffna town, but they intensified the fighting in both the Northern and Eastern Provinces, sometimes killing large numbers of Sinhalese in public places. The IPKF grew to 50,000 and remained at that level, claiming to have killed 1,500 Tamils by the end of 1988 at a cost of over 800 Indian casualties.

Meanwhile, a violent Sinhalese nationalist movement, the JVP

(People's Liberation Front), which had failed in an earlier attempt at insurgency in 1971, emerged to exploit Sinhalese chauvinistic fears that they were going to lose the Tamil provinces and that the Indians would use their intervention to impose their influence and control over the island – an historic fear of the Buddhist Sinhalese. The JVP, despite their Marxist rhetoric, used Nazi techniques of intimidation in the hope of paralysing the administration of the country in order to seize power. They conducted a vicious campaign of assassination, killing some 1,500 people between the announcement of the Indian agreement (August 1987) and the end of 1988. Most of the victims were members of the ruling United National Party (UNP) the local government officials, but later an increasing number of workers in essential public services were murdered or threatened.

The presidential election, due under the Constitution before the end of 1988, was held on 19 December and President Jayewardene, aged 83, decided not to run again. Of the three candidates, two ran neck and neck – the Prime Minister, Mr Premadasa (UNP) and a former Prime Minister, Mrs Bandaranaika (Sri Lanka Freedom Party: SLFP). Both declared beforehand that they would ask the IPKF to leave, but neither named a date. This would clearly depend on quelling the JVP insurgency, centred in the southern half of the country, as this was tying up almost the entire Sri Lankan army, which could not possibly handle both that and the Tamil insurgency in the north and east if the 50,000 Indians left.

The JVP declared the democratic process of the election to be a fraud, and condemned all three candidates. They did their utmost to disrupt the election by paralysing bus and rail transport and electric power in many southern districts, intimidating the population by murdering about ten people per day throughout the six-week run-up to the election, and warning them that anyone who went to the polling stations would be shot on sight. They did indeed shoot thirty on polling day but despite this, though the turn-out was lower than normal, especially in the south, 55 per cent of the electorate voted; a remarkable tribute to their courage. It was also a great achievement by the Sri Lankan army, whose brigade and battalion commanders had been proved in the fire of five years' fighting the Tamils, and were supported by effective emergency regulations (based on those used successfully in Malaysia in the 1950s and 1960s). The fairness of the poll was endorsed by an international monitoring team and Mr Premadasa was elected with a small overall majority (50.4 per cent, Mrs Bandaranaika getting 44.8 per cent, and the third candidate 4.8 per cent.

Premadasa took over as President on 2 January 1989. Concili-atory overtures to the JVP, however, were rebuffed and they continued their violence through the run-up to the Parliamentary Elections on 15 February, killing an average of 20 more people each day. Some were also killed by vigilante groups supporting the UNP. Despite this, a courageous 63.6 per cent turned out to vote, returning the UNP with a comfortable majority of 125 of the 225 seats. The Tigers ordered a boycott, but two other Tamil parties won 23 seats. The same two parties had also won 51 of the 72 seats in the joint Northern/Eastern Provincial Council elections held in November 1988 under IPKF protection.

On 1 June, after two months of secret negotiations with the Tigers, Premadasa asked for the complete withdrawal of the IPKF by the end of July, and four weeks later the Tigers announced that, if the IPKF withdrew, they would participate peacefully in the democratic process.

Rajiv Gandhi replied that such a rapid withdrawal was imposs-ible, suspecting that Premadasa had promised the Tigers a free hand in ousting the Council dominated by the elected Tamil par-ties. While keen to get the IPKF out, Gandhi was not prepared to abandon this democratic system (which had, by agreement, been installed at a cost of over 1,000 Indian soldiers' lives) to be swept away by force during India's general election year. The IPKF therefore launched an intensive drive to disarm and destroy the Tigers' organization before leaving.

Premadasa had vainly hoped that his demand for an Indian withdrawal would defuse the JVP campaign and the intensive wave of Sinhalese nationalism which supported it, so that he could redeploy his army in the north and east, in alliance with the Tigers, but the JVP continued strikes and murders unabated. Whatever happens, violence seems likely to continue with the JVP, or between Tamil, Muslim and Buddhist in the east or between rival Tamils in the north.

The Sikhs

Up until the middle of 1988 at least 5,000 Hindus and Sikhs had been killed in northern India arising from the communal violence which began in the Punjab in 1982, and more than 1,500 in the first eight months of 1988 alone. This must be seen in the context of communal violence in India as a whole, between Hindus and Muslims and high-caste and low-caste Hindus; and in separatist violence by Gurkhas, Nagas, and others. Casualties run into hun-dreds every year, sometimes one hundred or more in a single incident. The Sikh violence is mainly urban-based, though it extends to massacres of Hindus in the villages and in buses on the roads. It could be covered in either Part IV or Part V but is included here because of its similarities with the communal violence in Sri Lanka.

The 16 million Sikhs comprise 2 per cent of India's population of nearly 800 million; nearly half of these are in the state of Punjab, where they have a narrow (51 per cent) majority. This majority used to be bigger, but there has been an immigration of Hindus seeking work and an emigration of prosperous Sikhs seeking business opportunities in Delhi and elsewhere in India. It is this decline in the Sikh majority that the militant Sikhs are trying to reverse, by terrorizing Hindus to leave, and by provoking a Hindu backlash against Sikhs elsewhere so that more Sikhs return. They also demand independence for a new state of Khalistan.

The Sikh militants operate in a loose cell structure in about six main organizations, which mix open violence on the streets with individual murders and massacres. The most important is the All India Sikh Students Federation (AISSF), whose militancy is influenced by there being 100,000 unemployed graduates in Punjab.

The first terrorist killings were in 1980 but began in earnest when the leading militant, Sant Bhindranwale, established his headquarters in the sanctuary of the Golden Temple in Amritsar in July 1982. He continued to direct operations from there until the Indian government (which had suspended the Punjab state government and imposed direct rule in October 1983) sent in the army, which assaulted the Golden Temple on 5 and 6 June. Bhindranwale was found dead inside and another 400 Sikh militants killed. This was highly emotive, not only because the Golden Temple is the Sikhs' holiest shrine, but also because 10 per cent of the Indian army are Sikhs, many of whom took part in the assault.

As a direct result of this the Prime Minister, Mrs Indira Gandhi, was murdered by two of her own Sikh bodyguards on 31 October. In the Hindu backlash, over 2,000 Sikhs were killed in New Delhi in the next three days.

On 22 June 1985, 329 passengers and crew were killed in a mid-air explosion of an Air India jet, which had taken off from Montreal (see pp. 171–2) and the cycle of violence and backlash was given another twist. On 24 July Rajiv Gandhi, who had been elected Prime Minister in place of his mother, signed the 'Punjab Accord' with Sant Longowal, the leader of the moderate Sikh political party, Akali Dal. On 20 August Longowal was assassinated, but elections for the new state government went ahead on 25 September and Akali Dal were returned with a large majority over Rajiv's Congress (I) Party, which was clearly what he hoped would happen.

Part of the Accord was that Chandigahr, the joint capital of Punjab and Haryana, would pass exclusively to Punjab as its capital in January 1986. Haryana's Chief Minister, however, succeeded in getting this postponed and on 26 January Sikh militants reoccupied the Golden Temple, later declaring an independent state of Khalistan. On 30 April the state police and paramilitary forces reoccupied the Temple.

Violence thereafter escalated further, 330 people being killed in the first half of 1987. On 11 May 1987 Rajiv Gandhi again suspended the Punjab state government and resumed direct rule. During the second half of 1987, the police killed more than 300 terrorists. This did nothing to quell the violence, and over 1,000 more people were killed in the first four and a half months of 1988 before 15 May, when the army was once again sent in to occupy the Golden Temple, and 125 Sikhs surrendered. Predictably Sikh terrorists reacted by killing another 138 Hindus, police, and officials between 16 and 31 May.

At the time of writing there seems no prospect of either a political or a military solution. The bestiality of the massacres, mainly by indiscriminate shooting into crowds in the streets or in buses, and of the Hindu backlash, will ensure that passions remain high and the Sikh terrorists will continue to enjoy substantial support. There is also a risk of more incidents overseas, especially in Canada and Britain, where there are large Sikh and Hindu immigrant communities. The blowing up of the Air India jet from Montreal in 1985 gave a foretaste of this.

Afghanistan and Kurdistan

The North-West Frontier of Pakistan and Afghanistan has a long tradition of a particular type of highly effective rural guerrilla warfare. It is dependent on their rocky mountainous terrain and their tribal structure, and has been mirrored in the Kurdish areas of Iran, Iraq, Syria, and Turkey, and to some extent in the southern part of the Arabian Peninsula (Yemen and Oman).

In recent years the conflict has been intensified by the Soviet invasion of Afghanistan and by the flow of money from opium and heroin trafficking (described in Chapter 10). The character of fighting, however, continues to be shaped on the unchanging character of the people and the terrain.

Generally the tribesmen have been operating against regular armies of governments from which they want to be independent, such as the British and now the Pakistanis in the North-West Frontier, the Russians in Afghanistan, and the three countries between which Kurdistan is split.

Generally the regular armies have had to depend on roads for the movement of heavy weapons, ammunition, and supplies, because without these the guerrillas, in their own terrain on equal terms, could beat them. This applied both in the last century, with wagon trains and today, when helicopters, despite their other values, cannot move or maintain tanks or artillery. The wars remain focused on control of these roads and of the villages through which they pass. Tiny groups of tribesmen with snipers' rifles and (now) shoulder-fired missiles have been able to wreak havoc on wagon trains and mechanized convoys on the roads (even tanks can seldom move far into the rocky hills) and the helicopter gunships have brought a change of degree rather than kind from the biplanes of the 1920s. The shoulder-fired missiles have to some extent neutralized even this change of degree.

Success for the road-based armies has always depended on two things; on occupation of the commanding heights flanking the road by leapfrogging infantry trained in mountain warfare skills matching those of the guerrillas (and often recruited from rival tribes); and on intelligence. New technology has improved airborne-surveillance even of the elusive mountain guerrillas but the decisive intelligence must come mainly from the villages on which the guerrillas rely for supplies – one of the lessons which does seem to apply world-wide. Because of strong tribal cohesion and loyalty, no government's writ has extended into these villages beyond doing deals with the leaders.

Soviet intervention in Afghanistan followed a violent feud between the two Afghan Communist factions (Khalq and Parcham) which had united to depose the military regime of General Daoud (also Soviet-aligned) in 1978. The main reason was anxiety less a collapse of government allowed an Islamic Fundamentalist faction to seize control which might encourage similar risings in the neighbouring Muslim Soviet republics.

At its peak, the Soviet army deployed over 100,000 troops in Afghanistan but they had little success. The population was overwhelmingly against their occupation and even some sizeable towns, such as Kandahar and Gulbakar, fell into rebel hands for considerable periods. The Soviets tried equipping their convoys with self-propelled anti-aircraft guns (2SU–23–4) which, unlike the tanks, could fire at high elevations at the tribesmen in the hills, and the war provided useful combat trials for their helicopter troop carriers and gunships – the Mi–26, the Mi–24 Hind, and the Mil Mi–8 Hip. They had problems, however, in using them in the mountains and had many accidents, especially in the winter.

The Mujahideen guerrillas, too, were constantly getting better equipment, especially surface-to-air missiles and training in their use. They had much support from Muslim countries, especially the Arab oil states, and from China. They were based in Pakistan, where there were some 3 million Afghan refugees – about 25 per cent of the population. The guerrillas' weakness was that they were deeply split between various moderate and fundamentalist factions. The most effective militarily has been the Jamiat-i-Islami group led by Ahmed Shah Massoud but there has been no clear unity of aim between this and the other groups.

The withdrawal of Soviet troops in 1988–9 is unlikely to bring an end to rural guerrilla conflict. Whatever type of government emerges, there will be some guerrilla groups who oppose it, and even if a majority of the Mujahideen groups formed a coalition and took power, there would still be dissident groups in the mountains. Unless ex-King Zahim Shah were to be called back by them (and most groups would probably rally to him to bring peace), the eventual government may well be just what the USSR went in to prevent – an Islamic Fundamentalist regime. And, as Iran and Lebanon have shown, this is not a force for peace.

Seven million Kurds live in a similar environment in the mountains, rising in places above 10,000 feet, straddling the borders of Turkey (2.5 million), Iraq (2 million), Iran (2 million) and Syria (0.5 million). The country where they create most problems is Iraq, where they amount to nearly 20 per cent of the population, speaking their own language, and living in a largely autonomous region overlapping the oil-field areas around Mosul and Kirkuk. The Iranians and the Syrians have for years exploited this situation to disrupt and embarrass Iraq – especially the Iranians since the Gulf War began in 1980. There are about 15,000 Kurdish guerrillas under arms and the majority of these operate in and into Iraq from mountain bases which the Iraqi government cannot hope to control.

One of these movements, the Kurdish Socialist Party of Iraq (KSPI), has used the tactic of abducting expatriate workers, partly to extort ransoms for their funds, but primarily to obtain publicity. More than thirty of these from seven west and east European countries, and others from the USA and Canada, were kidnapped in 1981–3. Though none was harmed, the KSPI gained world-wide publicity for their cause.

The Turks and Iranians have been ruthless in suppressing their own Kurdish minorities while the Iraqis, under the pressure of the Gulf War, tried to some extent to appease them. Following the cease-fire with Iran in August 1988, the Iraqis turned the full force of their army and air force, allegedly using mustard and nerve gases, against their Kurds. By the end of September it was estimated that 60,000 Kurds, mainly women and children, had fled to Turkey. The Iraqis may be able to subdue them for a time, but the problem will not go away, because the Kurdish guerrillas, like the Afghans, are not easy to break in their own territory.

Sudan

The Sudanese People's Liberation Army (SPLA) is based in the southern (black, animist and Christian) half of the country and aims to end the domination of the Islamic Arab north by bringing about a secular, civilian, one-man-one-vote democracy. Since 52 per cent of the population of the Sudan are black, compared with 39 per cent Arab, this would (if one-man-one-vote could ever be organized in the remoter parts of the south) mean in effect control by the south instead of the north. For this reason, the north may continue to resist. The SPLA are supported by Ethiopia and they started operating, as an amalgam of other movements, in 1983. They are led by a former army officer, Colonel Dr John Garang, and have about 20,000 fighters.

The Khartoum government's administrative structure in the south is tenuous, and is more in the nature of a military occupation, with army posts in the main towns and armed convoys between them. Large areas are totally controlled by the SPLA. The army's primary aim has been to sustain the progress of two development projects being conducted mainly by expatriate companies: the oil pipeline and its associated refinery at Bentiu, and the Jonglei Canal.

These two projects are vital for the economic development of the Sudan. They were resented by the SPLA on the grounds that the money would go to the north, and they also saw an opportunity to weaken the government by disrupting its economy. One of their methods was similar to that used by the Kurds in Iraq: in November 1983 they kidnapped four Frenchmen and three Pakistanis working for a French consortium on the Jonglei Canal and on the same day they kidnapped two British engineers doing preliminary work for Chevron on the Bentiu oil refinery. All the hostages were released within a few days carrying lists of SPLA demands which included ceasing work on the projects. Early in

1984 further attacks killed a number of local workers and there were eight more kidnaps of expatriates. Two, from the Chevron project, were condemned to death but managed to escape in July 1985 after more than a year in captivity. The other six, from the Canal project, were taken to Ethiopia and were released on 28 January 1985, after payment of a large ransom in cash, medical supplies, and other equipment to a total value of $4.4 million. Work on the Bentiu and Jonglei projects remains virtually at a standstill.

Apart from these abductions of expatriates (there were several more in 1987, mainly of aid workers and missionaries) the operations of the SPLA had concentrated mainly on the more conventional targets of rural guerrillas – the army and disruption of communications. Soldiers are regularly killed in ambushes and by road mines. These also have a continuing effect of frustrating any kind of economic development.

Stability was further undermined in May 1988 by a bomb attack on a Khartoum club frequented by expatriates, mainly British and Americans, killing seven (including five British). Responsibility was claimed by the Palestinian Abu Nidal Group.

The year 1988 was one of social, political, and military turmoil in which 250,000 Sudanese died in a famine, largely because the civil war disrupted the transport of relief supplies. Both sides were suspicious that food convoys or air deliveries would be used by their enemy to gain an advantage, since the rebels controlled the countryside, many of the towns, and most of the roads in the south, while the government used its control of the air to supply its beleaguered garrisons. In May 1988 Sadiq el Mahdi, who had been Prime Minister since 1986, formed a new coalition, combining his party (Umma) with the Democratic Unionist Party (DUP) and the Islamic National Front INF), a fundamentalist group insisting on strict Islamic law throughout the country. A ceasefire plan was drafted by the DUP and the SPLA and signed by the army, but it was later rejected by Sadiq, who could not get the INF to accept the relaxation of Islamic law in the southern provinces. The DUP thereupon withdrew from the coalition and the SPLA launched a new offensive. The army was furious and by March 1989 was under severe pressure. Fearing a military *coup d'état*, Sadiq set up a new Cabinet without the INF, comprising only members who accepted a policy of peace and religious tolerance.

In May 1989 the SPLA, holding the military initiative and anxious to facilitate the passage of relief food supplies, declared a unilateral cease-fire and called on the government to talk peace.

With the Army and the DUP also pressing for peace, Sadiq agreed and talks began in June. Garang, who went on a world tour to enlist international support, declared that he had no desire to secede or break up Sudan; he added that he wanted to be free to stand for Parliament in Khartoum, and could envisage a coalition with the DUP. He also made it clear, however, that peace would be conditional on a high degree of autonomy and agreement that strict Islamic Law would not be applied to the South.

On 30 June, Sadiq was ousted by a military junta led by Brigadier Omar el-Bashir. Sadiq and many other politicians were arrested and all officers of major-general or higher rank were placed under house arrest. The junta promoted el-Bashir to General, and declared him Prime Minister, Defence Minister and Commander of the Armed Forces. While he extended the ceasefire and announced that there would be negotiations for a peaceful settlement, el-Bashir also promised increased expenditure on the army. He was equivocal about Islamic Law and promised to hold a referendum on it if agreement could not be reached. Garang is unlikely to accept this because, although the Arabs are in a minority, substantial numbers of the other ethnic groups are Muslims and, if a nationwide poll could be organized, there might well be a majority for Islamic Law.

General el-Bashir also launched a campaign against corruption and profiteering, which earned him initial popularity but this quickly backfired when it led to supplies in shops drying up altogether. He clearly has no intention of restoring what he regards as a corrupt democratic system.

The coup was encouraged by Egypt, and was generally accepted with cautious approval. Despite misgivings about yet another military overthrow of a fragile democracy, many felt that el-Bashir was more likely than Sadiq to resolve the country's political and economic crises, provided he could find officials with the necessary economic expertise, and attract overseas capital.

The underlying problems, however, will remain intractable. Attempting to enforce Islamic law universally would ensure continuance of the civil war in the south which the government lacks the power to win, but failure to do so would strengthen the appeal of the strong fundamentalist groups in the north. And, after years of civil war, disruption and famine, the threat of an economic collapse will remain.

Chapter fourteen

Development of rural guerrilla warfare

This chapter deals with the way current and future developments, particularly technological ones, are likely to affect rural guerrilla warfare. The technological trends and developments were discussed in Part II (Chapters 3 to 8), and their effect on urban terrorism will be assessed in Chapter 17, in the light of urban political and tactical factors in Chapters 15 and 16. Where the effects on rural and urban terrorism are relatively similar (e.g. in certain weapons, access and perimeter protection and search techniques) these will be deferred to Chapter 17 with only a brief reference ahead in this chapter as it is better to go into detail only once, in the light of both rural and urban factors. This chapter will therefore attempt only to highlight the effects peculiar to rural conflict, on both terrorist and security force tactics and techniques.

The psychology of rural terrorism

The rural populations are psychologically very vulnerable to terrorism as encapsulated by Sun Tzu – 'Kill one, frighten ten thousand'. When there are terrorists prowling their villages at night, or liable to jump out of the bushes when they are at work in the fields, the people feel very insecure – far more isolated than someone moving amongst the bustle of a city or a shanty town. This particularly applies to local government officials, village policemen, and to villagers accused of co-operating with them. Amongst the most chilling of stories was the treatment of one village chief in South Vietnam. North Vietnamese guerrillas entered the village at night, assembled the villagers, subjected the chief to a public trial, then mutilated each of his children, and disembowelled his wife in front of him, castrated him, and let him go, *pour encourager les autres*. Current experience in Peru, Sri Lanka, and Punjab suggests that this kind of terrorism is growing rather than declining.

So is the ambushing of buses on country roads, in all these cases and also by various Arab terrorists and the IRA. This tactic is considered in Part V as an offshoot of urban terrorism. Extortion of protection money and revolutionary taxes is also practised by both rural and urban terrorists.

Growing rural affluence, as in the drug-producing areas of Peru, Colombia, and Lebanon, makes people psychologically more vulnerable, not only to extortion but also to physical intimidation, because before a better standard of hygiene and better medicine had reached them they were more philosophical about deaths in the family than they are now.

Protection of rural populations is difficult and expensive. Village officials and policemen under threat tend to live-and-let-live with the guerrillas. Electronic and photographic surveillance inside the villages (by well-concealed long-range automatic cameras backed by good lighting) can extend the eyes and ears of the police but are only as good as the people manning them. Good human intelligence, discussed later in this chapter, provides the best hope of protection and deterrence.

Target selection

Prime targets are, as described, the people in villages at work in the fields or on the roads, and also isolated police or army posts, attacked not only for intimidation but also for acquiring weapons and ammunition.

Second only to these is the infrastructure, which becomes more interdependent as it is developed, with transformer stations, power lines, pipelines, roads, bridges, and telecommunications, all vulnerable to sabotage and interdiction. Their protection draws security forces away from the ultimately more important protection of people.

Water supplies are no more and no less vulnerable than they always were to contamination or to biological agents to spread disease. Like nuclear weapons, however, the intensity of public reaction and consequently the limited credibility of the threat, are powerful deterrents to this type of attack, as was discussed in Chapter 5 (pp. 50–1).

Weapons

Weapon development was discussed in Chapters 4 and 5 . Submachine-guns with a high volume of fire and, in the future, multi-barrelled sub-machine-guns capable of firing 100 rounds per second, will be devastating in a road ambush. So will modern and developing shotgun systems firing buckshot or flechettes (see pp. 39–40).

The development of heavy machine-guns capable of penetrating lightly armoured vehicles at long ranges across valleys is particularly applicable to rural guerrilla warfare. So are hand-held guided missiles such as MILAN (see pp. 43–4).

The weapons which have most transformed rural guerrilla conflict in recent years, however, have been the guided anti-aircraft missiles such as the Soviet SAM 7 (costing less than $1,000) and the more sophisticated 'fire-and-forget' US Stinger, as provided to Afghan guerrillas (see pp. 44–6 and 139). These weapons are developing fast as the super-powers, the Arabs and the Israelis, are competing for the technological lead. Unfortunately many rural terrorist movements now have rich backers (e.g. Libya and the drug barons) who will be prepared to make a big investment to counter the advantage the security forces gain from helicopter gunships and troop carriers. Fougasses and road mines are discussed on pp. 146–7.

Incapacitating gases (if they can be effectively developed) and blast weapons to stun could be used with less risk to passers-by in a rural than in an urban setting – e.g. to counter a road ambush with stun grenades fired from an armoured vehicle, or dropped from a helicopter. This would, however, have few advantages and many disadvantages compared with firing lethal weapons in those circumstances.

Security of premises and installations

Vulnerable premises in rural guerrilla conflicts range from isolated army or police posts to large installations, oil refineries, airfields, and defended villages, with perimeters several kilometres long. Quarries, mines, and other places where explosives may be stored are especially important to protect; so are transformers and pumping stations and bridges. Isolated guards to defend these are notoriously vulnerable, and long delay before help can come makes protection especially difficult.

Energy distribution and cross-country telecommunications are particularly vulnerable to interdiction. Buried pipelines and cables are less vulnerable, but usually prohibitively expensive, especially in rocky and mountainous terrain. Technological development can help in two ways: by automatic detection, cut-outs, and valves to limit damage; and by extension of grid systems so that breaches can be bypassed.

Equipment available and under development for access control, identification, perimeter security, surveillance, alarms, and electronic monitoring and recording of movement were discussed in Chapter 8 and their application will be further discussed in Chapter 17. Village security, enhanced by strong, well-lit perimeters, with surveillance and alarm systems, is probably the most important aspect of this.

Personal and travel security

Personal and travel security presents very difficult problems. It will be argued in Chapter 17 (p. 192) that it is unwise for 'amateurs' to carry firearms unless they are as well trained and psychologically prepared to use them effectively as the terrorists are; also that an inadequate bodyguard may increase rather than decrease the risk. Facing rural guerrillas in isolation, however, may necessitate being armed, in which case any local government official or estate or works manager who has to move about may of necessity need to carry a gun and therefore to be trained to achieve the high standard of skill and reflex action needed to survive an exchange of fire. The same goes for their drivers and bodyguards, whose greatest contribution, as in an urban setting, will be to advise them on how to keep out of trouble.

Road bombs and fougasses are a favourite weapon of rural terrorists against selected assassination targets or security force patrols. They often comprise huge charges, often of improvised explosives placed in culverts, or charges in roadside bushes or parked vehicles. They are most commonly fired by remote control cable or radio signal but they may also be detonated by a bullet fired from several hundred yards away to close an electric circuit between two metal plates (see pp. 48–9). They can also be fired by the electromagnetic field from a passing metal vehicle, but this method lacks selectivity. There is, however, some scope for ingenuity in finding characteristics peculiar to the type of vehicle which the terrorist wishes to select (see p. 49).

Road mines detonated by the pressure of the wheel of a passing vehicle have been in regular use for fifty years, with little development. They are particularly attractive for terrorists in rural areas where most of the roads are made of dirt, gravel, oil-bound sand, or laterite in which it is easier to bury them than in tarmac or concrete. On rural roads, even this surface is often one way, so the mines in the verge can catch vehicles pulling over to pass. Booby traps are commonly added. Plastic and wooden mines can defeat the metal detector but a well-trained dog can sniff most explosives.

In practice, the use of probes, sharp eyes, and sensitive fingers to detect where the soil or road surface has been disturbed has always been and still is the best means of finding mines, and pulling them out of the ground with a long piece of cable is the best guard against booby traps.

An efficient portable sniffer, sensitive enough to pick up the vapour from buried explosive and to give an immediate reading without the need to take it away for analysis probably offers the best alternative to dogs in the development of mine detectors, and possibly neutron bombardment. As with other forms of detection, whether of persons or material, it will pay to develop multiple means rather than rely only on one.

Alarms in isolated security force posts, homes, and installations, though valuable if only as a morale booster and a deterrent, are less effective in rural than in urban areas because of the response time for help to come. Transmitters and beacons can be effective but the range needs to be long so there is a limit to miniaturization. A powerful beacon concealed in the car should be able to sound the alarm when a victim is kidnapped but, to enable him to be tracked thereafter it may be necessary to conceal a beacon in something which the terrorists might allow him to keep. They might be suspicious of a radio or pocket calculator or video computer game, but less so of a heart pacemaker.

The possibility of a breakthrough in a VTOL, STOL, and micro-lite air travel for short distances was discussed in Chapter 8 (pp. 84–5). This could have a particular application to security in rural areas.

Search techniques

Techniques for searching for bombs and guns were described in Chapter 6. Those for detecting buried mines (see previous section) have the greatest relevance to rural guerrilla conflict and the detection and jamming of radio-controlled roadside bombs by the leading vehicle in a convoy could be valuable, though it would not defeat the more common method of firing them by land line.

In areas where the processing of narcotics (coca to cocaine, opium to heroin – see Part III) is closely linked with terrorism, for example in Colombia, Pakistan, and Burma, the use of well-trained dogs and possibly chemical sniffers with military patrols in searching villages and farms could greatly improve the detection of processing laboratories.

Intelligence

Rural guerrillas face an inherent dilemma: they cannot activate and dominate the rural population without making regular contact with them, either in the villages or at work in the fields. Such contacts are much more difficult to conceal in rural communities where visitors are noticed. This dilemma can be exploited by the security forces to acquire intelligence. Guerrillas living outside the villages may be hard to catch, but if they or their cadres live mostly inside the villages there will be people who know them and can be given incentives to tell what they know, coupled with reassurance that they and their families will be guaranteed security, if necessary in a new home, if they do.

The initial persuasion of a witness to give information usually comes when the intelligence or police officer speaking to him has good background intelligence and possesses powerful bits of evidence with which he can surprise and confront his witness – e.g. that some specific person well known to the witness is involved with the guerrillas. If the interrogator has immediate access to a mass of data by having with him an 'expert system' data bank in his own intelligent computer or terminal, as described in Chapter 7 (pp. 69–70), he is still more likely to be able to throw the witness into confusion by exposing lies or evasions, and by appearing to know everything already.

Another source of such evidence is modern surveillance equipment, especially long-range high-resolution cameras (still or video). These can produce reliable and undeniable evidence of personal contacts in a small village community, and the sudden presentation of such a photograph or video clip can have a powerful effect on the course of an interrogation. Given judicial authority, the bugging of the home of a known cadre, or of a house where he meets his cell members, can produce audiotape evidence of such contacts, and of the processes of organization and intimidation, which are valuable knowledge for use in interrogation.

Another technique used with success in the past is to conceal a secret circuit in some normal piece of electrical equipment, such as a radio receiver, which is, with the aid of someone recruited as an agent, inserted in the right place in the distribution chain to be sold or delivered to a suspected guerrilla leader or cadre. This circuit will transmit signals which can enable its location to be tracked, leading the security forces to the suspect's home or headquarters and, if he is mobile, to track his movements. This was achieved with the radios and tracking equipment available thirty years ago. It should have far greater potential, now and in the future, with the proliferation of electrical gadgets even in remote rural villages and the much greater sophistication of surveillance equipment.

Equipment under development for better identification and detection of impersonation was described in Chapter 8. Its use has equal application to both rural and urban conflicts so it will be discussed in Chapter 17.

The security forces

Rural guerrilla units can expect to have the advantage over the security forces only when they have the initiative, for example in an ambush or in a surprise hit-and-run attack on an isolated police post. In other circumstances the army or police, better armed and with better opportunities for training, will usually have the advantage if they can bring the guerrillas to battle. In the twelve-year Malayan Emergency the army and police killed or captured 5.7 guerrillas for every man they lost and, even in the worst year (1950) the ratio was 2.5 to one.

The problem is to find them or to predict their movements; this is a matter of good intelligence, and the best intelligence comes from human sources. Though these can be assisted and supplemented by hardware, no surveillance equipment has yet been invented which can equal the human eye and ear, and the human ability to differentiate between true and false.

The primary task of the security forces in rural guerrilla conflict is therefore to build up the confidence of rural communities in their own security, and in the inevitability of final defeat for the guerrillas so that they co-operate in giving information. This means, above all, enabling a permanent police presence, day and night, to be maintained and protected in every village.

A major factor in this is confidence in the rapid arrival of a reaction force if the village or the police post is attacked. The development of more reliable alarm systems and of rapid helicopter transport and gunship support should make this easier now and in the future than in the past.

The organization and accountability of the security forces – army, police, and intelligence services – will be discussed in Chapter 17.

Public support

The fastest change in rural areas has been and will be in accessibility to information. The spread of the cheap transistor radio began the process in the 1960s, by opening up even the most remote villages in Latin America and Asia for the first time to the influences of the outside world. This process has continued apace and within a few years most villages will be exposed to the more compelling influence of television. Even if sentimentalists were right in thinking that remote peoples would have been better left with their subsistence agriculture and 'happy' isolation (in fact a blend of boredom, back-breaking toil, and high infant mortality) that argument is now irrelevant because, as soon as the transistor radio apprised them that there were more comfortable ways of life, the demand for these became insistent. So did the demand for more information, and especially for television. While the fifty-channel flood into urban homes will not be repeated in the remote areas where rural guerrillas thrive, access for propaganda – government, dissident, and foreign inspired – will be steadily increased. In this competition for the hearts and minds of the people, governments will need to seize their technological opportunities to win it.

The other field in which governments must use their advantage is intermediate technology, to enable rural peoples to raise their own standard of living. If their rising expectations are not met, the people will not unreasonably accept the view put to them by the agit-prop teams.

Intermediate technology is less fashionable than high technology but offers immense opportunities for inventiveness in developing cheap, simple, and reliable equipment for the next step up the ladder. People walking half a mile with buckets to get stagnant water need, first, hand pumps in the village and then, when they have learned to operate and maintain engines, deep wells with motor-driven pumps. In places where the monsoons make mud tracks impassable they need all-weather roads – not a few miles of concrete or tarmac but many more miles of easily maintained roads of compacted local material – and culverts and bridges to keep the roads from flooding.

Given confidence that their standard of life, as well as the security of their villages and their families, will steadily improve if stable government is maintained, the people will not be interested in agit-prop, and rural guerrillas will be unable to take root.

Part five

Urban terrorism

Chapter fifteen

Urban terrorist organizations

The urban guerrilla heritage

Though there have always been assassinations and kidnaps
throughout history, the first calculated political terrorist campaign
was that by Irgun Zvai Leumi (IZL) in Palestine in the 1940s.
The term 'urban guerrilla' was not coined until 1967, after the
failure of Che Guevara and his rural guerrilla *Foco* Theory in
Bolivia, whereafter Latin American revolutionaries decided that,
in place of the unresponsive peasants, they must redirect their
efforts at the intellectuals and urban proletariat in the cities. This
philosophy was expounded in Brazil in 1969 by Carlos Marighela
in a series of tracts which became known as 'The Minimanual of
the Urban Guerrilla'.

Urban terrorism has proved a very effective way of destablizing
democratic societies and provoking an authoritarian take-over.
This was well illustrated in Uruguay in 1972 and Argentina in
1976; and in Turkey where, in 1980, urban terrorists killing twenty
people a day on the streets provoked a military coup which was
widely welcomed by an exasperated public. To his credit, General
Evren kept his word and restored parliamentary democracy two
years later. Even if some western observers are critical of the
limitations of that democracy, the urban terrorists have not so far
reappeared and a large number have been reprieved and rehabili-
tated in society.

International terrorism in its present form is a relatively recent
phenomenon; it is largely urban (though some rural guerrillas do
also receive foreign support – see Part IV). It was begun more or
less simultaneously in Brazil, Guatemala, and Uruguay and by the
Palestinians in 1968. The Palestinians, frustrated by their failure to
make any impact on Israel and by the loss in 1968 of every
adjacent frontier other than that with Lebanon, sought publicity
for their cause by attacks on aircraft in Europe, including hijack-

ing, a form of urban terrorism which killed relatively few people but certainly did gain enormous publicity. Latin American revolutionaries from 1968 to 1973 attempted to deter western countries from supporting their governments by kidnapping diplomats (about fifty in all). When this failed to have the desired effect they turned to seizure of embassies, which reached a peak in 1979–81, but this too failed and has been largely abandoned. Attempts to coerce governments by kidnapping their nationals in Lebanon, by Shia Muslims inspired by Iran, did have a big effect on the attitudes and policies of France and the USA.

The Palestinians

Yassir Arafat's Palestine Liberation Organization (PLO) is by far the richest terrorist organization in the world, receiving massive funds every year from the Arab states, some given willingly, e.g. by Libya and Iraq, and some partly as a form of protection money, by rich and vulnerable oil states. James Adams, in *The Financing of Terror*, estimates the PLO's assets as $5 billion, and their income as $1.25 billion, and says that they are organized as a multinational corporation with investments all over the world.

Their main constituent part is Arafat's own Al Fatah, which was about 9,000 strong when it was based in Lebanon in 1982. Since 1983, when it was temporarily expelled by President Assad of Syria after the Israeli invasion, it has been much dispersed and weakened – but its investments and income are intact.

Al Fatah is not really a guerrilla or clandestine movement. It fights almost entirely within the Middle East, mainly fighting other Arabs in Lebanon, because the Shia community always resented the PLO's many refugee camps in South Lebanon and, now that some have come back, fighting still flares up from time to time. Al Fatah has not fought the Israelis much, nor have they carried out international terrorist operations, though some of the smaller constituent organizations of the PLO – e.g. PFLP, PFLP(GC), and DFLP – certainly have. So have some militant groups within Al Fatah itself, notably Black September in the early 1970s and Black June in the late 1970s, the latter finally breaking away under Abu Nidal, to be based first in Iraq, then in Syria and then in Libya. The Abu Nidal group is now wholly disowned by the PLO and has devoted most of its energies in the 1980s to killing mainstream PLO representatives around the world and carrying out assassination projects for other Arab leaders who have been prepared to give them money or sanctuary.

Apart from these more militant groups, the mainstream PLO

rank-and-file live as a kind of Home Guard in the refugee camps, being paid from Arafat's ample coffers and defending the camps against whoever attacks them. During their occupation, after initially rounding up several thousand of them as prisoners, the Israelis seldom attacked the camps themselves, but turned a blind eye or positively encouraged rival Arab groups to attack them.

Palestinian international terrorist activities (hijacks, etc.) have been carried out almost entirely by the smaller groups (Black September, PFLP, Abu Nidal, etc.) and the number involved in this kind of activity have probably seldom exceeded 200 at any one time. Tragically, from the Arab point of view, the remainder, up to nearly 20,000 at times, have largely spent their time either in their camps, training and drawing their pay, or fighting each other and other Arabs.

The only achievements they can claim are the enormous publicity they have gained from their international terrorist actions (their techniques are discussed in Chapter 16); and from Yassir Arafat's appearances as the appointed spokesman of the exiled Palestinian people at the UN and, through his seventy recognized offices in capitals over the rest of the world. He has gained some sympathy in the Third World (where Israel is regarded as a US puppet) and from some European countries such as Greece; even the USSR, which has been prepared to provide arms because the PLO is a thorn in the side of the west, seems now to be finding them something of a nuisance.

The PLO will certainly not disappear. Even if the Arab states were to cut back their contributions, they would be able to live for years on their investments. If they were ever to achieve their aim of becoming the government of a West Bank and Gaza state, there has been much scepticism about the sincerity of their renunciation of their aim of using this as a springboard to take over the whole of Israel which is in places only nine miles wide between the hills of the West Bank and the sea. It is therefore extremely unlikely that the Israelis will ever allow a Palestinian West Bank state to become independent of their security control.

It seems, therefore, virtually certain that the present impasse will continue, with several million Palestinians, several thousand of them armed and paid as soldiers, somewhat grudgingly given house room by other Arab states. Their militant elements will keep up the spirits of the others and international terrorist acts will keep them in the limelight in the rest of the world. These individually make an impact, but collectively make it unlikely that the PLO will get the independent homeland they want in this century – if ever.

Lebanon

Lebanon has no central government. President Gemayal controlled only a few areas in East Beirut and North Lebanon and his multi-denominational 'Cabinet' had not met in full since 1985. His Sunni Muslim Prime Minister (Rashid Karami) was assassinated in June 1987, and his resignation in 1988 left the situation even more unstable.

Since 1975 Lebanon has been plagued by continuous civil war between various Arab militias, punctuated by two temporary occupations of South Lebanon by the Israeli army in 1978 and 1982–5. Since 1982 the Syrian army has occupied most of North and East Lebanon plus most of Beirut itself since February 1987, when it was invited in by common consent to control the violence in the city, though not in the southern suburbs controlled by the most violent militia of all – Hezbollah. Under the rather loose Syrian control, the rival militias operate very much like the mainstream, the PLO, as described above, living openly as private armies defending their own areas against the others. The PLO have themselves moved back into southern Lebanon since the Israelis withdrew. The militias are, as described in Chapter 10, largely financed by drug-trafficking, partly from opium and hashish cultivated in the Beka'a Valley (the main base of the Syrian army) and partly from heroin imported from southern and eastern Asia.

The main militias are Christian, Shia Muslim, Sunni Muslim, and Druze.

Christian

Lebanese Forces (LF) (General Aoun) East Beirut and northwards; 4,500 with 30,000 reservists; anti-Syrian (but tolerated occupation until 1989).
Marada Zghorta (North Lebanon); pro-Syrian.
South Lebanon Army (SLA) (Antoine Lahd) Israeli border; 1,000; Israeli sponsored; anti-PLO.

Shia Muslim

Amal (Nabih Berri) West Beirut and around Tyre (rival strongholds); 6,000 with 10,000 reservists; anti-PLO.
Islamic Amal (Hussein Musawi) Baalbek (Beka'a Valley); 600; Iranian sponsored.
Hezbollah Baalbek and Beirut southern suburbs, where western hostages are believed to be held; 3,500; Iranian sponsored.

Sunni Muslim

Murabitoun   (Ibrahim Koleilat) West Beirut; much weakened by fighting; about 400, mostly underground; Libyan links.

Towhid   (Sheikh Said Shaban) Sunni fundamentalists; North Lebanon; weakened by attacks by Syrian army and Syrian-sponsored Alawite militia; about 1,000, supported by a few hundred PLO.

PLO   (see pp. 154–5) about eight factions, based on refugee camps around South Beirut, Sidon, and North Lebanon; returning since 1985, perhaps about 5,000 in all in 1988.

Druze

Progressive Socialist Party (PSP)   (Walid Jumblatt) Chouf Mountains south-east of Beirut; 5,000 with 12,000 reservists.

Terrorism in Lebanon

Terrorism in Lebanon has taken three main forms. First, internecine shooting by militia on the streets, reminiscent of big criminal gang fights in Chicago supplemented by artillery fire. Second, the use of huge car bombs, sometimes internecine and sometimes (by Hezbollah in 1983) against western embassies and the Multinational Peacekeeping Force. Third, the kidnapping of large numbers of individual western hostages – more than twenty were held in South Beirut in the summer of 1989. (These techniques are further discussed in Chapter 16.)

For a number of reasons there is little prospect of an end to terrorism in the next few years. First, because of the historic determination of the Christian/Sunni/Shia/Druze communities to fight for their identity and their land (most of those killed are fellow Lebanese and refugee Palestinian Arabs). Second, because the Palestinians have nowhere else to go which has frontier access to Israel and their presence will always be resisted, both by the Israelis and by the mainstream of Shia Muslims. Third, because the militias are heavily financed by the drug traffic, which the Syrians are unlikely to stamp out because they probably see no way of replacing the 30 per cent of Lebanon's GNP which it provides.

As with Latin America, the Caribbean, and south and east Asia, the biggest contribution which the west could make would be to starve the militias of funds by cutting off the demand for drugs in western societies.

157

The role of Iran, Syria, Libya, and Iraq

Iran sponsored Hezbollah in Lebanon by sending about 1,000 of its Revolutionary Guards into the Beka'a Valley in 1982 to assist the Syrian army in fighting the Israeli invasion. Their task then spread to inducing the withdrawal of the US, French, Italian, and British Multinational Peacekeeping Force by suicide car bomb attacks on embassies and military bases in 1983 (see Chapter 16), and thereafter to kidnap individual western hostages in Beirut as bargaining counters. Iran has also sponsored terrorist attacks by Arabs for similar aims in other countries. Iran is unlikely to depart from its fundamentalist aim of expelling all infidel influence from Islam, though it may temper its actions for pragmatic reasons in the aftermath of the Gulf War and the death of Khomeini.

Syria has sponsored some murderous attacks all over the world by the Abu Nidal Group (though this is now probably based in Libya) and by various Palestinian splinter groups. Its Embassy in London was caught red-handed in April 1986 in the mounting of an attempt by Nezar Hindawi to blow up an Israeli aircraft taking off from London Airport (see pp. 173–4) and was suspected of similar support for Arab terrorists attacking US targets in Europe in the same period. Syria, however, like Iran, may now be realizing that, for political and economic reasons, it will pay to maintain at least a working relationship with the west, so this kind of support for terrorism may decline. So long as President Assad remains in power, however, he will have no scruples about indirectly using international terrorism as a weapon if he believes that it will further his aims at the time.

Libya has carried out direct terrorist acts by using its agents (often with diplomatic status) to murder anti-Gadafi Libyans in London, Paris, and so on. On one occasion (in 1984) a bad shot from the window of the Libyan Embassy in London, fired at Libyan demonstrators across the street, killed a British policewoman. Libya has also avowedly helped to arm and finance the IRA, both in Northern and Southern Ireland, particularly by smuggling large consignments of arms, ammunition and explosives to them, especially Semtex which is notoriously difficult to detect. Libyan agents were also involved in assisting terrorist attacks on US targets in Europe in 1986, though this has largely ceased since the USA bombed Libya in retaliation. Gadafi is unlikely to change his ideas and is relatively young, but he too may be deterred by economic problems or by fear of retaliation; he is also amongst the least secure of the Arab leaders sponsoring terrorism, both internally (especially if oil income falls) and externally, as he has few friends amongst other Arab governments.

Iraq desisted from international terrorism during the Gulf War, but was a frequent sponsor or supporter in the past, culminating in an Iraqi masterminding the seizure of the Iranian Embassy in London as part of the run-up to the Gulf War in April 1980. President Sadam Hussein, like Assad and Gadafi, would have no scruples whatsoever about using these techniques again if it suited him.

Also emanating from the Middle East is the Abdallah Group (FARL), a Marxist group based in north Lebanon and frequently operating in France up till 1986. Its leader, Georges Abdallah, is now serving a life sentence in France. Both of these groups have a strong family base and there are other Arab families, such as the Hindawi and Hamadi brothers, who have formed secret terrorist cells around them, operating internationally over the Middle East and Europe. Cells cemented by family ties have a high degree of cohesion and security.

The IRA and ETA

The IRA and ETA have a number of characteristics in common. Each has enjoyed the support, active or passive, of about 10 per cent of the population of its own province and negligible support in the country as a whole. This can be measured by the support for their associated political party, Sinn Fein and HB respectively. In the Republic of Ireland, Sinn Fein was able to attract under 2 per cent of the vote at the 1989 general election, even though they had declared that they would take up any seats they won in the Dáil. (In the past, their refusal to take up the seats had probably deterred many from voting for them.) On this occasion, they won no seats, nor any in the previous election either.

In the past twenty years, about 2,700 people have been killed in Northern Ireland – about 60 per cent by the IRA, with two-thirds of them civilians – out of a total population of 1.5 million. Nearly 700 have been killed in the Basque provinces of Spain in the same period – just over 500 by ETA, with half of them civilians – out of a total population of 2.25 million.

Both extort a large proportion of their funds by protection money of various kinds, mainly by threatening people with damage to themselves, their families, or their property if they do not subscribe. The IRA apply this at all levels in the construction industry, from managers to labourers. One means is to coerce them into tax and social security frauds, for which building sites, with their constant flow of casual labour, are particularly suitable. They also run businesses such as taxis, first forcing the buses and normal commercial taxis off the road by intimidation (or sometimes allowing them to ply in return for a large licence fee or revolutionary tax). Their own loyal cab drivers subscribe a proportion of their earnings and the profits of the whole enterprise go into IRA funds.

Racketeering – a term covering all these activities – provides the great majority of the funds for both the IRA and the Protestant paramilitaries. The Protestants are reputed to extort more: £10 million a year compared with the IRA's £5 million.

The IRA are based mainly in well-defined areas, in which most of the 10 per cent who support Sinn Fein are concentrated; in West Belfast, Derry, and a number of outlying areas, near the borders, such as South Armagh. In these areas they used to operate a relatively overt military structure of battalions, companies, and platoons, with commanding officers, adjutants, intelligence officers, and quartermasters. The identity of these officers was generally known to the loyal supporters, from whom they called out volunteers to act as rank-and-file, sometimes for one-off operations and sometimes continuously. The best of the volunteers in due course graduated as officers. By 1978, however, lack of discretion was resulting in the arrest of too many officers, so they reorganized into more traditional clandestine revolutionary cells or Active Service Units (ASUs). Each of these had its hard core of officers, who picked their volunteers more carefully. An active service unit was usually about eight to twelve strong, though extras could be recruited for particular operations if needed.

After about ten years' active service, by which time they might have wives and children, the hard core often move on to higher command and organization or political and propaganda work with Sinn Fein – as godfathers.

Thus the present structure comprises four levels: the godfathers; the hard core; the volunteers; and auxiliaries, who are active supporters willing to act as drivers or look-outs or, for example, to carry a gun or part of a gun to a hard-core sniper so that he can go to his fire position with nothing incriminating, and leave similarly clean, in case he is picked up in the street.

The importance of this is that most of the hard core – perhaps sixty to eighty in all – are well known to the police but cannot be convicted without evidence: they are experts in avoiding the risk of being caught with evidence. The volunteers and the auxiliaries take those risks in the knowledge that, even if convicted, their sentences will be light. Above all, the skilled and experienced hard core must be conserved.

When frustrated in Northern Ireland (e.g. by the series of public relations disasters from November 1987 into 1989, when large numbers of civilians were killed in bungled bombing operations) they send ASUs to Britain and western Europe, usually to attack either leading politicians or military personnel off duty in England, Germany, or the Netherlands. Typical examples were the bombing of the Grand Hotel in Brighton when Mrs Thatcher and her Cabinet were sleeping there in 1984, or of soft military targets like the sleeping quarters of the Army Postal Services at Mill Hill in London, airmen off duty in pubs in the Netherlands, or bombs placed on the perimeters of the Royal Corps of Transport and Topographical Survey barracks in Germany – all in the summer of 1988. There was not much risk in attacking targets like these.

There have seldom been more than one, occasionally two, ASUs operating at any one time in England and similarly in Germany or the Netherlands. In England they sometimes recruit auxiliaries locally from amongst the local Irish communities. In the Netherlands and Germany they receive some help, in the form of safe houses, locally registered vehicles, currency, and so on from Dutch and German extremist movements which have a common purpose in attacking NATO targets.

Although the total numbers killed in 1987 and 1988 were larger than in other recent years, they have declined to an average of less than one-fifth of their peak of 467 in 1972 and less than one-third of the average of 295 for the five years 1972–6. Since 1977 the average has been 85 per year, with the lowest figures of 64, 54, and 62 in 1984/5/6. After Sinn Fein's rejection by 98 per cent of the voters in the Republic of Ireland in 1986, the hardliners who preferred the bullet to the ballot box gained an ascendancy and killings rose to 93 in 1987 and the same again in 1988, but the killing in itself had little effect other than to keep the IRA in the news. It remained six times safer (in terms of homicides per thousand) to live in Belfast than Washington DC and, allegedly, twenty-four times safer than in Forth Worth, Texas.

Police co-operation on the border under the Anglo-Irish agreement is good, and probably goes as far as is politically feasible. Joint patrols in a zone both sides of the border, though desirable, would arouse outrage amongst both hardline republicans in the South and hardline unionists in the North, and might therefore be counter-productive. Anglo-Irish relations improve every time there is an incident involving vicious or reckless slaughter of civilians, such as at the bombing of the Remembrance Day service in Enniskillen in November 1987 or the firing of 150 bullets at point-blank range into the car of two unarmed building workers, both over 60, who had done some maintenance work at a police station. Eventually incidents such as these and the general alienation of the public on both sides of the border and overseas may lead the 'ballot box' faction in the Sinn Fein leadership to prevail over the 'bullet' faction, but their conflict and therefore a continuation of the killing at something like its present level is likely to continue.

Other west European terrorists

In January 1985 the German **Red Army Faction (RAF)** and the French **Action Directe (AD)** declared an anti-NATO Alliance and murdered a French General and a German industrialist. During the next two years, the RAF murdered six more people, including an American serviceman whom they had kidnapped for the sole purpose of stealing his identity card to enable them to get into a USAF base to plant a car bomb, which killed two civilian workers. The other victims included another industrialist and a senior foreign office official. AD followed a relatively similar pattern, murdering the chairman of Renault in November 1986 and carrying out a number of bombings of Jewish targets in France. In February 1987 the two founders of AD (Jean Marc Rouillon and Nathalie Menigon) were arrested. They had been previously arrested in 1980 but were unwisely released as part of an amnesty granted by the new President Mitterand. A number of other AD leaders were also arrested in 1987 and the movement has since been inactive. A sister movement in Belgium – the **Combatant Communist Cells (CCC)** – has also been inactive since its leaders were arrested in December 1985.

These three movements were typical of a number of movements which grew up in Europe from 1968 onwards (though AD was not founded until 1979). AD had a hard core of about twenty and CCC was smaller still. The RAF killed thirty-six people in eighteen years (1970–87) and AD fewer than that; the CCC did about eight bombings of NATO-related targets in 1984–5. The RAF and AD both co-operated with Arab terrorists, especially AD in attacks on synagogues and Jewish stores and restaurants in Paris. The RAF has proved the most resilient, having three times survived the arrest of most of its leaders, in 1972 (including Baader, Meinhof, and Ennslin), 1976, and 1978–80. It has a hard core of about 20, with about 200 'militant activists' – part-time saboteurs, semi-clandestine – who bomb installations of the 'military-industrial-complex' (MIK). There is also a 'legitimate fringe' of about 400 sympathizers who provide logistic support, couriers, and so on. The RAF attracts very little sympathy amongst the general population but their professionalism as clinical killers and in clandestine survival may prolong their existence; a fourth generation of leaders could emerge. This kind of movement, however, is probably on the way out.

The **Red Brigades (BR)** in Italy started at the same time as the RAF (1969). Though originating in a university, they had considerable success in organizing support in factories, chiefly by kidnapping junior managers and holding them until the company agreed to demands on behalf of the workers for better pay, reinstatement of people made redundant, etc. For the first three years they did not kill, but thereafter they became increasingly murderous and from 1972 to 1983 they killed about 145 people. During the same period Italian right-wing terrorists killed 193, mainly in a small number of mass bombings, e.g. 85 at Bologna railway station in 1980. Right-wing terrorists generally operated in small *ad hoc* groups with no hierarchical organization.

BR had a strongly hierarchical organization. At the bottom were the 'brigades', which were no more than small semi-clandestine cells of five or six, each supposedly responsible for organizing support and direct action in a particular university, district, or factory. The brigades were organized into about seven 'columns', in big cities or industrial complexes (e.g. Rome, Milan, Turin). The leading members of the columns formed a BR executive, monitored by a number of 'fronts', which reviewed political, strategic, and logistic factors. There was much overlap between them, and this was not good either for efficiency or for security.

In practice, most of the important operations, were conducted by a hard core of leaders in the column HQs, and the brigades were really just subversive propaganda and recruiting cells. This hard core numbered about fifty. As with most terrorist groups they started planning and preparing their major operations well in advance – usually three to six months ahead.

BR reached its peak in 1978, when they kidnapped and murdered Italy's most distinguished statesman, Aldo Moro, former Prime Minister and expected to be next President. This, however, prompted the Italian government to introduce more effective anti-terrorist laws, increase police powers, and improve intelligence organizations. Particularly successful was the provision for lenient treatment for repentant terrorists, *pentiti*, who were prepared to give information or evidence to assist the police. This scheme was initiated by General Dalla Chiesa in 1980 and by 1985 there were 389 *pentiti*, of whom 78 gave positive and valuable information. In 1982–3, 482 Red Brigadists were arrested, at which stage BR officially abandoned the armed struggle and large numbers of members, while not prepared to give information to the police, dissociated themselves from violence (*dissociati*).

By the end of 1988, only a small dissenting group was still operating – the Fighting Communist Party (BR-PCC). They committed a number of murders but, with the arrest of twenty-one of their surviving suspected members in Rome in September 1988, they ceased to be an effective political force. There is no doubt that the new measures introduced in 1979–80, and particularly the *pentiti* system, have proved highly effective and have resulted in the saving of many hundreds of lives.

In France, the **Corsican National Liberation Front (FLNC)** is a separatist movement which did major damage by bombing, mainly in Corsica but sometimes on the mainland, from 1978 to 1988, though they generally avoided loss of life. Targets were mainly government buildings, police stations, banks, and French holiday homes in Corsica. On 31 May 1988 FLNC declared a truce and began discussions with the French government with a view to greater autonomy.

The **Revolutionary Cells (RZ)** mark a relatively new departure in terrorist organization. They were founded in Germany in 1974 and they reject the traditional revolutionary structure of cells reporting to a hierarchy of higher cells up to a central committee. The RZ consists of about 300 part-time semi-clandestine saboteurs, organized in independent cells of five to eight, with no central structure. The cell members are mostly the sons and daughters of prosperous middle-class parents and live at home, or sometimes with groups of friends in apartments or squats. Each cell is autonomous, getting ideas for possible operations from the fringe press or just picking targets spontaneously by reading newspapers and watching television. They have no directives, and need no safe houses, no logistic organization, and no couriers. They are therefore very difficult for the police to detect or penetrate. They have done great damage to industry by arson and bombing, usually attacking in the early hours of the morning as they know that killing and injuring people alienates the public.

The **Autonomous Groups** in Germany are even more diffuse, and differ from the RZ in that members form a cell for a specific operation and then disperse. They attack mainly logistic or infrastructure targets, such as electricity pylons, the railway system, and construction plant working on airfields. Again they aim for material damage, not killing or wounding. About 90 per cent of the politically motivated acts of violence in Germany in 1986 were perpetrated by Autonomous Groups.

All these three German movements – RAF, RZ, and the Autonomous Groups – have a similar Marxist-Anarchist ideology, anti-NATO and attacking MIK targets. The most dangerous to life is the RAF. The other two, however, may survive for longer as they are so hard to keep under surveillance and to catch. For this reason, dissidents in other European countries may emulate the autonomous organization and philosophy.

The Japanese Red Army

The Japanese Red Army (JRA) is probably the most fanatical and resilient terrorist movement the world has seen in the past twenty years, and has certainly been the boldest and most wide-ranging in international operations. Largely dormant since 1977, it showed strong signs of revival 1986–8. It is a small movement (about forty-five strong) with no pretensions to popular support; it is based largely with the Arabs in the Middle East, who have provided it with funds ample for its needs; and with the North Koreans, who played a significant part in its revival, almost certainly in the hope that the JRA would disrupt the 1988 Olympic Games in Seoul. This aim was frustrated by intensive security measures in South Korea and Japan, but if the momentum of the revival survives this set-back, the potential of the JRA should not be underestimated. Its bases in the Middle East and North Korea are secure and, at the time of writing, its two most experienced and determined leaders, Fusako Shigenobu and her brother-in-law, Junzo Okudaira, are still at large, with a network of contacts in the Middle East, Asia, and, to a lesser extent, in the USA and Europe. These two leaders and their comrades have moved freely between these countries in recent years without getting caught, though several other important members were arrested in 1987–8 in Japan, the USA, and the Philippines.

The JRA was founded in 1968, as part of the world-wide explosion of student-based revolutionary movements such as the RAF and BR. From the start it set its sights on world revolution, giving itself the task of leading and motivating other revolutionary movements in other countries. On 31 March 1970 nine JRA members led by Takamro Tamiya hijacked a Japanese Airlines (JAL) aircraft to North Korea where they were given sanctuary and set up a base.

The JRA in Japan, however, was torn by vicious internal strife,

165

culminating in 1972 with the torture and murder of twelve of its members 'to eradicate bourgeois tendencies'. Their bodies were discovered when police besieged the JRA's mountain stronghold near Karuizawa in February 1972 and arrested the fourteen surviving members. The JRA did not reappear in Japan until the mid–1980s.

As well as the cell in North Korea, another cell led by Fusako Shigenobu had gone to Lebanon to offer its services to the Popular Front for the Liberation of Palestine (PFLP), so they too escaped arrest in Japan. On 30 May 1972 three members of this cell carried out a massacre of twenty-six airline passengers in the baggage reclaim hall at Lod Airport in Israel, on behalf of the PFLP. Using guns and grenades which were in their hold baggage, they fired indiscriminately, sixteen of their victims being Puerto Rican pilgrims on their way to Bethlehem. Two then killed themselves (one was Shigenobu's husband, Tsuyoshi Okudaira). The third, Kozo Okamoto, who was the brother of one of the hijackers who went to North Korea in 1970, was captured and sentenced to life imprisonment. He was later released by the Israelis in Lebanon in 1985 as part of a prisoner exchange deal.

At his trial in Israel in 1972, Okamoto gave a revealing account of the international network involved in the operation. After some weeks of general training in Beirut the three terrorists were briefed for the specific operation on 16 May and practised with the type of weapons they would use. On 22 May they flew via Paris to Frankfurt where they were issued with false papers, and thence to Rome where they were given suitcases containing Kalashnikov weapons and grenades purchased from Czechoslovakia. They boarded a French Airlines aircraft in Rome Airport after a body search, but their hold baggage containing the weapons was not searched.

Okamoto said that the JRA cell had joined the PFLP because 'the Arab world lacks spiritual fervour so we felt that through this attempt we could stir up the Arab world'. He added that he had intended to die like the others and made his statement only on the promise that he would be allowed to shoot himself. There was an element of mysticism in his testimony (e.g. 'We three soldiers wanted to become three stars of Orion. Some of those we killed have become stars in the sky. The revolution will go on and there will be many more stars.')

Thereafter the JRA carried out a series of spectacular international operations, usually in co-operation with the PFLP. On 20 July 1973 a JRA/PFLP team hijacked a JAL 747 thirty minutes after take-off from Amsterdam, and, after various refuelling stops in the Middle East, landed in Libya. They demanded the release of Okamoto, which the Israelis refused. The Libyans denounced and imprisoned them, but released them a year later. On 31 January 1974 two JRA and two PFLP terrorists, after an abortive attempt to set fire to a Shell oil installation on an island off Singapore, hijacked a ferry, taking passengers as hostages, and were besieged by Singapore harbour police. The Singapore government held firm so, on 6 February, five PFLP terrorists seized the Japanese Embassy in Kuwait with sixteen hostages, including the Ambassador, demanding the release of the Singapore team. Kuwait and Singapore wanted to stand firm but the Japanese government persuaded them to agree to safe custody for both the hostage-taking teams, who were released to Aden and thence back to Lebanon. Again, this revealed a formidable ability to exploit their international network of contacts.

On 26 July 1974 one of the Singapore team, Yutuka Furuya, was arrested at Orly Airport in possession of forged passports, coded letters, and money. He proved to be a courier from Shigenobu to a JRA cell set up in Paris to kidnap rich Japanese businessmen in Europe. French police located the cell and made eight arrests but, as they could pin no crime on them under French law, they were deported, the leader going to the Netherlands.

On 13 September 1974 three JRA terrorists, one of whom was Shigenobu's brother-in-law Junzo Okudaira, seized the French Embassy in The Hague, taking eleven hostages including the Ambassador, and demanded the release of Furuya. There is evidence that the Venezuelan terrorist, Carlos, then heading the PFLP commando in Paris, financed and participated in this raid. The French gave way and Furuya and the hostage-takers were flown to Syria and handed back to the PFLP.

Similar international incidents continued until 1977. Two JRA members, one of whom had taken part in the French Embassy seizure, were arrested in Stockholm and deported to Japan on 13 March 1975; they were, however, soon released when the JRA seized the US consulate in Kuala Lumpur in August 1975, along with three others arrested in the 1972 police raid on the Karuizawa base, including Norio Sasaki, an explosives expert, and Kunio Bando, both of whom remain free an active to this day. On 28 September 1977 a JAL DC8 was hijacked to Bangladesh, with passengers from sixteen countries on board. The Japanese government gave way, releasing six more of its JRA prisoners and a ransom of $6 million, with which they and the hijackers were flown from Bangladesh to Algeria and thence back to Lebanon. One of those released from prison in Japan was Hiroshi Sensui, a convicted criminal who had made friends with JRA fellow prisoners, and thereafter became an important JRA leader until his arrest in the Philippines in 1988.

The lull in JRA operations after 1977 was probably due largely to the death of Wadi Haddad, the leader of the PFLP military organization, in 1978. The mainstream PFLP leader, George Habash, had become disenchanted with international terrorism, and Shigenobu may have turned increasingly to Ahmed Jebril and his PFLP (General Command). Shigenobu and her JRA cell left Lebanon (probably to go to Europe) when the Israelis invaded in 1982 but returned in 1983, settling into the Syrian army base in the Beka'a Valley. After a period of ideological discussion and retraining, the JRA resumed terrorist operations in 1986 in conjunction with the Anti-Imperialist International Brigade (AIIB), which has links with Iran and Shia terrorist groups. The JRA were suspected of participation in the spate of bombings in Paris in 1986.

On 14 May the AIIB claimed responsibility for mortar attacks on the US and Japanese Embassies in Jakarta during the Tokyo Economic Summit meeting. A JRA veteran, Tsutomu Shirosak, is known to have taken part. In November 1986 the Mitsui manager in the Philippines, Nobuyuki Wakaoji, was kidnapped for ransom and, though this was thought at the time to be the work of a criminal gang, the Japanese National Police Agency later announced that they believed the JRA were involved.

On 15 April 1987 there was a mortar attack on the US Embassy in Madrid, after the JRA had declared its support for the AD/RAF anti-NATO Alliance (see p. 162), and further mortar attacks followed on the British and US Embassies in Rome during the Venice Economic Summit in June 1987. In all these Embassy attacks, in Jakarta, Madrid, and Rome, a very similar improvised mortar tube was used to project the bombs, usually from a hotel window, and there is strong suspicion of JRA involvement.

With the approach of the Seoul Olympics, there was increasing evidence of JRA activity being revived in Asia, including Japan itself, unquestionably sponsored by North Korea. In November 1987 Osamu Maruoka, a veteran of a number of JRA attacks in the 1970s, who had become second-in-command of the movement, was arrested in Tokyo. His interrogation and documents found on him revealed that he had travelled from Japan to Switzerland in June 1987 and thereafter to Hong Kong, Singapore, China, and the Philippines. He was carrying $39,000 and an air ticket to Seoul.

In April 1988 Yu Kikimura, who had in 1986 been arrested

in Amsterdam on arrival from Greece carrying explosives and deported to Japan, was re-arrested on the New Jersey Turnpike carrying $3,649 and three large bombs in his car, with a New York map showing likely targets. Documents revealed that he had entered the USA on 8 March 1988 and had since then travelled 10,000 km in his hired car; also that he had travelled in Europe and had access to Swiss and German bank accounts.

Two days later, in Naples, there was a bomb attack on the US Officers' Club in Naples. A Japanese couple resembling Fusako Shigenobu and Junzo Okudaira were seen leaving the area afterwards in a car with a man of Middle Eastern appearance, and a similar trio was seen outside Naples railway station. It later transpired that Okudaira had spent five nights in a Naples hotel and had checked out a few hours before the bombing.

On 6 May 1988 Yasuhiro Shibata was arrested in Tokyo. He had entered Japan from North Korea in April 1985, and had transferred $80,000 to a Japanese bank account since August 1987. Then, acting on information from Japan, the Philippines police in June 1988 arrested Hiroshi Sensui in a clinic in Manila where he had undergone plastic surgery, and he was extradited to Japan. There was evidence that he was planning to set up a JRA Latin American base in Brazil. The arrests of Maruoka and Sensui revealed that the JRA explosives expert, Norio Sasaki, had been in contact with both of them and had visited Manila several times from Singapore, where the JRA had stored explosives and bank deposit boxes. Maruoka told his interrogators that JRA members had arranged such bank deposit facilities in a number of countries and a search in Singapore revealed a box containing explosives and detonators. These had already been there for eighteen months, and could have become highly dangerous if left for a long time. There may be others in this condition.

Evidence since these arrests suggests that the JRA has links to Chosen Soren (or Chongyon), a pro-North-Korean residents' association in Japan, which is suspected of issuing forged passports, including those used by the two North Korean agents who placed a bomb in a Korean Airlines aircraft in November 1987, killing 115 passengers and crew. Shibata had been based in Pyongyang before coming to Japan in 1985, and documents found in his flat revealed contacts with more than 100 left-wing activists sympathetic to Chosen Soren. There is little doubt that his mission in Japan was recruiting.

Though it has made no progress towards its long-term aim of world revolution, the JRA has been successful in achieving spectacular short-term successes in terms of propaganda and humiliation of governments, especially the government of Japan in the 1970s. In that decade it showed remarkable skill in selecting hostages, creating coercive situations, and conducting negotiations. Its members also ranged more freely on the international stage than any other movements have ever done, as illustrated at Lod Airport in 1972, Singapore and Kuwait in 1974, Paris and The Hague in the same year, Stockholm and Kuala Lumpur in 1975, and Bangladesh in 1977. Their resurgence in 1986–8 has shown a similar flair for flexibility on an international scale, and leading JRA members such as Shigenobu, Okudaira, Sasaki, and Bando are still at large, despite frequent world-wide travels while being on numerous wanted lists for sixteen years.

Their success has emanated from their two inviolable sanctuaries in Lebanon and North Korea. Their dedication, ruthlessness, and fanatical readiness for self-sacrifice – all Japanese qualities abundantly proved in the Second World War – have clearly made them the most valuable hired assassins in the world and both the Palestinians (who are immensely rich – see pp. 154–5) and North Koreans have been very ready to hire them. Subsidizing forty-five terrorists, with their weapons and their travel, does not require a very large diversion from government budgets, and Syria, Libya, and Iran may well have contributed too.

How far their revival will survive their failure to make any capital from the Seoul Olympics (for the South Korean government, despite heavy expenditure on security, made a huge profit) remains to be seen, but there will be no room for complacency until the dedicated leaders still at large have joined Maruoka, Kikumura, Shibata, and Sensui in custody, because they will go on commanding a good price as terrorists for hire, and will regard this role as their most effective contribution to changing the world.

Chapter sixteen

Urban terrorist techniques

Damage to property

A number of contemporary groups using political violence prefer to avoid inflicting human casualties for fear of alienating public sympathy. These include FLNC, RZ, and the Autonomous Groups (see Chapter 15) and some of the more militant environmental and animal rights groups. They set their bombs and incendiary devices to go off during the night and sometimes warn the authorities or firms that, unless they concede to their demands, the next bombs will be set off in hours of peak activity, with maximum casualties, though this threat is seldom carried out.

The devices for precisely timed delay or remotely controlled firing are adequate for their needs. The likeliest changes are in their selection of targets. Maximum disruption can already be caused by putting a major computer system out of action, but the greater interdependence of business and industry and the growing mass and complexity of computerized records will make high technology industries, finance and insurance companies increasingly vulnerable. Hardware, software, and communications will all be vulnerable and disruption by hacking or feeding in fake programs may be more effective than bombing or burning. The development of more reliable technology and procedures for computer security will provide the best answer.

Bombs to kill

The worst recorded single terrorist bomb outrage was on 23 June 1985, when Sikh extremists planted a bag containing a bomb in the hold of an Air India jumbo jet flying from Montreal to India via London, which exploded in mid-Atlantic, killing 329 people. It was almost certainly fired by a delay fuse (not an altitude fuse) because it went off near the end of the Atlantic flight. On the same day, a bag being unloaded from an Air Canada aircraft exploded (killing two baggage handlers) in Tokyo Airport where it had touched down en route for India. There was evidence in this case too of Sikh involvement in Canada, and the bag was presumably labelled to Tokyo rather than India to divert suspicion, and intended to explode over the Pacific. The subsequent investigation suggested that in both cases, a Sikh 'passenger' appears to have checked in with hold baggage but not to have boarded the aircraft, a serious lapse in routine airport and airline security which cost – from two bombs – 331 lives. These lives might also have been saved if hold baggage had been subjected to vapour detection by hand-held sniffers (see p. 58) before checking in, as described for Singapore Airport on p. 188.

The Lockerbie air disaster on 21 December 1988 further underlined the need for tighter control of all cargo and passenger hold baggage, when Pan American Flight 103 was blown up at 31,000 feet by a terrorist bomb in the forward cargo hold. All 259 passengers and crew were killed, and the centre part of the aircraft with its fuel tanks hit the Scottish town of Lockerbie, killing 11 of its inhabitants, bringing the death toll to 270. There was initially some doubt as to whether the bomb was in passenger baggage loaded on to a feeder aircraft at Frankfurt and transferred in bulk at London Heathrow Airport to Pan Am 103, or as baggage of a passenger checking in at Heathrow, or with unaccompanied cargo loaded by Heathrow Airport staff; it was later confirmed that the bomb was in a bag loaded at Frankfurt. The measures needed to reduce the risk of disasters like these are discussed on pp. 185–90.

The bloodiest series of bomb attacks was perpetrated in 1983, when Hezbollah terrorists in Lebanon bombed the French and US Embassies in Beirut on 18 April 1983, killing 50 people, and then the US and French bases of the Multinational Peacekeeping Force (MNF) invited in by President Gemayal, when 240 US Marines and 60 French parachutists were killed, on 23 October 1983. A further 11 bombs were exploded in December 1983 on targets in Kuwait, including the French and US Embassies – a total of over 350 killed in 15 attacks. In the two biggest, the attacks on the French and US MNF bases, suicide drivers were employed to drive huge truck bombs into the heart of the target, and were then blown up with their trucks by another Arab with a remote-control device.

The most serious aspect of these bombings was that they led to the withdrawal of the MNF, an indisputable surrender to terrorism which encouraged further terrorist acts, not only by bombing but also by kidnapping US and other western hostages.

Bombing is also the main technique used by the IRA in attacking police and military targets (including off-duty police officers and part-time Ulster Defence Regiment soldiers), reserving shooting for civilians who are not likely to be armed. Bombing involves very little risk to the bomber. The tilt fuse (see pp. 49–50) in a bomb fitted with magnets, can be slipped underneath the body of a car or in the wheel arch, and the safety device removed, in a few seconds, putting not only the intended victim but also an indiscriminate number of passers-by at risk, with the murderer safely out of the way. It does not need a brave or adventurous person to kill in this way, so it is likely to grow in popularity amongst terrorists unless public disgust convinces them that it is counter-productive.

The same could be said of the remote-controlled bomb planted in a small boat used by Lord Mountbatten and his family on vacation to fish in an estuary in County Sligo in the Republic of Ireland. This was an attractively safe way to kill a man of 79 and a young Southern Irish boatman with him, but in this case it did prove counter-productive. Admiral Mountbatten had been a Commander-in-Chief in the Second World War, much respected both in Europe and the USA and, at the age of 79, was unlikely to harm the IRA in the future. The public anger in the Republic of Ireland was such that the murderer was eventually caught. Contributions from the USA to the IRA also fell and have not staged any lasting recovery.

The precise delay fuse (see p. 48) made a spectacular début in the bombing of the Grand Hotel in Brighton in an unsuccessful attempt to murder Mrs Thatcher and her Cabinet (though five other people were killed). As for most terrorist operations against major defended targets, planning for this one began long in advance – in 1981 with a two-year target date for the Conservative Party conference in October 1983 – but the hotel in that year proved unsuitable so it was postponed until the 1984 conference. Again, world-wide public disgust created a climate in which the murderer was eventually caught and convicted. Since then, more meticulous and efficient searching (primarily by explosive-sniffing dogs) combined with good background intelligence has thus far prevented any repetition of this type of attack by the IRA.

Perhaps the most cold-blooded bombing technique on record was that attempted by the Syrian-sponsored Nezar Hindawi at London's Heathrow Airport in April 1986. He first made a Southern Irish chambermaid pregnant in a London hotel, and returned to the Middle East. He later returned, promised to marry her in Israel, and said he would arrange flights. He came into the

UK disguised as a member of a Syrian airliner crew, carrying a Syrian passport and papers, which the Syrian government admitted issuing. He lodged in the official Syrian aircrew accommodation in London. He told the girl he had booked her on an El Al flight but that he, as an Arab, would have to fly by an Arab airline and would join her there.

In the taxi on the way to the airport he gave her a holdall, asking her to take it with her. It contained a bomb, which was not detected by the normal Heathrow X-ray baggage check. An Israeli guard employed by El Al at the boarding gate, however, thought it was suspiciously heavy and searched it. There was a flat plastic explosive charge in a false bottom and an ordinary calculating machine, in working order, which proved to contain an additional electric circuit to fire the bomb, which would have exploded at high altitude killing all the passengers, including Hindawi's unsuspecting girlfriend and his unborn child.

When the operation was prevented by the El Al guard, the Syrian Embassy helped Hindawi to hide, but he was arrested and convicted. Britain cut off diplomatic relations and expelled the Syrian Ambassador.

The continuing miniaturization and growing reliability of electronics will provide the likeliest development of bombs in coming years. It will become easier to conceal minute and sophisticated precise delay or remotely controlled firing mechanisms within the increasing number of pocket computers, etc., which people will carry. The development of more precisely guided vehicles will obviate the requirement for suicide drivers. But the use of nuclear, chemical, and biological weapons will be neither more nor less likely than in the past (see pp. 50–1), as the restraints on their use are social and psychological rather than technological.

Guns and missiles

Murder by shooting is the favoured method used by terrorists to pick out individual targets when they want to avoid the counter-productive indiscriminate casualties which may be caused by bombs. Developments most likely to affect this technique are the use of laser sights, which enable terrorists to hit their target at short ranges without either aiming or even showing the gun (see p. 36). Further development of silencers so that the silenced gun is short enough to fit into a smaller bag may facilitate this; so could the application of the G11 type of three-round burst with light caseless ammunition (pp. 27–30) to sub-machine-guns.

For longer ranges, sniper rifles with night vision aids (image indentification and thermal imagery) will become more effective, possibly with a lock-on facility which, given accurate night range-finding, will aim the weapon for the correct trajectory. This could be effective for a night sniper hoping to hit a target in a predetermined spot (e.g. the entrance to a building or a footbridge) from a window some distance away.

For longer range still (in daylight) the heavy machine-gun with armour-piercing ammunition may be further developed for use against lightly armoured vehicles (e.g. VIP limousines or armoured Land Rovers).

Recent years have seen increasing use of expensive and sophisticated surface-to-surface and surface-to-air missiles (SSM and SAM) by terrorists, generally of Soviet or east European origin and redirected by Arab governments, notably Colonel Gadafi's. Continuing development of these weapons for use by regular armies will ensure that new and more efficient versions will become available for terrorists. Lighter hand-held missiles with more accurate and foolproof guidance systems (e.g. MILAN see pp. 43–4), and heat- or metal-seeking weapons will reduce the advantages of armoured vehicles enjoyed by security forces. The elimination of smoke and flash (see Armbrust – p. 42) will increase the chances of a getaway by ambush teams or terrorists firing from windows.

Similarly the helicopter will become increasingly vulnerable to hand-held SAMs of the Javelin and Stinger types (see pp. 45–6).

Intimidation and racketeering

'Necklacing' is a particularly vicious form of terror used primarily against elected or appointed local officials in 'black-on-black' violence in the townships in South Africa. A rubber tyre is filled with petrol and ignited round the neck of a victim who is bound so that he cannot shake it off. The screams and the writhing agony have an especially daunting effect on the community and exercises terror in its most literal form. Whether or not the cause is justified, this kind of cruelty must be unreservedly condemned, and is probably likely to repel rather than attract support.

Intimidation is not always as extreme as necklacing. It can start, as Hitler's Brownshirts showed in the 1930s, around the homes and shops of Jews, first warning them to get out and then harassing them until they did so, daubing their walls with slogans or breaking the windows or shouting or telephoning abusive messages throughout the night. This is the technique used by some animal rights activists against laboratory workers testing new pharmaceutical products or hospital supplies on animals – following the Nazi technique, with 'animal torturer' instead of 'Jew' in the slogan. They carry it further by putting paint-stripper on cars and sometimes starting fires with petrol bombs. On four occasions in 1982 they posted letter bombs to leading politicians and in 1986 they attached magnetic bombs under research scientists' cars. The leader of the Animal Liberation Front (ALF) encouraged his members by writing that it was a perfectly feasible aim to drive the great majority of laboratory staffs to abandon their jobs by this kind of intimidation.

The ALF also, in November 1984, attempted to punish a large confectionery manufacturer, Mars, for financing dental research at Guy's Hospital. They delivered two poisoned chocolate bars to the BBC and a Sunday newspaper asking them to warn the public not to eat Mars bars. No one was poisoned because, apart from these two, the other forty or fifty bars smuggled on to the shelves of retail outlets contained only a leaflet claiming that they were poisoned when they were not, but a number of children were terrified when they saw the leaflets after they had eaten one of the bars. This did not endear the ALF to the public but the incident did cost Mars (who, for safety, withdrew and destroyed all the 3,000 tons of bars which had left the factory) about £3 million.

Product contamination or the threat of it are, however, much more often used to intimidate companies into paying a ransom than for political coercion.

More lethal forms of intimidation have been used by political terrorists in Spain and Northern Ireland. ETA have extorted large sums in revolutionary taxes from businessmen in the Basque country by threatening death or damage to property if they do not pay. In Northern Ireland in 1987 it was estimated that £15 million was raised by terrorists in this way (see pp. 159–60).

In the Republic of Ireland the IRA is alleged to have extorted money from a corporation by threatening to kidnap executives or staff if they refused to pay. (The Irish Government located the bank into which the money was paid and seized it.)

Guerrillas in Angola and southern Sudan have also attempted to disrupt government development projects by abducting expatriate workers and holding them for several months, in order to deter people from working on the projects and to coerce the contractors into abandoning them (see pp. 139–41).

There are numerous means of intimidating corporations and individuals to convince them it is not worthwhile to continue what they are doing, or to extort money to finance further terrorism, both by rural and urban terrorists. Much of it probably goes unreported so it is a technique which must be expected to continue.

Future techniques are likely to centre increasingly around EDP, computer, hardware, software, and communications, as described on p. 171. The potential cost can be so enormous that corporations may well be intimidated into changing their policies (e.g. by ceasing to trade with Israel or South Africa) or paying ransoms by the threat of such disruption without it ever actually taking place.

Kidnapping

More conventional forms of kidnapping of individuals to secret hideouts, usually in urban areas, have been widely used for extorting money (for either criminal gain or funding further political activity and terrorism) or political concessions, including changes in governments' policies and release of prisoners. It is, in fact, one of the most ancient and most international of coercive techniques, and was very prevalent in medieval times. The abduction of sons and daughters as victims (whether as mature heirs or infants) has long been found to be the most effective form of coercing the most robust of leaders and business executives. The Anglo-Saxon origins of the word 'kidnap' were to seize (nab) a child (kid). It has been especially applied in recent years by criminals in Italy.

The techniques used for abduction and incarceration of a hostage vary greatly with the environment. In Lebanon, where there has since the late 1970s been no effective government or law enforcement (see Chapter 15) it has been very easy for militia groups to seize victims in the streets and conceal them in the honeycomb of apartments in the areas of Beirut which they control. In a more orderly environment, a complicated plan with many months of preparation may be needed.

The most lucrative political kidnapping on record fell into this latter category. In 1974 a Marxist-Peronist movement, the Montoneros, kidnapped Jorge and Juan Born, the two sons of an ageing father who had built up the biggest firm in Argentina, Bunge Born, which he was looking forward to handing on to them. The brothers were in early middle age with children at school, and lived as neighbours. The terrorists placed them under discreet surveillance and observed that, though heavily guarded, they usually left home together at about the same time in order to escort all their children together to school in the suburbs of

Buenos Aires. They took three cars, one dropping the children and the other two proceeding on into the city, the two brothers in the back of one car followed by another escort car with more bodyguards.

The Montoneros employed about fifty terrorists in all. Nineteen did the actual kidnap, working in five teams. They selected a site on a broad tree-covered boulevard with narrow parallel service roads on each side. On a signal that the convoy had left home, they set up diversion signs blocking the main boulevard for tree-lopping and diverted all traffic into the service roads, where two trucks were used to collide with the two cars. Terrorists, dressed as policemen, shot dead the chauffeur and escort in the brothers' car, 'arrested' and beat the other bodyguards, handcuffed them under their car, and drove the brothers away. The bystanders, not surprisingly, preferred to look the other way. Another twenty to thirty terrorists were involved in guarding the hideouts and in logistic duties. A command cell conducted the negotiations and extorted $60 million from the old man before releasing his sons seven months later.

A group of similar size kidnapped the British Ambassador to Uruguay, Sir Geoffrey Jackson, in 1971. In this case he was able to detect at least three of the surveillance teams: one posing as a young couple with a baby picnicking in a park opposite his home; a couple on a motor scooter who regularly tailed his car on its various routes to the Embassy, sometimes cutting in to test the chauffeur's reactions; and a 'courting couple' in a doorway opposite the Embassy gate. For the abduction they staged an 'accident' with his car in a narrow street and employed four or five more teams to block all the access roads leading on to the getaway route to give them a clear run. He estimated that about thirty others took part in the roster of guards during his eight months in captivity.

There may therefore be from five to ten different cells operating, each from three to eight strong: a reconnaissance cell, perhaps doubling with one or more surveillance cells; a snatch squad, usually about five strong; a number of diversionary teams as in the cases described; possibly a shuttle team with a van to which the victim is quickly transferred so that the snatch squad does not actually take the victim to the hideout; this team may also serve as the logistic team to supply the hideout; there may be several cells sharing the task of guarding; and there will be a command cell to plan and control the operation and to negotiate and distribute any ransom obtained; there may well be a separate cell with the necessary criminal and banking contacts to launder the money.

In a well-ordered clandestine political movement, these cells will be isolated from each other as much as possible, with only the cell leaders (or perhaps even the leader of a group of cells) having contact with one particular member of the command cell. Each cell will know only who and what it needs to know.

This all refers to kidnaps by political movements containing an ample supply of volunteers who do not expect to be paid more than their keep and are unlikely to give way to offers of rewards to betray the movement.

Criminal gangs are much more economical with manpower. For a well-guarded target, they may still spend six months in reconnaissance, surveillance, and planning, but they may employ only five or ten people at most, since each one will expect a large slice of the ransom if he is going to resist police rewards to give information.

The longest political kidnap on record (though some of the hostages in Lebanon may exceed this) was that of William Niehous from 1976 to 1979 in Venezuela, by the Red Flag movement. He was held for 1,219 days. He survived the ordeal, both physically and mentally, and was sustained, as Sir Geoffrey Jackson was, by a strong religious faith. He did his best to develop a human relationship with his captors in the correct belief that this would make them less likely to kill him. He was eventually rescued when a patrol came across the hideout accidentally.

Another model of survival was Leon Don Richardson, kidnapped by the left-wing EGP (Guerrilla Army of the Poor) in Guatemala in 1981. He is founder and chairman of a multinational metal group based in Australia and Hong Kong, and was kidnapped by eight armed terrorists while visiting a subsidiary in Guatemala. He was held for about 100 days and most of the negotiation, both with him and a colleague in Australia (Tom Dundon), was done by an extremely unpleasant woman who spoke fluent English with a Canadian accent. She referred to him contemptuously as a 'piece of merchandise' and from this and other indications he shrewdly deduced that he was of more value to them alive than dead. He thereafter took the initiative, alternately aggressive and agreeable to his guards, and gained psychological dominance over them. This, coupled with superb negotiating techniques used by Tom Dundon and his advisers, and excellent police co-operation, resulted in the kidnappers' cutting their losses and releasing him without taking the risk of collecting a ransom. (This and about sixty other case studies, are discussed in more detail in Clutterbuck, *Kidnap, Hijack and Extortion*, 1987.)

One case which demonstrated a new and grisly technique was the kidnap of Gerard Jan Heijn, vice-chairman of a retail chain in the Netherlands, in September 1987. The kidnappers in fact killed him on the first day but they cut off his finger either just before or just after he died and put it in the freezer. Several weeks later, they sent it to his family and the doctors judged that it was 80 per cent certain that he was alive when it was cut off. On the strength of this, despite no other proof of life, the family paid a ransom, in full co-operation with the Dutch police. Though it was too late to save Mr Heijn, this did enable the police to arrest the principal kidnapper, who confessed to the crime, and a number of suspected accomplices were also arrested.

Both criminal and political kidnapping have proved effective enough in achieving their aims to make it likely that this form of crime will continue. Huge ransoms have been paid, prisoners have been released, and there is at least a strong suspicion that the Hezbollah in Lebanon, as creatures of Iranian fundamentalism, have successfully induced the French, German, and US authorities to modify or change their policies in various ways in order to get hostages released.

The technological developments likeliest to help kidnappers are in the fields of tapping communications (Chapter 3), and possibly in as yet unknown development of drugs with which to make hostages more ready to talk. Most developments (including the latter) are, however, more likely to assist in countering kidnapping and some of these are discussed in Chapter 17.

Hostage seizure

The term 'hostage seizure' is used to differentiate the holding of hostages in a known location (e.g. in an embassy) from kidnapping to a secret hideout. Most hostage seizures are domestic, to apply pressure on families, acquaintances, or colleagues. They are sometimes used by criminals on the run in a desperate attempt to evade capture.

Political hostage seizures are done to attract publicity, though hostage-takers have occasionally been given safe custody to a chosen location, sometimes even with a ransom, in order to spare the lives of hostages (e.g. at the Dominican Embassy in Bogota in 1980). On one occasion (in Iran in 1979–81 – see opposite) the government actually co-operated with the hostage-takers and this, of course, added a unique new dimension. Normally, however, the police will surround the premises in overwhelming force, and thereafter have the initiative. It quickly becomes clear that the hostage-takers (and the hostages) are totally dependent on the police for their food, their survival, and their eventual destiny, so the only thing left for them to gain is publicity. They probably knew this all the time, so that is usually their primary aim.

The seizure of the Iranian Embassy in London in 1980 was a typical example. In April 1980 six anti-Khomeini Iranians of ethnic Arab origin seized Khomeini's Embassy in London, together with twenty-six hostages. The police surrounded the Embassy within a few minutes. The terrorists made some extravagant political demands (e.g. the release by Khomeini of ninety-two prisoners in their province) but neither they nor anyone else expected these to be granted. After five days of constructive negotiation (during which five sick or pregnant hostages were released) the terrorists shot one of the Embassy staff and threatened to shoot others at forty-minute intervals until they were granted safe custody out of the country. The British Army SAS Regiment therefore raided the Embassy and rescued the remaining hostages (except one whom the terrorists shot during the rescue) and killed five of the terrorists – all except one, who succeeded initially in masquerading as a hostage. The real aim, however, was publicity. Literally hundreds of press and television cameras and reporters converged into Hyde Park, which was across the road from the Embassy. When one of the hostages (a British BBC technician) obtained the time of transmission of a BBC World Service broadcast and ensured that the terrorists heard it, their delight was unrestrained, and most of the tension was lifted. Though all but one of the terrorists chose to die rather than surrender, they did so in the knowledge that their case had been brought forcibly and dramatically to the attention of the world.

The seizure of the US Embassy in Tehran by Islamic fundamentalists on 4 November 1979, with over fifty staff who were entitled to diplomatic protection, was not specifically ordered by Khomeini but, as he condoned it within a few days and thereafter deployed large police and military forces to prevent the lifting of the siege, the Iranian government must be condemned as responsible for the 444-day detention of the hostages and thus for the most flagrant breach of the Vienna Convention and of civilized international behaviour in history. After a bungled rescue attempt, the US government negotiated the release of the hostages by releasing some of the Iranian assets frozen when Khomeini had deposed the Shah earlier that year. Unfortunately, now that the precedent has been created and Iran appears to have lost nothing from the episode, it must be assumed that, when they judge that their vital national interest justifies it, other unscrupulous leaders may emulate his example.

The only technological developments likely to assist hostage-takers in selecting targets and planning their seizures are improved techniques for bugging, eavesdropping, and hacking. Technological developments should generally strengthen the hand of those responsible for security of premises and access control, and this will be discussed in Chapter 17.

Hijacking

Hijacking an aircraft, train, or ship is another form of hostage seizure; the premises seized happen to be mobile, but it is generally known where they are. Moreover, wherever it occurs, the environment is 'urban' rather than 'rural' in its nature; the aircraft, train, or ship is a miniature extension of urban life. The types of pressures exerted on the hostages and on those negotiating for their release are similar to those in urban rather than rural situations; so are the techniques used by the terrorists.

The primary aim of most hijacks, as of other hostage seizures, is to gain publicity for a political cause. Occasionally individuals have used hijacks to escape from or get to some specific place. Only rarely have they achieved political blackmail or ransom.

The heyday of hijacking was the period 1969–72, when the average was eighty per year (a peak of ninety-one in 1969 – mainly to Cuba). In January 1973 the introduction of the 100 per cent search at the airport boarding gates reduced this to an average of thirty from 1973 to 1981. Since 1982 the annual average has been reduced to fewer than twenty – less than a quarter of the peak. The chances of an aircraft's being hijacked are now one in half a million (twenty in 10 million take-offs).

Hijacks do, however, have a political effect greater than almost any other terrorist act because of the dramatic treatment they receive from the media, and especially on television. The most notorious example was the hijack of a TWA Boeing 727 (Flight 147) from Athens to Beirut in June 1985. Most of the 145 passengers, plus the crew, were Americans and after a number of women, children, and other nationals were released, there were 108 hostages. One young American had been murdered during the flight. The hijackers were Shia fundamentalists demanding the release of over 700 Shia prisoners captured during and since the Israeli invasion of south Lebanon in 1982. The US television channels surpassed themselves in arousing and exploiting American emotions in order to attract viewers, which enormously strengthened the hijackers' hand and made negotiation almost impossible. Eventually President Reagan shrewdly sensed that there were only two people who had any possible influence over the hijackers and were themselves anxious lest a terrorist triumph would increase the disruptive power which the fundamentalists were already able to exert: these two were Nabih Berri, leader of the moderate Shia Militia, and President Assad of Syria. Faced with the passion and publicity generated by the media, Reagan made the best deal that he could, saving the lives of the remaining hostages, but the hijackers went free.

A similar publicity bonanza dogged the handling of the hijack of a Kuwaiti airliner in April 1988, again by Shia fundamentalists, first to Iran, thence to Cyprus, and finally to Algiers. Again, many of the world's television stations behaved appallingly, with conjecture or leakage of possible negotiating ploys or rescue preparations, giving the terrorists the initiative and the publicity they wanted. The hostages were saved (except for two, murdered and contemptuously thrown out on to the tarmac in front of the cameras) but, once again, the murderers were given safe custody back to an ecstatic welcome in Lebanon.

This kind of media irresponsibility is the biggest single encouragement to hijacking, which must therefore be expected to continue. The coming multiplicity of competing television channels is likely to make this worse. Even if reckless use of the media so as to put lives at risk were made a criminal offence, this would have little practical effect because both hijacking and television transcend national frontiers and jurisdiction.

In other respects, technological developments are likely to improve the opportunities for preventing and handling hijacks, and these are discussed in the next chapter.

Chapter seventeen

Developments in countering terrorism

Security of premises and installations

Travel and personal security are of little value unless the individuals under threat can work, live, and sleep in a secure environment. The current and developing technology for the protection of premises was discussed in Chapter 8.

Access control through authorized entrances for staff, visitors, and vehicles depends not only on technical aids but more still on training and the alertness of security staff in applying them. Would-be intruders, hoping to reconnoitre or carry out a terrorist attack, will use every possible trick to deceive the guards.

No barrier is impregnable and the principle of concentric rings, procedural and physical, to give warning and impose delay, was set out in Chapter 8; the importance of developing alarms with a lower false alarm rate (FAR) was particularly stressed. This is a field in which there will almost certainly be progress in coming years.

In some countries, more sophisticated bullet-proofing of office buildings is becoming necessary, and flexible armour such as Kevlar will be useful. In one multinational company office in a Latin American city, for example, as well as bullet-proofing of all windows on lower floors, the executive suite and conference room on the top floor have flexible Kevlar curtains which can be drawn across all windows at the touch of a switch, in the event of suspicion that terrorists have occupied rooms in other high buildings within firing range.

Security of computer centres and of computer hardware, software, and communications, will become increasingly important as the degree of interdependence and reliance on EDP increases year by year. Bugging, hacking, computer fraud, and the detection and countering of all these is a developing science in itself, with a continuing battle of both inventiveness and wits comparable to the historic leapfrog between armour and the weapons to penetrate it.

Airport and airline security

The technological aids available or under development for aviation security were discussed in Chapter 6 (explosives detection, pp. 57–60) and Chapter 8 (access and embarkation control, identification and prevention of impersonation, pp. 78–80). The urgency of tightening security against both hijacking and aircraft sabotage has been highlighted by the massive mid-air bombs in the Air India and Pan-American aircraft in 1985 and 1988 and the TWA and Kuwaiti Airlines hijacks in those same two years (described in Chapter 16).

There are essentially three avenues for getting a bomb into the hold or cabin of an airliner: concealed in cargo or kitchen supplies loaded on the ramp by airport staff; in hold baggage checked in by embarking passengers or checked through from linking flights and transferred in bulk across the ramp by airport staff; or smuggled into the cabin by passengers in their hand baggage. The same procedures needed for preventing passengers getting bombs into the cabin in their hand baggage should also prevent them from smuggling weapons aboard for a hijack.

Ramp security should be the easiest to enforce, since it is wholly under the control of the airport authorities and of staff employed by them. The first essential is watertight control of every means of access to the ramp through maintenance areas, cargo sheds, and kitchens, etc; from the terminal buildings; and from outside the airport. Second, every one of the people issued with passes giving such access – engineers, cleaners, kitchen, fuel and cargo handlers – must be security vetted. Third, such staff should be subject to monitoring by metal and explosive detectors and, where needed, hand search. All cargo should also be similarly monitored. Vapour sniffing should detect drugs and other contraband as well as explosives.

Hold baggage should also be monitored by multiple means: X-ray, vapour sniffing (by plant or dogs), neutron bombardment, and new methods as they are developed (see Chapter 6); also by testing in a bomb-proof vacuum chamber in which reduced barometric pressure will fire an altitude-operated fuse. These need cause virtually no additional delay *given the necessary expenditure on plant and operating staff*. Batches of luggage can go through a continuous flow system of such checks – X-ray, vapour sniffing, neutron bombardment – one after the other and thence into the barometric vacuum chamber and out for loading.

At some airports or for some flights additional security measures for hold baggage may be needed because of the situation in the country of the airport (e.g. Lebanon, Israel, Northern Ireland, certain Latin American countries and, at various times, Turkey, India, and Sri Lanka); or because the airline itself may be a particular target (e.g. El Al); or because of the destination or the types of passengers likely to travel (e.g. flights to the Middle East or Northern Ireland, or flights widely known to carry US servicemen). A common precaution in such cases is for all hold baggage, after going through all the X-ray, vapour and other checks to be laid out beside the gangway, all the passengers identifying their own as they board, no item being loaded unless so identified. Even this will not guard against the suicidal bomber, nor against naive travellers who have agreed to pack a hermetically sealed 'gift' in their bags to deliver for 'a friend'. Only a 100 per cent hand search can overcome these two.

Both identification at the gangway and, still more, the hand search do add considerable delays and labour costs, and will therefore be unpopular with airports, airlines, and passengers unless they are done universally. Whether it is achieved by identification of baggage at the gangway or by meticulous documentation and cross-referencing between boarding cards and baggage tag numbers, the essential is an infallible means of reconciliation so that no aircraft takes off unless the owner of every bag in the hold is on board.

A very useful precaution, affecting both hand and hold baggage, and improving security against both bombing and hijacking, is the X-ray and sniffing of *all* baggage at the entrance to the terminal building before check-in. At Singapore's Changi Airport this is done by airport police using a fast and simple X-ray tunnel and hand sniffers, in the presence of the passenger. Any bag giving any cause for doubt has to be opened by the passenger and hand searched. No gun or explosive is known ever to have got through this – but in Singapore other forms of security are also good (see p. 188).

Procedures for check-in, search, boarding, and transit of passengers and their hand baggage is the most important of all, and the most difficult to make perfect. As well as the reconciliation of passengers with their baggage, there must be leak-proof sterilization of the air side from the ground side: the departing passengers, having once been checked through the 'passengers only' barrier, must have no conceivable means of getting out of it undetected, excepting only through the door of the aircraft on which they have been allocated seats. Moreover, from wherever they are last searched to the aircraft door, they must have no access whatever to disembarking passengers.

There are generally seven or eight stages (the first only at a few airports):

1 Preliminary search of passengers with all their baggage at the terminal entrance.
2 The 'passengers only' barrier, with boarding card check.
3 The passport check, which may be combined with stage 2.
4 The search tunnel and magnetometer arch, where passengers and their baggage are searched. The tunnel should in future include X-ray explosive sniffer and neutron bombardment, and the arch should also include at least one explosive detector (probably a sniffer) in case the passenger has concealed it on his or her person.
5 The general departure lounge, where airports earn much of their revenue from duty free and gift shops.
6 The pipeline from the general departure lounge to the individual boarding lounge.
7 The entrance to that boarding lounge.
8 The exit from it, by a single boarding gate leading only through a tube or a bus or a supervised walk across the tarmac to the aircraft door.

In many airports there is a dangerously weak point in stage 6, when departing and arriving passengers use the same two-way pipeline to or from the boarding gate *after* the departing passengers and their baggage have been searched. It is thus easy for an arriving passenger to pass a bag to a passenger about to embark, e.g. in the corridor or in a toilet. If collaborating terrorists know this, one could bring in a bag containing guns or explosives from an airport where security is known to be lax and pass it to the other. Thus the passenger and hand baggage security of any airport with such a single pipeline is reduced to that of the worst airport from which any incoming flight has originated or refuelled in transit – unless the embarking passengers are finally searched *after* passing through that pipeline.

Another notorious weakness, for which both airlines and airports may be at fault, lies with transit passengers. At many refuelling stops, transit passengers are allowed to leave their hand baggage on board the aircraft while they go out. It may then be easy for a *disembarking* passenger to leave a bag containing a bomb under a seat or in the overhead rack, so that it is assumed to belong to one of the transit passengers. This was one suspected explanation when a bomb exploded under a seat in a TWA aircraft over Greece on a Cairo-Athens-Rome-Athens-Cairo shuttle on 2nd April 1986, and four passengers were sucked out of the aircraft to their deaths. There may also, in some airports, be mingling between passengers in transit or embarking on different flights in the same lounge – especially if the airport wishes to expose them all to the lures of its lucrative gift shops.

One of the best systems is at Singapore Airport (where they also have the extra 'hurdle' of the search at the terminal entrance – see p. 186). There is in addition a full passenger and hand baggage search at stage 7, at the entrance to every individual boarding lounge. This entrance leads directly from the general departure lounge where arriving, departing, and transit passengers can all congregate with access to shops, etc. Anything passed between passengers should be detected when the embarking and transit passengers all pass through the search process on entering or re-entering their individual boarding lounge. Here too, however, it is up to the airlines not to allow transit or disembarking passengers to leave hand baggage in the aircraft.

A good alternative to this is that at Geneva Airport (and a number of others) where the embarkation and disembarkation pipelines are on different levels, and are totally insulated from each other between stage 2, the 'passengers only' barrier, and stage 8, the aircraft door. As with every security measure mentioned in this book, a series of 'multiple hurdles' is best, but each, of course, costs money and may cause passenger irritation. Other improvements of a wider nature should also in future improve airport security – for example, machine-readable passports, visas, and 'international air travel permits', prevention of impersonation and the use of the developing fine-grained parallel computer systems to detect suspicious passengers and links between them (see Chapters 7 and 8).

In the medium term it would be wise to redesign the layout of most airport terminals, over the next few years. Stages 1 to 4 should be integrated, with ticket and baggage check-in, into a single tightly controlled complex through which the passengers flow with all their baggage. To check in, passengers would enter a one-way corridor from which there would be no return. Having checked in and received a boarding card, they would move on down the corridor, with their heavy baggage on a parallel conveyor through a tunnel with multiple checks such as X-ray, vapour sniffer, and neutron bombardment (also, in due course, other forms of explosive detector). Passengers would link up with their hold baggage in a search room. If the tunnel had revealed anything which could itself be, or could conceal, part of a gun or bomb, the heavy baggage would be opened and searched in its owner's presence. Passengers and their hand baggage would also pass through metal, X-ray, and vapour checks and also be hand searched if necessary. The hold baggage would then continue through the loading flow while passengers are checked (and, if need be, interrogated) at a passport and immigration barrier. The only exit from this pipeline would be into the general departure lounge.

When their flight was called the passengers would walk, as they do now, to the boarding lounge for that flight, at the entrance of which they and their hand baggage would again pass through metal detectors, X-rays, sniffers, etc. (as already happens in Singapore) to detect any gun, plastic grenade, and so on which might have been passed to one passenger by another. This would also simplify the airport layout by enabling transit passengers to wait in the general departure lounge – again, as in Singapore. Transit passengers would, however, be required to take *all* hand baggage off the aircraft and present it for search when they re-enter the boarding lounge for their flight.

Both for the immediate and medium-term measures, the extra costs of installation, equipment, and security staff will have to be reflected in higher airport landing charges and thence, inevitably, in the price of airline tickets. This, together with earlier check-in times and passenger inconvenience, makes it essential that the International Air Transport Association (IATA) should collectively enforce a common standard. If one airport has higher charges or involves more passenger inconvenience than others, some airlines and some passengers will be driven away to its competitors and, as has been pointed out earlier, one airport with poor security increases the risk to every other airport to which aircraft fly from it.

IATA can enforce these standards on airports only if the airlines and their parent governments collectively insist on it, and boycott airports which do not. The starting-point for this must be the seven countries of the Economic Summit (the USA, Japan, Canada, France, Germany, Italy, and the UK) who, between them, operate 80 per cent of the non-Communist world's commercial air traffic. Those seven countries should require IATA to monitor and enforce standards at every airport at which their scheduled flights land, and should agree universally and collectively to boycott any airport which fails to rectify faults revealed by this monitoring. Faced with the prospect of a boycott by 80 per cent of their potential traffic, the airports would have little option but to conform. Other responsible governments and airlines, for example, Dutch, Belgian, Spanish, Swiss, Scandinavian, Indian, Pakistani, Japanese, Australian, New Zealand, and Latin American, would almost certainly agree to support such a boycott and, in the present political climate, there is a good chance that the USSR and eastern European countries would join too, so the boycott could become virtually 100 per cent.

Search techniques and research

As well as vapour sniffing and neutron bombardment, research must continue into other possible methods of detecting explosives, such as the measurement of dielectric properties and the application of thermal imagery. There may be many more as yet undreamed of. This raises difficult and delicate problems, since there will inevitably be competition between countries and between manufacturers, leading them to keep their most promising developments to themselves until they have enough of a lead to go into production and grab the market. Here again, the IATA countries (especially the Summit Seven) must stand together. The best way would be to put money into a large pool of research funds, to be allocated only in exchange for the right of IATA to monitor the use and the resulting dividends from each allocation, so that the availability of the product and the profit are fairly distributed, with a reasonable premium for those whose research contributed most. The industrial world should by now be sufficiently adult to do this in the face of the common terrorist threat, as allies do in major wars.

The prospect of detecting explosives would be greatly enhanced if the majority of countries of the world, including all the main industrial countries, agreed to a comprehensive system of tagging explosives, especially detonators (see pp. 56–7).

Detection of electronic devices is developing fast, because of growing concern about bugging, hacking, industrial espionage, and computer fraud. It should be possible to apply some of this technology to detection of electrical firing devices, notably the precise delay fuse (like a video timer) of the type used in the bomb attack on the Grand Hotel in Brighton in 1984 (see p. 48); also to the detection and jamming of radio-controlled firing mechanisms (see p. 60).

Supplementing all of these, there is still much scope for developing aids to the normal senses (sight, smell, hearing, and touch) of human searchers. A typical example of this is the use of fibre-optics to enable an operator to insert the 'eye of a camera' through narrow and tortuous gaps to see round corners or under or behind objects before they can be safely removed (see p. 55).

The watchword for search techniques must be multiplicity. Reliability will lie in placing many hurdles of different kinds across the path.

Personal and travel security

Individual victims of terrorists – politicians, officials, businessmen, or targets for intimidation – are most at risk when they are travelling, especially by car, and to a lesser extent by air. The essence of travel security is unpredictability, particularly regarding time and route. The majority of kidnaps occur on the road between home and work. A kidnap or assassination requires more organization than is generally realized (e.g. see pp. 178–80) and the kidnappers need to know that their target will pass a selected spot suitable for a kidnap and getaway within a definite time bracket. If strict discretion is maintained over the movements of potential targets and they vary their time, route, type of car, and so on, the chances are that the kidnappers will turn away and look for an easier target.

Similar discretion is advisable over air or sea travel, and especially regarding the date and time of arrival at the seaport or airport, since this will clearly reveal the time and place of the start of a car journey. The IRA twice attempted to ambush (with huge roadside car bombs) the cars of judges who had failed to conceal the fact that they were returning from holiday to Northern Ireland via Dublin at a stated time; in one case (in 1987) the IRA killed the judge and his wife; in the other case (1988) they confused the judge's car with that of another man travelling on the same ferry and killed him instead, with his wife and child.

Though not comparable in importance with the value of unpredictability, various equipment can be installed to improve security for car travel. Light armour is widely used by VIPs, but is not proof against heavy machine-guns or missiles. Internal locking, two-way radio, alarms, and tracking systems are other valuable aids, but the use of multiple aerials (and armour) may reveal to a sophisticated observer that the car is a special one. Unless the VIP is instantly recognizable (e.g. a president or senior minister) greater safety may be achieved by travelling in an unostentatious car and changing it frequently (e.g. using a series of company fleet cars of the type normally used by junior executives).

Security against aircraft hijacking is in the hands of airports and airlines (see pp. 185–90). All that individuals who are potential targets can do is to avoid airports or airlines with a bad security record, report lapses if they notice any, and ensure that neither they nor their staff reveal which flight they are using. Potential targets should also be as inconspicuous as possible during check-in and boarding, and especially so if the aircraft they are in is actually hijacked.

The most intriguing possibility for safer VIP travel will be opened if there is a revolutionary breakthrough in the power-to-weight ratio of engines – similar to the breakthrough of the steam engine in the late eighteenth and the internal combustion engine in the late nineteenth centuries. There is no scientific reason why some similar discovery, either in design or in fuel, should not occur, with reduction in size and weight comparable to the miniaturization of computers achieved successively by transistors, printed circuits, and microchips. Given a very small engine capable of generating a jet with a powerful enough thrust, the personal microlite or vertical take-off aircraft could become both practical and cheap. With the air at low altitudes filled with such traffic, it would be almost impossible for terrorists to pick out their targets or to predict when and where they are likely to be.

Weapons

It is generally unwise for potential victims of terrorists to carry guns unless they are not only fully trained to use them but also psychologically prepared to shoot to kill without hesitation. The terrorist certainly will be trained and 'psyched up' to shoot; he or she will also hold the initiative whereas the victim will be surprised and shocked; the terrorist will also be covered by other terrorists similarly prepared. The likely effect of the victim's drawing a gun will be to get himself shot before he can use it. If it is decided that an armed response to possible terrorist attack may be necessary, this should be provided by fully trained bodyguards. Even the most dedicated bodyguards, however, may be a liability if they are hopelessly outnumbered and outgunned (terrorists are usually armed with sub-machine-guns and are seldom single-handed). In fact, the most valuable contribution of trained bodyguards is that their advice may keep their principal from ever getting into a dangerous situation.

As was pointed out in Chapters 4 and 16, developments in personal weapons are likely to help the terrorist rather than the counter-terrorist, because they may be easier to conceal, and because higher rates of fire and laser sights will favour the aggressor with the initiative rather than the defender restrained by the principle of minimum force and firing only in response.

Nevertheless, the first weapons designed to be concealed in a briefcase were to help bodyguards to avoid drawing attention to themselves (to be fired by 'aiming' the briefcase, not with a laser sight). And sophisticated night vision equipment may assist the security forces and may help both in pre-empting a night attack and in preventing the escape of terrorists after it.

Development of heavier weapons such as HMGs, mortars and hand-held guided missiles, while necessary for conventional armies, will be wholly to the advantage of terrorists. So will that of indiscriminate weapons such as grenades, bombs, and mines.

Aids to training in the use of weapons, such as simulators and 'pop-up' target ranges, are unlikely to be available to terrorists as they are not compatible with a clandestine life-style, so security forces should be better trained individually in quick response and accurate fire. Indeed, for the same reason, terrorists will generally have practised less often with live ammunition than soldiers or armed police officers, and this will to some extent mitigate the surprise factor mentioned above.

Non-lethal incapacitating weapons, which temporarily disable friend and foe alike, are one of the dreams of security forces for dealing with hijack, hold-up, or hostage situations but at present the problem of achieving an instantaneous knock-out effect, to prevent the terrorist from shooting or throwing a grenade, has not yet been solved. One conceivable line of research was mentioned in Chapter 5 (pp. 51–2).

The security forces

Protection of the population from guerrilla warfare and terrorism depends above all on good intelligence. Intelligence organizations vary between countries: the commonest weakness is lack of co-ordination between rival political, police, and military intelligence services. In Britain the intelligence community comprises the Secret Intelligence Service (MI6), the Security Service (MI5), and the Police Special Branch, co-ordinated by various committees and supplemented by other intelligence agencies (e.g. military, industrial, economic, topographical, and scientific).

An intelligence service must operate secretly. If the sources from whom it gets its information suspect that their identities may be widely accessible, the information will at once dry up. There have been numerous examples of this, especially in Italy in 1976–8. The dilemma for governments lies in the need for intelligence services to be accountable to the public. This is best done by making the directors of the service accessible to a supervisory committee (normally from the legislature or the judiciary). These directors should also, within reason, be accessible to politicians and to journalists who are prepared to honour 'off-the-record' or 'non-attributable' information. The front-line intelligence officers must, however, be accessible to no one who does not need to know them; for if their faces are known it is an easy matter to follow them to their informants whose confidentiality may be literally a matter of life and death. The directors must be answerable for the actions of their subordinates but not required to reveal their identities unless they are charged with an offence.

Working from all this information (including that of their own Special Branch) the police are the primary arm of law enforcement and guardians of public safety. In dealing with guerrilla warfare and terrorism, the army may be called in to support them but only very rarely (e.g. in Northern Ireland from 1970 to 1976) has the army in the UK taken over prime responsibility for security from the police. In many countries, especially the less developed ones, the army more often dominates.

Many police services have specialist riot and anti-terrorist squads. Personnel in these squads should regularly be rotated back to normal police duties; otherwise the squads may take on a character of their own, and are likely to lose contact and sympathy with the public.

Specialist anti-terrorist squads ('commandos' or 'rescue squads') are sometimes found by the police or by the army or by a 'third force' (as in Germany). In France the 'Intervention Group' (GIGN) is provided by the National Gendarmerie, and handles both criminal and political terrorist interventions. This gives it the advantage of having taken part in several hundred rescue and other operations with live ammunition, whereas the German (GSG9) and British (SAS) forces deal only with political terrorists. This advantage is offset by the fact that the resolution of a criminal case (e.g. the holding of a hostage in a house) demands great restraint and the minimum use of force, for which police firearms officers are trained, whereas intervention against heavily armed terrorists who have shown their readiness to shoot freely and to kill without mercy demands a military attack, with fire and movement, to capture or kill them before they kill any more victims. The training of a person's reflex actions for these two roles is very different, and it may be difficult for the same person to perform with confidence in one role on one day and the other role next day. The GIGN, however, have been successful in both.

The tactical handling of rescue forces requires skilled judgement and timing, as was illustrated by the contrasting stories of two rescue attempts, in Malta in 1985 and in Karachi in 1986.

On 23 November 1985 three Palestinian terrorists hijacked an Egyptian Boeing 737 en route from Athens to Cairo and forced it to land at Luqa Airport in Malta. After their ultimatum had been rejected, the hijackers shot ten passengers (two dead and eight wounded) and clearly intended to carry out their threat to shoot more. An Egyptian commando force landed and as soon as it was dark, eleven hours later, attempted a rescue, but, under the pressure of the threat to kill more passengers, their preparations had been inadequate. They entered through the belly door into the cargo hold, where they placed a charge to blow an entrance through the floor of the cabin above. This was intended as a diversion from the main attack over the wings. There was some confusion and the aircraft caught fire. There is some doubt as to whether the fire was caused by the commandos' explosive or by a terrorist grenade, but fifty-seven more passengers died, most of them from inhaling smoke fumes. Only one hijacker survived and he was later sentenced to twenty-five years' imprisonment for murder of the two passengers before the rescue attempt.

At 6 am on 5 September 1986 a Pan American 747 was seized on the ground while refuelling and embarking transit passengers at Karachi Airport. Despite intelligence warnings, four Arab hijackers dressed in the uniform of airport security guards, waving fake passes, were allowed to drive their van on to the ramp (an inexcusable lapse in security – see p. 185) and stormed up the gangway through the embarking passengers, one of whom they shot (presumably to terrorize the rest). The aircrew, acting on Pan Am standing orders, escaped by ropes from the flight deck, making it impossible for the aircraft to take off. The Pakistani commando force arrived and were told to be ready to mount a rescue operation in the early hours of the following morning – about twenty-four hours after the hijack. Presumably with the story of the Egyptians in Malta in mind, they were ordered to make detailed preparations and rehearse on an aircraft set aside for that purpose on the other side of the airport. The aircraft captain (now in the Control Tower) warned that the aircraft's generators would run out of fuel at about 9 pm, but nothing was done to prevent or make allowance for this. At 9 pm the aircraft lights dimmed and went out. The hijackers, thinking that this indicated an impending attack, panicked and starting shooting the passengers in the dark. They killed another 16 (making 17 in all) and wounded 127 more. The rescue force took fifteen minutes to reach the scene and it was twenty-five minutes before they had collected ladders to enter the aircraft.

It is easy to criticize the Egyptians for going in too hastily and the Pakistanis for taking so long to respond to the crisis. The best answer is for a rescue force to get two separate teams to the site as quickly as possible. One team should make an immediate plan to go in if it becomes necessary, say if the terrorists start killing hostages. That team should remain at instant readiness for this, using every hour they have thereafter to improve their plan, find better means of access, and assemble equipment. Meanwhile, the second team should study the site, make a model or mock-up if possible, and develop and rehearse it until it is time to relieve the first team. The first team, after a rest, then use the time available to improve the plan further with the mock-up. But there is always one team ready for instant response.

This is the approach used by the British SAS, who have earned a very high reputation and are in immense demand to train other national forces all over the world, especially in Commonwealth countries. There are SAS units trained in the same way (and with common origins in 1941) in Australia and New Zealand. The main reason for the excellence of the SAS is their system of selection. Unlike GSG9, they do not recruit directly. They get their men from other regiments of the British army in which they have served for at least two years and have gained outstanding appraisal reports. The SAS get so many applicants that they need consider only the outstanding ones. These are then invited for intensive tests – physical, mental, and psychological – in Hereford where, on average, only one in ten is selected, the other nine being returned to their regiments. Those who get into the SAS are therefore the *crème de la crème* of the army, and this is the foundation of their morale.

Within the SAS, one squadron provides the rescue force for six months at a time, and has a year or more on other duties in between (e.g. in Northern Ireland) so that it does not get stale. That squadron finds three rescue teams, each of a troop (about twenty-three men). At any time of the day or night, one of these teams is at instant readiness, with a helicopter standing by. A second team is training in barracks, ready to follow up. The third team is stood down or on leave. They are kept at 100 per cent fitness, physically and psychologically, and at concert pitch in their reflexes and weapon handling. This is maintained by regular exercises in their ricochet-proof 'killing house', where they practise rescues with live ammunition, with one of their number in turn acting as a 'hostage' surrounded by figure targets representing terrorists. This breeds mutual confidence. Their morale is comparable to that of some national football squads, in which every man has got there by giving every ounce of his body in every match in every team during his progress to selection, and goes on doing so in his determination not to be dropped.

Intelligence

Intelligence and personal surveillance are the most promising fields for development of effective counter-terrorist aids, provided that they are regarded as supplements to human intelligence and not as substitutes for it.

Computerized data banks of personal information and information about personal possessions (e.g. cars, weapons, homes, clothing) and personal habits (e.g. the *modus operandi* of known criminals and terrorists) are already of great value to police forces in quickly identifying links between apparently unconnected pieces of data. These computer systems are increasingly linked internationally between police forces, and their potential was discussed in some detail in Chapter 7. Thus far, however, they have been used only for data about known or highly suspected criminals or terrorists and there is a strong political and public reluctance to allow their use to be extended to data on people about whom there are no grounds for suspicion. This concern is healthy and justified, because it is at present almost impossible to guarantee that an individual police or intelligence officer who has memorized such information cannot communicate it undetected by word of mouth to someone not authorized to receive it. So long as this is the case, there will always be people (e.g. criminals or members of unscrupulous credit companies) who will be prepared to offer attractive bribes for such information.

It is therefore especially urgent to develop parallel means of preventing or, should prevention fail, of detecting abuse. Otherwise, the community will continue to be denied the full use of one of the most effective weapons in protecting it against terrorism. These safeguards will be all the more necessary if there is a major upsurge in the use of terrorism, because public opinion will then demand and accept much wider recording of personal data, as has already happened in Northern Ireland, and the opportunities for abuse of it would be likely to cause both an erosion of civil liberties and, in due course, a backlash against it.

An upsurge in terrorism would also necessitate the recording of a wider range of information, the issue of identity cards (discussed, see next section) and registration of where people live, including notifying the police of overnight tenants, which is already done in a number of European countries. A great deal of this information is, ironically, already recorded by private companies for people holding cheque cards and credit cards, but this is not perceived to carry the same risk of abuse as if it were held on a national computer.

Tight safeguards are also necessary for other aids to police detection, such as tapping and taping of telephone calls and bugging; also of electronic monitoring and tagging (discussed in the next section).

The devastating influence on terrorism of the whole process of drug-trafficking, from the rural cultivation areas to the streets of prosperous countries, was assessed in Part III. It was concluded that it must primarily be fought on the streets of the USA and western Europe. Further development of means of detecting drugs and possibly also of detecting drug addicts must be given high priority, and the traffickers and addicts must be identified and taken off the streets.

Identification and prevention of impersonation

The development of means of identification and detection of impersonation is an essential basis for crime prevention and for arrest and conviction of criminals and terrorists – the best of all deterrents against further crime. The technological means available or under development were examined in Chapters 7 and 8. These include the issue of machine-readable identity cards and passports or visa cards, of which harmonization within Europe will be essential when national frontiers are virtually abolished in 1992. Germany has pioneered this, and her system should be adopted by others. Once again this very necessary step for public safety is restrained not so much by technological problems as by concern for civil liberties, but in this case the concern is less justifiable. Concealment of identity is not a proper civil liberty; as practised by criminals and terrorists it deprives the rest of the community of their civil liberties and sometimes also of their property and their lives. Social reasons for concealment of identity (e.g. by a philanderer deceiving his wife) do not justify leaving the way open for others to conceal it for what are almost always unlawful purposes. The technology is already available and becomes cheaper every year.

Impersonation has no moral justification at all, and is a direct abuse of someone else's civil liberty. Again, it is almost invariably used for a nefarious purpose. The technology available or under development for preventing it was discussed in Chapter 8. The most effective and economic method currently available is by digital recording of unique fingerprint data either in a microprocessor incorporated in an identity card (the 'smartcard') or in a computer memory or, ideally, in both. This and other methods (such as DNA and vein patterns) were described on pp. 79–80. Used in conjunction with the computerized intelligence system discussed earlier in this chapter, these techniques could greatly enhance the prospects of detecting criminals and terrorists in advance.

Where appropriate, this same data can be used for electronic monitoring of people's movements in places where crimes or terrorist acts may be contemplated. This is already done in restricted areas of high security establishments so that if anything occurs which needs investigation there is a precise record of who entered and left the restricted area and at what times. The extension of this to other areas does create obvious risks of abuse of privacy. It may, however, be properly used in conjunction with tagging of convicted criminals or terrorists who have been released or (if they are allowed freedom of movement) of drug addicts. The technology of tagging is discussed on pp. 81–2.

Interrogation and justice

Conviction both prevents and deters terrorism and crime, and depends upon hard evidence such as will leave a judge and jury in no reasonable doubt of guilt.

Once enough evidence has been obtained for the police to arrest a suspect for questioning, the preparation of a case for prosecution and successful conviction depends on the building of a structure of interlocking facts and statements from witnesses. From the moment of arrest, the suspect is the most important witness; the suspect's demeanour and reaction to questions are, or should be, material evidence. The suspect has an absolute right of silence, but the community – as later to be represented by a judge and jury – should also have an equal right to place whatever interpretation they judge fit on any refusal to answer questions. This is as valid a part of their judgement of guilt as the answers or demeanour of a witness under cross-examination in court. For this reason, every interrogation should be recorded on audiotape and, if the police consider the case to be a serious one, also on videotapes. These tapes also provide a safeguard against improper interrogation. They are already used by police, and sealed copies are given at once to the suspect. These must be shown to be identical to any tape later presented in evidence, and it is now technologically possible to ensure that neither the police copy nor the suspect's copy can be tampered with undetected. These procedures will now make it possible to change the terms of the standard caution without any danger to a person who is innocent. The caution should now be

> These questions and your answers will be recorded on tape of which you will have a copy. You are not obliged to answer the questions but, if you do not do so, this fact may be drawn to the attention of the court and the judge and jury will draw whatever conclusion they think fit.

The basis for successful interrogation and for subsequently presenting convincing evidence is the interplay of proven facts with statements and answers given by the suspect and other witnesses, both during interrogation and in court. This structure is built up both from prior background intelligence and subsequent investigation, both of facts and of witnesses. It is the spotting of discrepancies that detects a liar and convinces a jury. Confronting people who are lying with facts at variance with what they have said will disconcert them and lead them to tell further lies which can also be detected. For this purpose the maximum possible use must be made of fact-gathering resources now available, including long-range high-resolution cameras (both still and video), identification, and detection of impersonation. Where appropriate, evidence of movement produced by electronic monitoring can be valuable in detecting discrepancies. All of these techniques have been described above, and must be used to best advantage if society is to curtail the alarming growth of crime in recent years, and to control the threat to life and denial of liberty created by terrorism.

One more reserve power must be held in readiness. Trial by jury has over the centuries been a guardian of freedom and justice; it can, however, be made unworkable by intimidation of both juries and witnesses. This has already necessitated the suspension of trial by jury for terrorist offences in the Republic of Ireland (since 1962) and in Northern Ireland (since 1973). In recent years in England, 'jury-nobbling' has become rife, and so has the intimidation of witnesses. There have also been a number of notorious cases in which juries have returned perverse acquittals out of pure terror of the consequences of a guilty verdict. It is, of course, the richest criminals and terrorist organizations which can afford to apply either bribes or threats for this purpose – especially those financed by massive fraud or drug-trafficking.

To counter this, Parliament should legislate to empower a judge, in advance of a trial, to direct that neither the witnesses nor juries should be seen in court by anyone except the judge and (in the case of witnesses) by the jury. Sadly, the proof of connivance of some lawyers with crime and terrorism, especially in Germany and to some extent in the UK, precludes the otherwise desirable right of the lawyers also to see the faces of the jury and witnesses. CCTV technology now makes this perfectly feasible. The jury would sit and the witnesses would give evidence in rooms which were quite separate from the court (they need not be in the same building) with a system of cameras and screens to be controlled by a court official so that the appropriate people can or cannot see the faces of the others. Everyone would see the judge and the accused. No one at all would see the jury. They, however, would see the faces of the witnesses. Everyone, including the public, would hear the voices, but the public would see only the judge, the court officials, the lawyers, and the accused. The identity of the jurors would be disclosed to no one. Their selection and their deliberations would be monitored by an 'Ombudsman' organization appointed by Parliament on the recommendation of the Judiciary.

No one *needs* to see the jury's faces though they, to judge whether they are lying, do need to see the faces of witnesses and of the accused. This is precisely the position of, say, politicians being interviewed on television. They can be seen by the viewing public, who can make up their own minds, by judging their words and their demeanour, whether the politicians are telling the truth. In fact, with faces close up on camera, the viewers can probably make a more informed judgement than if they were looking across a large room. Politicians, however, cannot see their viewers, nor do they know who or where they are, nor do they need to. But the public are the 'jury' the politicians have to convince.

Part six

Conclusions

Chapter eighteen

Nightmare scenarios

None of these scenarios need ever materialize. They are presented as a warning of how fragile is the barrier which holds back the flood. Totalitarian countries are largely free from terrorism because terrorists can expect no publicity, and they know that they can be arrested secretly and disappear without trace. In pluralist societies, however, terrorism is very easy. Anyone can plant a bomb, provided that they do not mind if it kills people indiscriminately as well as their intended target, and provided that they are not really afraid of the likelihood or consequences of being caught. If pluralist societies do not act firmly, casualties from terrorism could quite suddenly reach alarming levels.

The drug barons

By 1995 the consumption of hard drugs in the USA and western Europe had reached four times its 1990 level. The process began in 1991 when the US government 'decriminalized' the use of soft drugs (cannabis, amphetamines, etc.) and maintained a stock of heroin and cocaine to be provided under supervision to registered addicts at a relatively low price. A number of west European countries followed suit. A parallel was drawn with the repeal of Prohibition in the USA in 1933.

The result was a disastrous increase in addiction, first to soft drugs, and then increasingly to heroin and crack. The increase was mainly amongst affluent 'Yuppies' seeking relaxation and excitement to counter the stresses of their increasingly hectic business life. Street values of drugs fell, but consumption soared. When governments tried to turn off the tap of official supplies, the drug-traffickers maintained their profits by further increasing the flow and the spread of addiction. Violent crime, both by drug addicts and amongst rival trafficking gangs, grew alarmingly. The gangs ran hit squads, and terrorist murders of police officers and of politicians, officials, and journalists who spoke out against drug addiction became commonplace.

The huge increase in demand from western countries broke any serious attempt by the governments of Bolivia, Peru, and Columbia to control the cultivation and processing of coca. It became the undisguised mainstay of the economy of all three countries and any politician who attempted to curb it at best forfeited any hope of re-election and more often was assassinated. The drug barons became richer and they were able to seize the commanding heights not only of the economy but also of politics and the media. In conjunction with jet-setting colleagues in Miami, the Caribbean, and Amsterdam, the 'narcotic multinationals' widened and diversified their activities under all-embracing titles like 'the Pan-American General Trading Corporation', but they made no serious attempt to conceal their main activity. They established huge media empires, gaining control of most of the growing number of television channels (both cable and airwave) which, with cheap receivers and the burgeoning coca-based prosperity of the population, reached almost every household in the cities and most in the rural areas. They gained growing popular support both for their defiance of the west and for the prosperity they had created; they set up large charitable funds with ample resources for sport sponsorship and running recreation centres, clinics, and schools. They financed political parties and leaders who could facilitate the continued expansion of their wealth and power. By 1995 all the countries had elected populist presidents, all sporting 'People's' or 'Socialist' labels, but all closely associated with and dependent upon the drug barons who held the real power. They continued to finance SL in Peru and FARC in Colombia, which became reminiscent of the notorious *tons-tons-macoute* in Haiti, enforcing discipline by state terror.

Their power and influence spread across the Caribbean and thence to the affluent post-industrial societies where their tentacles reached into the streets and trendy night-clubs of the USA and Europe. Anyone who stood in their way, from Bolivia and the Bahamas to London and Los Angeles, could not expect to live for long. Though the Medellin and Cali cartels continued to compete, and to some extent replaced the traditional democratic political parties, there was a degree of live-and-let-live to maintain the trade, and together they amounted to a gigantic terrorist multinational empire.

The Christian fundamentalists

This scenario is based on a marriage between political terrorist movements and liberation theology. The story began in 1992, when left-wing activists in Mexico, frustrated by their inability to shift the one-party government, set up a clandestine terrorist organization, for which they provided a launching fund by kidnapping a series of expatriate multinational executives for whose release they collected more than $100 million, lodged untraceably in the international banking system. With this money they established a cadre organization in the shanty towns and villages, backed by regional terrorist groups, able in most cases to live clandestinely in the villages. These groups were able to extort large revolutionary taxes and protection money from both expatriate and Mexican firms. The movement was well supplied with arms and explosives, initially through Cuba, and later increasingly from Libya as a means of embarrassing the USA.

Encouraged by their success, the Guerrilla Army of the Poor (EGP), operating in the northern part of the Guatemala, also built up their funds by a series of kidnaps and ransoms, as did the Red Flag movement in Venezuela, aided by M19 and ELN from Colombia. Nicaragua, exhausted by her long civil war, played no direct part but acted as a transit area for supplies of arms. Cuban advisers operated with the guerrillas.

Meanwhile a growing number of left-wing priests, in order to retain their flocks in the poorer parts of the cities and rural areas, expressed sympathy and later organized active support for the terrorists. It was easy enough to justify this by selective quotations from the Bible and to apply them to rooting out the evils of capitalist exploitation and government corruption.

This suited the political terrorist movements very well. It greatly widened the base of their support and gave them an appeal to liberal opinion in the USA and western Europe, whose Congresses and Parliaments became reluctant to prop up the governments with economic and military aid. At a fraternal conference in Nicaragua, the leaders of the movements pledged mutual support and agreed to play down the Marxist line and base their platform on 'the fundamentals of Christianity as expressed in the Bible. He who has lived by the sword shall die by the sword.'

They killed selectively, picking unpopular victims who suited their image (corrupt officials, oppressors, exploiters); after the initial fund-raising kidnaps, these victims were almost entirely local, because every murder of an expatriate would encourage foreign aid to the governments. They avoided large-scale massacres for the same reason but, by 1995, there was an average of twenty terrorist murders every day in most of the big cities and a continual trickle of deaths and abductions in rural areas. Local officials and police officers lost heart, and increasingly turned a blind eye. Journalists dared not speak out for fear of their lives. The rest of the world was shocked when, early in 1996, the Rand Corporation published statistics showing that nearly 100,000 people had been killed by terrorists in the region during 1995.

At this stage, with large guerrilla armies being organized in liberated areas, the only likely alternative to civil war seemed to be a Castroite or Sandinista-style revolution incorporating the whole of Mexico, Central America and Venezuela. The guerrilla leaders represented this as a militant revival of true Christian values and persuaded western governments and multinationals that they had less to fear from this than from continued civil war against corrupt government. With a steadily rising oil price in the 1990s, they felt confident that Christo-Marxist fundamentalist dictatorships would be as viable as Khomeini's Iran had been.

An independent Ulster

The newly elected British government in 1993 announced that an election would be held in Northern Ireland in 1994, after which the new Stormont Government would be given the choice of reunification with Ireland, remaining part of the UK (though with massively reduced subsidies), or becoming an independent country. This action was taken in the light of growing exasperation amongst the British public, more with the militant Protestants than with the IRA, whose activities had been much reduced by arrests and convictions arising from revised rules of evidence and investigation and of rewards for information. The Reverend Ian Paisley had been killed in an IRA bomb attack in 1992, and a new younger generation of populist leaders exploited the momentum created by his leadership (and by his death) to found a New Ulster Protestant Party (NUPP). This had close links with the Protestant paramilitaries, who fed it with funds from increasing racketeering and intimidation. There was a growing demand in the British electorate to let them stew in their own juice.

The NUPP was elected, on a platform of an independent Ulster, and the British set a date to complete withdrawal in twelve months. After some initial sectarian rioting and blood-letting, both the IRA and the Protestant paramilitaries decided to conserve their strength for the main battle which they knew would follow the British disengagement. The Dublin government made it clear that they had no intention of intervening or of pressing for unification unless, as they had always set down as a condition, the majority of the Northern Irish population had voted in favour of it, which clearly they had not.

The 1995 the newly independent NUPP government took over. Though there were some resignations, the RUC generally decided that it was its duty to maintain order and an expansion programme was launched. Much the same applied to the eight battalions of the Ulster Defence Regiment, which expanded to eleven battalions and formed the basis for a full-time regular army. This was supplemented by fourteen reserve battalions formed out of the Ulster Defence Association and various other Protestant organizations, some of which had been preserving weapons under floorboards since 1912 and carrying out clandestine organization and training in readiness. 'Doomsday' dawned on 1 June 1995. The fourteen reserve battalions were all mobilized full-time for the first three months, with provision for some to revert to part-time service thereafter, so the NUPP initially deployed twenty-five battalions in support of the RUC.

Their first act was to detain all suspected members of the IRA and INLA and to proscribe Provisional Sinn Fein – many of whose leading members were also detained as IRA suspects. Most of the hard core had, of course, crossed into the Republic before Independence Day, and continued to direct operations from there. Within 'Ulster' (which the new government claimed as its title despite the continued exclusion of three of the nine counties), however, the IRA leadership was taken over by inexperienced and extremely violent young men. The NUPP at once declared a state of emergency and, for a time, contained the attempted uprising, making many more arrests. The repression which they had to impose to survive, however, caused many of the more moderate Catholic population to rally round the IRA as their only form of defence. IRA recruiting and popular support in the Catholic areas rapidly increased. Moreover, the violence and rough justice of the NUPP repression caused a massive swing of sympathy to the IRA in the Republic and in the Irish American community. Arms, ammunition, explosives, and money poured in. The more violently the growing IRA fought, the more violent was the repression; and the more violent the repression, the greater the support for the IRA, both internally and externally. By the end of 1996, the number of people killed in terrorist violence had exceeded that in the worst year of the previous troubles (467 in 1972), rose to more than 100 a month in January 1997, and continued rising.

Conclusions

The Civil War in Ulster was fast approaching Latin American levels and no one could see any way to stop it.

Chapter nineteen

The price to pay

This chapter summarizes some of the more important suggestions considered in earlier chapters in the light of the changing environment of technology of the 1990s. It also reflects the balance between the rule of law and civil rights.

Coming to terms with the microelectronics revolution

Robotics and information technology will change the shape of society and the targets chosen for attack by guerrillas and terrorists, as was described in Chapter 3. Eighty percent of the people in prosperous post-industrial societies will be employed in service industries, many working at home with computer terminals and teleconference facilities.

Interdependence of business arising from centralization of data and reliance on telecommunications will change the choice of targets for saboteurs and terrorists, and the virtual supercession of cash by plastic money and electronic transfer will put a premium on extortion. Laundering money will become easier, linked with growing traffic in drugs and computer fraud.

The greatest social effect of the microelectronics revolution will increasingly arise from the information explosion. Most homes will have access to up to fifty television channels, including those by direct satellite from foreign stations outside sovereign control. They will compete fiercely for audiences by entertaining them, some just for high ratings for advertisers, others to influence political opinion. While authoritarian governments will manipulate this flow of information to tighten control over their populations, pluralist societies will become easier to destabilize (see Chapters 2 and 3).

Intelligence, identification, and civil liberties

Almost every adult in post-industrial societies carries at least one machine-readable identity card, in the form of a cheque or credit card. The rising level of sophisticated crime, the opportunities for major and petty fraud, and the disproportionate effects of terrorism on society now justify the compulsory issue of one more card – a machine-readable national identity card which would also be linked to social security records, making it much quicker and easier to draw benefits from these services. ID cards, and machine-readable passports and visa cards, will all become essential in 1992 when entry from outside into one EC country will authorize crossing into any other. The ability of the police to check who people are, any time anywhere within the EC, will be the only way of keeping track of criminals and terrorists who pass from one nation's jurisdiction to another's.

It now costs very little, about £2, to fit these ID cards, passports, and visa cards with their own microprocessors containing unique personal data (e.g. a digital recording of a fingerprint) to prevent impersonation. As a further precaution, these same data can also be recorded on the appropriate national computer (via the European link-up) to be activated by the card. The technology and the ethics of these things were discussed in Chapters 8 and 17. Ethically, no innocent person has anything to fear from this system and it will greatly increase his or her own security within the community. It is not a civil right to conceal identity, still less to impersonate someone else.

Such a system will be an important component in a good intelligence system. This also must, after 1992, be fully linked up within the EC. Linked national computers will need to record the same kinds of data as are already recorded on government computers for tax, social security, and vehicle licensing, and on commercial computers in banks, and credit and insurance companies. Expert systems and fine-grained parallel computers will increase the speed and efficiency with which these linked systems will be able to detect and draw attention to discrepancies concerning individuals, their cars, their homes, etc. Such discrepancies may prompt the police to hold someone when necessary to check further (see pp. 69–74).

Parallel with the development of this kind of personal surveillance will be the development of means to prevent or, failing that, to detect abuse of such information by officials who have access to it. The only inconvenience for innocent members of the public will be the brief delay for checking – a small price to pay for security (see pp. 197–8).

Judicial proceedings and the rule of law

One of the primary aims of terrorists is to make the liberal system of law unworkable by intimidating witnesses and juries. They hope thereby to have credible grounds for accusing the government of repression. It was in the face of this that trial without jury for terrorist offences was introduced in Northern Ireland in 1973 (as it already had been since 1962 in the Republic of Ireland). In Northern Ireland, however, the trial is conducted by a single judge, subject to full rights of appeal to a court of three judges. Justice would better be seen to be done if there were three judges at the trial itself, of whom two could be junior judges, stipendiary magistrates, or QCs temporarily seconded from the UK, though this would necessitate prolonged personal protection thereafter. An alternative would be the CCTV technique for safeguarding the identity of jurors and witnesses (described on pp. 200–1). This is now technologically quite practical.

There should certainly be a reinterpretation of the 'right to silence' (proposed on pp. 199–200), whereby the court can put its own interpretation on refusal to answer questions (presented as a tape recording at the trial), just as it interprets a failure by a person to provide a convincing explanation in court for something he is shown to have done. Again, only the guilty have anything to fear from this. It is already applied in certain cases in the Republic of Ireland and in Northern Ireland.

In dealings with terrorists who calculatedly try to make the law unworkable, it is all the more justifiable to offer incentives for evidence from informers and to give them whatever protection is needed. This provided the greatest single breakthrough in fighting the Red Brigades in Italy and thereby saved hundreds of lives. In Northern Ireland, absence of corroborative evidence led the Appeal Court to quash a number of convictions, though in many cases the Appeal judges made it clear that they themselves had no doubt of the guilt of the person convicted. A court in which the witness could feel confident of not being identified and, better still, a jury able to hear and see but not to be seen, would probably have overcome this problem.

As well as granting immunity or leniency for Queen's evidence, it is essential that any witnesses or informers likely to be at risk should be given protection and, if they desire it, provision of generous funds to enable them and their families to start a new life in a new place. The cost of this is negligible compared with the cost of the damage done by terrorism. It was certainly done in the first and most successful experiment in this field in Malaya. Both there and in Italy, few if any of the informers or other witnesses giving 'dangerous' evidence have suffered retribution.

Other forms of intimidation, such as demands for protection money and racketeering (see pp. 159–60 and 176–7) must also be firmly dealt with: first, by extending the same guarantees and protection to informers as above, and second, by freezing all the assets of people accused of this crime and those of their family and colleagues, and confiscating these if they are found guilty. The onus would be on the family to prove that they had obtained any money or property in their possession by legitimate means. This, again, has been done in Northern Ireland.

With the opening of frontiers in 1992, it will be necessary to have a harmonization of judicial systems in the EC, and an acceptance (with no loopholes for offences claimed as political) of the obligation to hand an accused person over for trial in the country where the offence was committed and for acceptance in any EC court of evidence of witnesses from any other EC country.

Other laws which help to fight terrorism

Legislation is needed for stricter control of the possession and movement of arms, ammunition, and explosives. This could be greatly improved by an agreement by civilized nations to tag all explosives with a colour code system which would identify their source and enable their progress to be recorded (see pp. 56–7). The number of countries (such as Libya) which would refuse to take part in such a system would be small, so that there would be a much narrower field of search when untagged explosives were found.

Registration of private security companies is inadequate in most countries, especially in Britain. The 100 largest British security companies, which handle 90 per cent of the trade, are voluntary members of the British Security Industry Association (BSIA) which does enforce professional standards of both management and guards. There are, however, at least another 600 small security companies which undercut costs by employing poorly trained guards at low wages which many of them are prepared to accept because they have criminal records, and perhaps also because they hope to supplement these wages by dubious use of the opportunities available in this business. Control could be exercised in one of two ways. Either all security companies should be required by law to register with the BSIA, accepting its monitoring of their recruitment and professional standards as a condition of being allowed to practise (like doctors being required to register with the BMA). Alternatively, this compulsory registration could be with a government body, which would serve the same purpose. The first is probably the better alternative, and would be welcomed by the hundred or so large and responsible security firms which are currently undercut by 'cowboys' to the benefit of criminals and terrorists.

Reckless use of the media in such a way as to put lives at risk should be treated like reckless driving. If an editor, reporter, or producer recklessly or wilfully reports a terrorist incident, or reveals measures to pre-empt it or to catch the terrorists, in such a way as to increase the risk to life, a court should convict him or her whether anyone was killed or not.

Emergency legislation

In November 1974, after IRA bombs killed twenty-one people in Birmingham, the Prevention of Terrorism Act became law within a week and, with only minor adjustments, has been renewed by Parliament every year since then. This would clearly not have been possible unless legislation had been held ready in draft for such a contingency. Other powers may be kept in force but not used, such as the power of detention without trial, introduced in Northern Ireland in 1971 but not used since 1976. If there were a major crisis (e.g. a series of massacres such as to create a risk that the population might take the law into their own hands), virtually the entire top line of the IRA's godfathers and hard core (sixty to eighty people – see pp. 160–1) could be detained.

Legislation which should be held ready in draft might include Tenants Registration, whereby every householder and innkeeper would be required to register the names and National Insurance numbers (or ID card numbers) of everyone resident in the house overnight. In some European countries this is already required by laws which specify periods within which arrivals and departures (permanent or temporary) must be recorded. This is very valuable, not only for keeping track of terrorist suspects or supporters, but also for detecting houses being used for sheltering them or for other unlawful purposes. Though this would be counter-productive in normal times, it might be justified and necessary in certain specified areas (e.g. Northern Ireland) if both the circumstances and public opinion demanded it.

If it were decided that the issue of ID cards was not at present

215

justified, then at least the necessary legislation, machinery, and materials for immediate implementation should be held in readiness, as they clearly were (along with ration cards, etc.) as part of the mobilization plans for the Second World War: such legislation would take account of the experience of other countries which have had to take such action. In France, for example, legislation was passed in 1986 to prevent people leaving the scene of a crime, enabling the police to demand proof of identification and to detain them if their identification was in doubt. If anyone declined to co-operate in providing such proof, the police could refer to a magistrate who had the power to order photographs and fingerprints to be taken.

Power to increase the permitted duration of detention for questioning should be held in reserve in case a concerted attempt to circumvent existing procedures, coupled with an upsurge of terrorism, were to make it necessary. In Italy, for example, calculated disruption by intimidation of the processes of investigation by magistrates led the government to extend the time and postpone hearing of the case for an indefinite period after the murder of Aldo Moro in 1978. They also permitted 'informal interrogation' (i.e. it was not admissible as evidence) without the right to have a lawyer present. Spain, after a spate of ETA murders in 1985, authorized detention of suspects incommunicado for up to ten days (reduced in 1987 to three days extendable to five).

Abuse of rights by lawyers may also need to be covered. In Germany in the 1970s, leading figures in the middle-class Red Army Faction included a number of lawyers who had not given sufficient proof of involvement to justify arrest. These lawyers, representing leading terrorist comrades under arrest or undergoing trial, skilfully disrupted the processes of investigation and court proceedings and, in the course of privileged prison visits to the clients, acted as couriers and channels for orders and communications; some also smuggled weapons and radios into the prison. The German government therefore legislated to bar from the courts any lawyer who had supported terrorist activities or disrupted legal proceedings, and applied stricter control to prison visits.

Laws to suspend jury trial or to safeguard the identity of jurors and witnesses (see p. 201) could also be held in readiness, in case intimidation or corruption (by criminals as well as terrorists) made this necessary to prevent interference with the course of justice. The 1986 package of laws in France enacted non-jury trial for terrorist offences by a *Cour d'Assises* comprising a president and six assessors (all judges – the French separation of the Judiciary and Advocacy allowing quite young 'examining magistrates' to act in this capacity).

France also tightened migration and extradition procedures on the Spanish frontier in 1983–4 at Spain's request. Again, the complexity of such legislation justifies holding it in draft.

Drugs and illegal money

Chapters 9, 10 and 11 identified the 300 billion dollar narcotics profit as the biggest single generator of terrorism and criminal violence in the world. Its evil effect spreads from the Third World countries in which the narcotics are cultivated and processed, to the affluent countries in which most of them are consumed, especially Europe and the USA, but spreading increasingly as affluence grows in the producing countries themselves. There is no anti-terrorist measure which can compare in importance with the need to stop the rising spiral of drug-trafficking.

While the USA and Europe (including the USSR) should give every possible co-operation to those producing countries willing to tackle the problems of drug cultivation, and the countries through which narcotics are transported, the only real cure will be in cutting off the demand from the addicts on the streets of the consuming countries themselves.

The cure proposed in Chapter 11 is to impose perpetual imprisonment (life-meaning-life sentences) for drug-traffickers, both to keep them out of circulation and to deter others, and to commit addicts to custodial hospital treatment until they are passed as cured, thereafter to be subject to regular blood tests and immediate return to detention in hospital at the first sign of re-addiction. The alternative could be the 'nightmare scenario' described in Chapter 18.

Coupled with drug-trafficking is the illegal money it creates, hand in hand with the illegal money created by fraud, counterfeiting, and extortion. In some countries the amount of illegal money in circulation is already having a dangerously destabilizing effect on the economy.

As well as tackling narcotics consumption, it will therefore be necessary to tackle the laundering of money from all these sources. Laundering is done primarily through electronic transfers between banks. While most western banks are legally obliged and willing to give access to customers' accounts if the police can produce evidence that they may contain money illegally obtained (see Chapter 3), it may be difficult to produce such evidence without first examining the account – a Catch 22 situation. A full right of access, subject to safeguards and monitoring by the Judiciary, must be extended internationally if this problem is to be solved. A further problem is that some Third World banks are willing to take any money without asking questions and to transfer it instantly by electronic means to another bank, after which the police trail will grow cold. To overcome this, western governments will need to legislate to ban their banks from any transactions with foreign banks which do not maintain proper records and make them available for scrutiny, subject to reasonable judicial safeguards.

Priorities for research

The most valuable research and development for fighting terrorism will be the development of computerized national intelligence systems with mutual international access for police of friendly countries, initially within western Europe, USA, Canada, Japan, and Australasia, then extending to other countries which accept and honour the necessary safeguards to prevent abuse. If Gorbachov's reforms progress, there is every likelihood of the USSR and other east European countries becoming trusted members.

In parallel with this, it will be equally important to develop reliable means of preventing or, if prevention fails, of detecting any abuse of computerized information such as would erode civil liberties. The first stages will be good management, vetting of those with access to the computer system and strict control, with automatic recording, each time they go in and out. There is great scope for computer research in solving this problem.

There is also need for continuing research into the prevention or detection of computer fraud and mischievous hacking. Potentially the damage can be enormous. At the same time, with the increasing speed of date processing, it should be possible to build into the international banking network a capability to trace any electronic transfer of money and to prevent a money launderer from escaping detection by rapid transfer of relatively small amounts to a large number of banks all over the world.

All of these things will be greatly enhanced by the development of artificial intelligence (AI) and, in particular, of expert systems and fine-grained parallel computers, which will be able to detect and draw inferences from links between apparently unconnected details of data much more quickly than is possible now. This whole field of development was examined in Chapter 7.

A closely connected field, in which computer development will play a big part, is the improvement of selection and vetting procedures and access control. Identification is a crucial part of this, and the prevention of impersonation (hitherto a major weakness in ID cards, key cards etc.) is now a high priority for research. Digital recording of fingerprint data on both a smartcard micoprocessor and a main computer memory will come close to 100 per cent reliability. Other promising alternatives (e.g. DNA and vein patterns) are also under development.

Airport and airline security research remains a high priority in view of the disproportionate publicity and political blackmail achieved by hijackers, thanks to the irresponsible capitalization of emotions to attract television audiences. Hijack prevention depends above all on good security management, but the essential technological task is to provide equipment that the airports and airlines can and will use without the risk of driving their passengers away to competitors. This was discussed in Chapters, 6,7,8, and 17.

Voluntary tagging would provide incentives in terms of convenience sufficient to attract most of those concerned, and there are various forms it could take, e.g. the already familiar wristband, a dressing on the hair, or skin pigmentation, renewed at intervals. This field of research was discussed in Chapter 8.

Equally important is the detection of narcotics and explosives. This becomes more urgent with each further development of metal-free guns and bomb-firing mechanisms. Vapour sniffing, neutron bombardment, measurement of dielectric properties, and thermal imagery were some of the current areas of development examined in Chapter 6. These same techniques could be applied to the detection of other materials.

Tagging of explosives was discussed earlier on pp. 56–7. The technology of multiple colour coding is well developed but for various reasons there is opposition to its use by manufacturers. Research is needed to overcome these objections.

Currently one of the greatest shortcomings of alarm systems is the high False Alarm Rate (FAR). Some interesting developments were discussed in Chapter 8, but this is another urgent field of research in which the manufacturer who achieves a breakthrough should reap huge rewards, as the demand is unlimited.

An enormous number of terrorist attacks against individuals take place on roads. VTOL, STOL, and microlite aircraft are not yet a reliable or economic alternative to regular road journeys but if there were a quantum leap to a dramatically lighter engine (see p. 85) we should be ready to make use of it.

Conclusions

Striking the balance

Guerrilla warfare and terrorism are, with very few exceptions, the recourse of tiny minorities who know that they could never get the majority to accept their views. While dissent can be constructive and stimulating, when it gives way to violence it must not be tolerated. The majority, as recorded by the ancient Greeks and the successors to their civilization, have always had to be prepared to forgo some of their own comforts and liberties when facing the challenge of people prepared to kill. But there is no rightful claim of a civil liberty to kill, wound, sabotage, impersonate, or intimidate. The claim by a minority of the right to kill must never be allowed to override the right of the majority to live in peace.

Sources and bibliography

Part I Fighting under the nuclear umbrella

1 Introduction and
2 The spectrum of political conflict

Bowden, T. (1978) *Beyond the Limits of the Law*, Harmondsworth: Penguin.
Clutterbuck, R. (1984) *Conflict and Violence in Singapore and Malaysia*, Boulder, Col: Westview; Singapore: Brash (1985).
Clutterbuck, R. (1986) *The Future of Political Violence*, London: Macmillan; New York: St Martins Press.
Dobson, C. and Payne R. (1986) *War Without End*, London: Harrap.
Jenkins, B. (1982) *Terrorism and Beyond*, Santa Monica, Calif: Rand.
Kitson, F. (1971) *Low Intensity Operations*, London: Faber.
Laqueur, W. (1977) *Guerrilla*, London: Weidenfeld & Nicolson.
Laqueur, W. (1987) *The Age of Terrorism*, London: Weidenfeld & Nicolson.
Marighela, C. (1971) *For the Liberation of Brazil*, Harmondsworth: Penguin.
Van Der Haag, E. (1972) *Political Violence and Civil Disobedience*, New York: Harper & Row.
Wardlaw, G. (1982) *Political Terrorism*, Cambridge University Press.
Wilkinson, P. (1986) *Terrorism and the Liberal State*, London: Macmillan.

Part II Technological Development

3 Terrorist targets in the 1990s

Alexander, Y. and Kilmarx, R. A. (Eds) (1979) *Political Terrorism and Business*, New York: Praeger.
Clutterbuck, R. (1986) *The Future of Political Violence*, London: Macmillan; New York: St Martin's Press.
Clutterbuck, R. (1987) 'The future of political violence and terrorism' *Journal of the Royal Society of Arts*, April: 376–86.

Sources and bibliography

Ellen, E. (1986) *Violence at Sea*, Paris: ICC Publishing SA.
Jenkins, B. (1982) *Terrorism and Beyond*, Santa Monica, Calif: Rand.
Jenkins, B. (1985) *Terrorism and Personal Protection*, Boston, Mass: Butterworth.
Richardson, L. (1986) 'The urgency of detergency (or how money laundering is carried out)', *TVI Report* 6, 3: 12–22 and 4: 43–50 (in two parts).

4 *Personal weapons* and
5 *Missiles, longer range weapons, and bombs*

Brasseys (1982–6) *Battlefield Weapons Systems and Technology Series*, London: Brasseys.
Dobson, C. and Payne, R. (1979) *The Weapons of Terror*, London: Macmillan.
De Leon, P. and Hoffman, B. (1988) *The Threat of Nuclear Terrorism*, Santa Monica, Calif: Rand.
Hogg, I. (ed.) (1986) *Jane's Infantry Weapons*, London: Jane's Publishing; also personal interview and correspondence.
Macksey, K. (1986) *Technology in War: The Impact of Science on Weapon Development and Modern Battle*, London: Arms and Armour Press.
Pengelly, R. (1982) 'G11: Worth waiting for?', *Defence Attaché* 1: 22–5.
Raschen, Col. D, G., OBE, Royal Military College of Science, Shrivenham, personal interviews and correspondence.

6 *Detecting explosives, bombs, and guns*

Bozorgmanesh, H. (1987) 'Bomb and weapon detection', *Terrorism: An International Journal*, 10, 3: 285–7.
Kindel, S. (1987) 'Off-the-shelf technology', *Terrorism: An International Journal*, 10, 3: 281–4.
Knowles, G. (1976) *Bomb Security Guide*, Los Angeles, Calif: Security World.
Morris, D. (1986) *Dogwatching*, London: Jonathan Cape.
Yallop, H. J. (1980) *Explosion Investigation*, Edinburgh, Forensic Science Society.
Yallop, H. J. (1980) *Protection Against Terrorism*, London: Barry Rose.
Also interviews and correspondence with Lt. Col. A. J. Wright, RE, and Major J. R. Wyatt, MBE, RE, at The Royal School of Military Engineering, Chatham.

7 *Intelligence and the microelectronics revolution*

This chapter is based mainly on visits and interviews with:
Professor Richard Gregory, of Bristol University, who has combined his medical and computer expertise to become the leading thinker in Britain on artifical intelligence;

Dr John Hulbert who, as Chief Superintendent of Police, developed
some highly original computer systems for police intelligence and
now runs his own computer research and development company,
Cogitaire;
Superintendent David Webb, who worked with John Hulbert in this
development, is now completing his own PhD;
Dr Masoud Yazdani, Lecturer in Computer Science at the University
of Exeter.
Writings by two of these, both understandable to the non-professional,
were consulted throughout:

Webb, D. (1987) 'Artificial Intelligence: Its potential to create an impact
in the fight against terrorism', Paper presented to a symposium at
the Office of International Criminal Justice, University of Illinois at
Chicago, August.
Yazdani, M. and Narayanan, A. (eds) (1984) *Artificial Intelligence:
Human Effects*, Chichester: Ellis Horwood.

8 Physical security

Clutterbuck, R. (1987) *Kidnap, Hijack and Extortion*, London:
Macmillan; New York: St Martin's Press.
Federal Bureau of Investigation (1982) *Crisis Reaction Seminar*, held at
the International University for Presidents, Maui, Hawai, 1982;
Washington, DC: FBI.
Jenkins, B. (ed.) (1985) *Terrorism and Personal Protection*, Boston,
Mass: Butterworth.
MacKenzie, G., McLoughlin, A. A., and Twiss, G. (1983) *The Security
Handbook*, Cape Town, Flesch.
Sitrep International, a periodical published every two months since
September 1987, with articles and manufacturers' details on new
developments in security equipment.
Moore, K. C. (1976) *Airport, Aircraft and Airline Security*, Los Angeles,
Calif: Security World.

Part III Drugs, political violence, and crime

9 *Cocaine,*
10 *Heroin and hashish,* and
11 *The consumers*

Adams, J. (1986) *The Financing of Terror*, Sevenoaks: New English
Library, ch. 9, 'The Narc-Farc connection'.
Browne, D. (1988) 'Crack', *Observer*, 24 July.
Control Risks, *Briefing Book*: monthly analysis of events in all countries
subject to security and political risks, published in London by
Control Risks 1984–9, available by private subscription.
'Drugs: Prevention begins in Peru', *The Economist*, 16 July 1988.
Goldsmith, C. (1987–8) 'Drugs: The threat to society' *Sitrep*

International, 1: 2–4, 2: 3–11, 3: 4–10, and 4: 4–11, September 1987 to July 1988 (in four parts).

Posner, G. (1989) *Warlords of Crime: The New Mafia*, London: Macdonald Queen Anne Press.

Part IV Rural guerrilla warfare

12   Rural guerrillas – Latin America,
13   Rural guerrillas – Asia and Africa, and
14   Development of rural guerrilla warfare

Anderson, J. (1987) *Sendero Luminoso*, London: Institute for the Study of Terrorism.

Asheshov, N., journalist resident in Peru, interview and correspondence.

Asprey, R. (1976) *War in the Shadows*, London: Macdonald.

Beckett, I. W. F. and Pimlott, J. (1985) *Armed Forces and Modern Counterinsurgency*, London: Croom Helm.

Bradford Burns, E. (1987) *At War in Nicaragua*, New York: Harper & Row.

Clutterbuck, R. (1984) *Conflict and Violence in Singapore and Malaysia*, Boulder, Col: Westview; Singapore: Brash (1985).

Clutterbuck, R. (1986) *The Future of Political Violence*, London: Macmillan; New York: St Martin's Press.

Clutterbuck, R. (1987) *Kidnap, Hijack and Extortion*, London: Macmillan; New York: St Martin's Press. ch. 16, 'Anti-development abductions'.

Control Risks, *Briefing Book*: monthly 1984–9.

Control Risks (1987) *South Asia: Political Forecast 1987–89*, London: Control Risks.

Corbett, R. (1986) *Guerrilla Warfare from 1939 to the Present Day*, London: Orbis.

Goldsmith, C. (1987–8) 'Drugs: The threat to society', *Sitrep International*, 1, 2, 3, and 4, September 1987 to July 1988 (in four parts).

Kitson, F. (1971) *Low Intensity Operations*, London: Faber.

MacKenzie, G., McLoughlin, A. A., and Twiss, G. (1983) *The Security Handbook*, Cape Town, Flesch.

Smith, M. (1988) 'Maoist supremo sets the course for Lima revolution', *The Times*, 30 July.

Tremayne, P. and Geldard, I. (1986) *Tamil Terrorism*, London: Institute for the Study of Terrorism.

Part V Urban terrorism

15   Urban terrorist organizations,
16   Urban terrorist techniques, and
17   Developments in countering terrorism

Adams, J. (1986) *The Financing of Terror*, Sevenoaks: New English
    Library.
Alexander, Y. and Kilmarx, R. A. (eds) (1979) *Political Terrorism and
    Business*, New York: Praeger.
Clutterbuck, R. (1987) 'The future of political violence and terrorism',
    Journal of the Royal Society of Arts, April: 376–86.
Clutterbuck, R. (1987) *Kidnap, Hijack and Extortion*, London:
    Macmillan; New York: St Martin's Press.
Control Risks, *Briefing Book*: monthly 1984–9.
Dobson, C. and Payne, R. (1982) *Terror: The West Fights Back*,
    London: Macmillan.
Dobson, C. and Payne, R. (1986) *War Without End*, London: Harrap.
Herz, M. (ed.) (1982) *Diplomats and Terrorists: What Works, What
    Doesn't*, Washington, DC: Georgetown University.
Jenkins, B. (1982) *Terrorism and Beyond*, Santa Monica, Calif: Rand.
Jenkins, B. (1985) (ed.) (1985) *Terrorism and Personal Protection*,
    Boston, Mass: Butterworth.
Lodge, J. (ed.) (1981) *Terrorism: A Challenge to the State*, Oxford:
    Martin Robertson.
Lodge, J. (ed.) (1987) *The Threat of Terrorism*, Brighton: Wheatsheaf.
Selth, A. (1988) *Against Every Human Law*, Sydney: Pergamon Press.
Steer, S. (1988) 'Maltese trial ends with 25 year sentence,' in
    International Law Enforcement Reporter, Washington DC, 412–4,
    Dec.
Wardlaw, G. (1982) *Political Terrorism*, Cambridge University Press.
Wolfe, J. B. (1981) *Fear of Fear*, New York: Plenum Press.

Part VI Conclusions

16   Nightmare scenarios and
17   The price to pay

Bowden, T. (1987) *Beyond the Limits of the Law*, Harmondsworth:
    Penguin.
Lodge, J. (ed.) (1987) *The Threat of Terrorism*, Brighton: Wheatsheaf.
Richardson, L. D. (1986) 'The urgency of detergency (or how money
    laundering is carried out)', *TVI Report* 6, 3: 12–22 and 4: 43–50 (in
    two parts).
Turner, S. (1986) *Secrecy and Democracy: The CIA in Transition*,
    London: Sidgwick & Jackson.
Wardlaw, G. (1982) *Political Terrorism*, Cambridge University Press.
Wilkinson, P. (1986) *Terrorism and the Liberal State*, London:
    Macmillan.
Wolf, J. B. (1981) *Fear of Fear*, New York: Plenum Press.

Index

Index